Restoring Justice:
An Introduction to
Restorative Justice

Restoring Justice: An Introduction to Restorative Justice

Fifth Edition

Daniel W. Van Ness

Karen Heetderks Strong

Routledge
Taylor & Francis Group

LONDON AND NEW YORK

First published 2015 by Anderson Publishing

Published 2015 by Routledge
2 Park Square, Milton Park, Abingdon, Oxon OX14 4RN

and by Routledge
711 Third Avenue, New York, NY 10017, USA

Routledge is an imprint of the Taylor & Francis Group, an informa business

Acquiring Editor: Pam Chester
Development Editor: Ellen S. Boyne
Project Manager: Julia Haynes
Designer: Tin Box Studio, Inc.

Library of Congress Cataloging-in-Publication Data
A catalogue record for this book is available from the Library of Congress.

British Library Cataloguing-in-Publication Data
A catalogue record for this book is available from the British Library.

ISBN 978-1-4557-3139-8 (pbk)

Dedication

We dedicate this fifth edition to all the thinkers, practitioners, policymakers, critics, and champions who shape restorative justice and keep it growing across the globe.

Contents

Comments on Previous Editions of *Restoring Justice*　　　xiii

Preface　　　xv

Online Resources　　　xix

Part 1: The Concept of Restorative Justice　　　**1**

1. Visions and Patterns　　　3
   How Patterns of Thinking Can Obstruct Justice

   Key Concepts　　　3

   An Ancient Pattern　　　6

   A Shift in Thinking　　　7

   The Declining Role of the Crime Victim　　　10

   Critiques Pointing to a New Pattern　　　12

   Conclusion　　　18

   Review Questions　　　18

   Endnotes　　　18

2. A Brief History of Restorative Justice　　　23
   The Development of a New Pattern of Thinking

   Key Concepts　　　23

   The Term *Restorative Justice*　　　23

   Explorers of Restorative Justice Theory　　　25

   Programs Offering Restorative Processes　　　27

   Incorporation of Restorative Justice into Criminal Justice
   　Systems　　　30

   Time Line of Significant Developments Related
   　to Restorative Processes　　　31

Conclusion   39

Review Questions   39

Endnotes   39

3.   Restorative Justice   **43**
        Justice That Promotes Healing

Key Concepts   43

Definition of Restorative Justice   43

Principles of Restorative Justice   45

Values of Restorative Justice   48

Restorative Justice or Restorative Practices?   50

Restorative Justice as Opposed to What?   51

Does Restorative Justice Work?   53

Restorative Justice: A Visual Model   54

Conclusion   57

Review Questions   58

Endnotes   59

Part 2: The Cornerposts of Restorative Justice   61

4.   Inclusion   **63**

Key Concepts   63

Restorative Justice and Inclusion   65

Inclusion for Victims   67

Inclusion of Offenders   75

Inclusion of Community Members   76

Conclusion   77

Review Questions   78

Endnotes   78

5.   Encounter   81

Key Concepts   81

Mediation   82

Conferencing   84

Circles   85

Impact Panels   86

Elements of Encounter   88

Issues   90

Conclusion   95

Review Questions   95

Endnotes   96

6.   Amends   99

Key Concepts   99

Apology   101

Changed Behavior   102

Restitution   103

Generosity   104

Issues Related to Restitution   104

Conclusion   109

Review Questions   110

Endnotes   110

7.   Reintegration   113

Key Concepts   113

Victims   115

Offenders   117

Reintegration   119

Building a Reintegrative Response   119

Reintegrating Communities 121

Conclusion 128

Review Questions 129

Endnotes 129

Part 3: The Challenge of Restorative Justice **133**

8. Making Restorative Justice Happen 135

Key Concepts 135

Build Support for Restorative Justice 135

Increase the Use of Restorative Practices 137

Develop a Credible Coalition 138

Pursue Strategic Goals 139

Revisit the Vision and Evaluate Impact 142

Realign Vision and Practice 144

Stay Connected 145

Expect Resistance 146

Conclusion 147

Review Questions 147

Endnotes 147

9. Toward a Restorative System 149

Key Concepts 149

The Conditions for a Restorative System 149

Five System Models and "Restorativeness" 153

Uses of Restorative Justice Processes in Contemporary
Criminal Justice 156

A Framework for Assessing the "Restorativeness" of
a System 160

Conclusion 167

Review Questions   167

Endnotes   168

10. Transformation   169

Key Concepts   169

Transformation of Perspective   170

Transformation of Structures   173

Transformation of Persons   174

Review Questions   176

Endnotes   176

Appendix   177

Select Bibliography   189

Index   211

Comments on Previous Editions of *Restoring Justice*

As a crime victim, victim advocate, and long-time supporter of restorative justice values and principals, I found *Restoring Justice* to be an excellent resource for anyone interested in the complex world of restorative justice history, processes, and ideas. Bravo to Dan Van Ness and Karen Strong for offering a balanced approach to restorative justice that understands "real" justice is about repairing the harm and healing those who have been harmed by crime: victims, offenders, and communities. *Restoring Justice* is a well-written and quite often inspirational book!

> Ellen Halbert, Director, Victim/Witness Division,
> Travis County District Attorney's Office, Austin, Texas
> Editor, the *Crime Victims Report*, a national newsletter

At each edition of *Restoring Justice*, Daniel Van Ness and Karen Heetderks Strong set the standard and make their volume one of the basic books—or perhaps *the* basic book—on restorative justice.

Their book reflects the richness of the restorative justice approach, through process analyses with clinical relevance, theoretical thinking with social ethical and social significance, principled exploration on juridical options, and a broad sociological context analysis. Van Ness and Heetderks Strong colour this broad interdisciplinary picture with their own visions and options. In doing so, they deliver a crucial contribution to understanding restorative justice principles and their proper implementation.

Restoring Justice is the result of intensive commitment to the values of restorative justice, balanced with a constructive critical mind for possible problematic implementations, and openness for unanswered questions and unresolved difficulties. It is a landmark in the restorative justice literature.

> Lode Walgrave
> Professor Emeritus
> Catholic University of Leuren

[In *Restoring Justice*, Dan Van Ness and Karen Strong] challenge researchers and scholars to move beyond measuring only recidivism as the ultimate outcome of evaluation, and victim and offender satisfaction as the primary intermediate measures. Based on this work, we may now instead build upon core principles to develop dimensions and measures of process integrity, as well as theoretical dimensions to assess intermediate outcomes for victim, offender, and community.

Gordon Bazemore
Professor of Criminology and Criminal Justice
Florida Atlantic University

Restoring Justice is the best, most thorough text on the most important development in the justice system in the last decade: restorative justice.… a seminal work.… this book does a wonderful job of describing the rationale, presenting the arguments, confronting the criticisms.… provides a measured, reliable statement on our need to restore justice.

Todd Clear, Professor of Criminal Justice
John Jay College of Criminal Justice

… a great introductory overview of restorative justice … easily understood while also providing significant depth.… draws together the significant insights in the field while making several new contributions… invites and encourages change without alienating people who are currently working in the field. I recommend *Restoring Justice* for both the novice and the seasoned restorative justice reader.

Ron Claassen, Director
Center for Peacemaking and Conflict Studies
Fresno Pacific University

… an exceptionally good job of clearly articulating the underlying principles and values of restorative justice, including many practical examples. This book will serve as a primary resource for scholars and practitioners involved in the restorative justice movement as it continues to expand.

Mark Umbreit, author of *Victim Meets Offender*
Professor, School of Social Work
University of Minnesota

Preface

Restoring Justice is an introduction to the theory and practices of restorative justice. Since the publication of the previous editions in 1997, 2002, 2006, and 2010, restorative justice has continued to develop worldwide. We have accordingly updated this edition to include the significant contours of these developments.

Our work on restorative justice began in the mid-1980s when the criminal justice advocacy organization we worked for undertook development of a model built on what was then a largely unknown and incomplete theory called restorative justice. The organization was Justice Fellowship, a criminal justice reform organization affiliated with Prison Fellowship Ministries.

The first step involved articulating what seemed to be the core principles of restorative justice. This took months of work and involved not only our team at Justice Fellowship but also criminal justice practitioners, researchers, elected officials, academics, theologians, and concerned laypersons. After working sessions and multiple drafts, we settled on three basic principles, similar to those proposed in Chapter 3. Then began a 3-year project to research and write systematically about the theory undergirding restorative justice, the principles and values guiding its application, and particular programs to bring it into being. These were developed using a similar approach of working sessions, multiple drafts, and external review. Our purpose then was to help Justice Fellowship focus its reform efforts by identifying significant public policy implications of this new theory.

Interest in restorative justice kept growing, and we worked with Anderson Publishing to revise and enhance our internal work to engage a broader audience. Since publication of *Restoring Justice* in 1997, the movement has both deepened and widened with substantial developments in the concepts, policies, and practices related to restorative justice.

At every stage of our journey with restorative justice, we have benefited from the insights, questions, research, writings, experience, and practical contributions of scholars and practitioners around the globe. Our best ideas are the result of interaction with the remarkably generous, creative, and courageous people in this field. Although these individuals may not agree with all of our conclusions, their contributions have enriched and strengthened our work and that of restorative justice advocates and practitioners throughout the world.

We especially thank former colleagues at Justice Fellowship who helped us research and write "Restorative Justice: Theory, Principles, and Practice," printed and copyrighted by Justice Fellowship in 1989 and 1990. Ideas and portions of these manuscripts are reflected in this book, by permission from Justice Fellowship and our co-authors. As we have prepared each edition of *Restoring Justice*, we have been continually reminded of the formative and highly meaningful interaction among these individuals as we worked together to challenge, articulate, and refine ideas about restorative justice and their implications. Thomas Crawford poured himself into the project, cultivating personal and intellectual excellence in the process. Lisa Barnes Lampman kept asking the tough questions and pressing for clarity. David R. Carlson played a crucial role in the formulation of the three original Justice Fellowship principles of restorative justice and the development of "Restorative Justice: Theory." Kimon Sargeant and Claire Souryal assisted in researching and writing "Restorative Justice: Principles and Practice." Dorothea Jinnah was invaluable as a precise, resourceful, and ever-thoughtful researcher and colleague. Thanks, too, to Ed Hostetter for his online searches and project help. We also thank Lynette Parker for her work in facilitating wide access to the excellent resources available at http://www.restorativejustice.org, both as a benefit to us in preparing this updated edition of *Restoring Justice* and as a resource to others, worldwide. We are indebted to these co-laborers (and others, too many to name) for their hard work and insightful perspectives.

We are grateful for those at Anderson Publishing Co. (now part of Elsevier, Inc.) who have been instrumental in bringing *Restoring Justice* to press and to the attention of readers since 1997. Mickey Braswell cajoled, encouraged, and constructively criticized as we completed the first edition and helped us see the need and potential for the subsequent ones. Ellen S. Boyne applied her adept editing and refining skills to good effect. Pam Chester and others have helped us understand the mysteries of marketing, translation rights, and adapting to changes in the requirements for publication. We have enjoyed working with them all.

Excerpts from other previously published works by Daniel W. Van Ness have also been used by permission in this volume. These works and publishers are as follows: "Preserving a Community Voice: The Case for Half-and Half Juries in Racially-Charged Criminal Cases," *John Marshall Law Review* 28, 1 (1994), is used courtesy of The John Marshall Law School. "New Wine and Old Wineskins," *Criminal Law Forum* 4, 2 (1993), and "Anchoring Just Deserts," *Criminal Law Forum* 6, 3 (1995), are used courtesy of *Criminal Law Forum*, Rutgers Law School. Adapted excerpts from "Restorative Justice" in *Criminal Justice, Restitution, and Reconciliation*, edited by Burt Galaway and Joe Hudson (1990); from "Restorative Justice and International Human Rights" in *Restorative Justice: International Perspectives*, edited by Burt Galaway and Joe Hudson (1996); and from "Legal Issues of *Restorative Justice*" in *Restorative Juvenile Justice: Repairing the Harm of Youth Crime*, edited by Gordon Bazemore and Lode Walgrave, are used with permission from Criminal Justice Press, P.O. Box 249, Monsey, New York 10952. The review of uses of restorative justice processes in the criminal justice system in Chapter 9 was drawn from a paper Van Ness prepared for the Workshop on Enhancing Criminal Justice Reform, Including Restorative Justice, conducted April 11, 2005, at the United Nations 11th Congress on Crime Prevention and Criminal Justice held in Bangkok, Thailand. The case study in Appendix 1 is reprinted by permission from Prison Fellowship International.

In the following chapters, we consider why so many people throughout the world believe that criminal justice is in need of a new vision, and we offer a brief history and timeline of significant milestones in the development of restorative justice. We present our understanding of the meaning of restorative justice and explore its conceptual and practical cornerposts. We then explore how restorative justice ideas and values are being (and might be) integrated into policy and practice. Finally, we outline issues that are commonly raised about restorative justice, and we summarize various perspectives related to each issue.

As will be clear in Chapter 2, we certainly do not claim to be the first or principal proponents of restorative justice. We are encouraged by the growth of interest in restorative justice worldwide, and the many and diverse examples of its development and practice. Therefore, it is our desire that this volume may benefit those who are exploring restorative justice and encourage practical implementation of its principles, values, and programs in a wide variety of contexts.

We are learners and sojourners in the work of restorative justice. Most of what we have come to understand, we received from others. We thank the generous people who have gone before us, including the aboriginal peoples of the world who have preserved restorative approaches for centuries, and also the wonderful people who travel the road with us today. Most of all, we are grateful to Jesus Christ, who steadily leads us into deeper understanding of, and appreciation for, true peace—shalom.

Daniel W. Van Ness
Karen Heetderks Strong
August 2013

Online Resources

Thank you for selecting Anderson Publishing's *Restoring Justice: An Introduction to Restorative Justice,* 5th edition. To complement the learning experience, we have provided online tools to accompany this edition.

Qualified adopters and instructors can access valuable material for free by registering at: www.routledge.com/cw/vanness

The Concept of Restorative Justice

1

Visions and Patterns
How Patterns of Thinking Can Obstruct Justice

KEY CONCEPTS

- Patterns of thinking—their strengths and limitations
- Ancient views of justice
- Government as "victim"
- Critiques of contemporary criminal justice
- Competing views of justice

The young woman watched intently as the man who raped her was sentenced to prison. But as the rapist was escorted from the courtroom, it was clear to Justice John Kelly that she was no less distraught than she had been throughout the court proceedings. So before the next case was called, Justice Kelly asked the victim to approach the bench. He spoke with her briefly and quietly about what had happened, and he concluded with these words: "You understand that what I have done here demonstrates conclusively that what happened was not your fault." At that, the young woman began to weep and ran from the courtroom. When Justice Kelly called the victim's family several days later, he learned that his words had been words of vindication for the woman; they marked the beginning of her psychological recovery. Her tears had been tears of healing.

A short time later, this Australian judge spoke at an international conference on criminal law reform held in London. Speaking to 200 judges, legal scholars, and law reformers from common law countries, he laid aside his prepared comments and spoke with great feeling about the need for criminal law practitioners to view themselves as healers. A purpose of criminal law, he said, should be to heal the wounds caused by crime—wounds such as those of the rape victim for whom even the offender's conviction and sentencing had not been enough.

The rehabilitation model of criminal justice has been by far the most influential school of thought in criminology in the past 200 years. Although the model fell into disrepute among criminal justice policymakers in the latter decades of the twentieth century, opinion surveys suggest that the desire to rehabilitate offenders remains strong among members of the general public and even many crime victims.[1] At a fundamental level, we recognize that criminal justice should consider not only whether accused offenders have violated the law but also why they have done so. However, even when rehabilitation programs are helpful in addressing the underlying problems that led to the decision to commit a crime, those programs fail to address all the injuries surrounding the crime. Crime is not simply lawbreaking; it also causes injury to others. Although it may be the manifestation of an underlying injury, it also creates new injuries. A purpose of criminal justice should be, in Justice Kelly's words, to heal those injuries.

As we will see, these injuries exist on several levels and are experienced by victims, communities, and even offenders. The current policies and practice of criminal justice focus almost entirely on the offender as lawbreaker, filtering out virtually all aspects of crime except questions of legal guilt and punishment. This is because a set of assumptions, or a pattern of thinking, structures our perception of crime and, consequently, our sense of what a proper response should be. Howard Zehr's description of paradigms is pertinent here: "They provide the lens through which we understand phenomena. They shape what we 'know' to be possible and impossible. [They] form our common sense, and things which fall outside … seem absurd."[2]

Patterns of thinking are necessary because they give meaning to the myriad bits of data we must deal with in life. Edward de Bono illustrates this using the example of a person crossing a busy road:

> *If, as you stood waiting to cross the road, your brain had to try out all the incoming information in different combinations in order to recognize the traffic conditions, it would take you at least a month to cross the road. In fact, the changing conditions would make it impossible for you ever to cross.*[3]

To avoid this problem, the brain uses "active information systems" to organize data into patterns of thinking that allow us to quickly make sense out of the chaos of information that would otherwise overwhelm us. A pattern of thinking is like the collection of streams, rivulets, and rivers formed over time in a particular place by the rainfall; once the pattern of water runoff is established, rainwater will always flow there, and nowhere else.

■ ■ ■ ━━

A fundamental weakness of patterns of thinking is that they limit what we perceive.

━━ ■ ■ ■

However, the reason for their usefulness is also a fundamental weakness of patterns: They limit the data we perceive. We see only what makes sense in the pattern; we simply do not recognize "absurd" information. Therefore, one sign that a pattern of thinking has become deficient is that we increasingly encounter troublesome data that do not fit. We are then forced to make a choice: disregard that evidence or seek a new pattern. For example, at one time scientists believed that the Earth was flat and that the universe revolved around it. However, as astronomers recorded the actual movement of heavenly bodies, this model became increasingly less satisfactory. When Copernicus proposed that the Earth revolves around the sun—not the other way around—his model offered a much more satisfactory explanation of observable data.

It is normal to think that the way we understand or do something is not only the right way but also the only way, until we encounter other approaches and recognize that they present alternatives. We may not adopt those alternatives, but the benefit to having encountered them is that we realize we have choices. This is why some people travel, read, watch television programs, go to museums, or listen to music. They are "broadening their horizons"—discovering that other people in other times and places have made different choices, and that those choices have had consequences. And even as they experience the differences, they also notice things they have in common, and they may come to a changed understanding of what it means to be human.

In other words, exposure to other ways of doing things helps us recognize patterns of thinking, allows us to reflect on alternative approaches, and offers us the opportunity to make choices.

Consider criminal justice. When we hear about a crime, we know that there are probably victims, people who were harmed by the crime. We also know that there are laws to protect those people, and that the offender should be caught and held accountable for breaking those laws. We are not surprised that criminal cases involve government prosecution of suspected offenders to determine whether they did in fact break the law. Nor are we surprised when guilty offenders are sent to prison as punishment or "given a break" and placed on probation. We may have opinions about whether the suspect was actually guilty or about the sentence, but we seldom, if ever, question the underlying assumptions of the process: Crime is lawbreaking; the focus after crime should be on the suspected offenders, and once found guilty they should have their liberty taken away or curtailed in some way.

Yet nagging questions surface from time to time, prompted by events or intuitions that do not fit neatly within the pattern. Perhaps the most profound and obvious ones have to do with victims of crime. Why are some so dissatisfied with how the criminal justice system treats them? Is it wrong when victims want to have a say in how the police conduct the investigation, or how the prosecutor presents the case, or what sentence the judge gives the offender? Why isn't it enough for them to sue the offender in civil court?

And what about the high rate of recidivism—repeat offending—among offenders? As we will see soon, the institutions of criminal justice were developed in large part to achieve rehabilitation. For two centuries, Americans and Europeans have experimented with a succession of programs to accomplish this purpose. Every such attempt has ended in disappointment. Why is that so, and isn't there something we could do differently to get better results? If not, then shouldn't we be trying something different?

What we suggest in this book is that the way we think about crime is inadequate. By defining crime as lawbreaking and then concentrating on the resulting adversarial relationship between government and the criminal offender, we fail to address—or even recognize—certain fundamental reasons for, and results of, criminal behavior. Adding new programs to an inadequate pattern of thinking is not enough if what is needed is a different pattern. That is what this book proposes.

■ ■ ■ ▬▬

Legal systems in the past expected offenders and their families to make amends to victims and their families.

▬▬ ■ ■ ■

It is not as though our current approach to criminal justice is the only one; there have been times and places when crime was viewed far more comprehensively—as an offense against victims, their families, the community, and society. The goal of justice was to satisfy the parties, and the way to do that included making things right by repairing the damage to those parties, whether the damage was physical, financial, or relational. This is different from an approach that defines crime solely as an offense against the government, and whose goal is crime prevention through rehabilitation, incapacitation, and deterrence.

Let us explore these patterns more closely.

An Ancient Pattern[4]

The legal systems that form the foundation of Western law did not view crime simply as a wrong to society. Although crime breached the common welfare so that the community had an interest in—and responsibility for—addressing the wrong and punishing the offender, the offense was not defined solely as a crime against the state, as it is today. Instead, it was also considered an offense against the victim and the victim's family. Consequently, offenders and their families were required to settle accounts with victims and their families in order to avoid cycles of revenge and violence. This was true in small non-state societies, with their kin-based ties, but attention to the interests of victims continued after the advent of states with formalized legal codes. The Code of Hammurabi (c. 1700 B.C.E.) prescribed restitution for property offenses, as did the Code of Lipit-Ishtar (1875 B.C.E.). Other Middle Eastern codes, such as the Sumerian Code of Ur-Nammu (c. 2050 B.C.E.) and the Code of Eshnunna (c. 1700 B.C.E.), provided for restitution even in the case of violent offenses. The Roman Law of the Twelve Tables (449 B.C.E.) required thieves to pay double restitution unless the property was found in their houses, in which case they paid triple damages; for resisting the search of their houses, they paid quadruple restitution. The Lex Salica (c. 496 C.E.), the earliest existing collection of Germanic tribal laws, included restitution for crimes ranging from theft to homicide. The Laws of Ethelbert (c. 600 C.E.), promulgated by the ruler of Kent, contained detailed restitution schedules that distinguished the values, for example, of each finger and its nail. Each of these diverse cultures retained an expectation that offenders and their families should make amends to victims and their families—not simply to ensure that injured persons received restitution but also to restore community peace.

This is suggested, for example, by the language of the Hebrew Scriptures, in which restitution played an important role.[5] In these writings, the word *shalom* was used to describe the ideal state in which the community should function.[6] It meant much more than absence of conflict; it signified completeness, fulfillment, and wholeness—the existence of right relationships among individuals, the community, and God. It was a condition in which, as Ron Claassen has said, no one is afraid.

Crime is the opposite of shalom, rupturing right relationships and creating harmful ones. Although restitution formed an essential part of the justice process, it was not understood to be an end in itself. The Hebrew word for restitution, *shillum*, derives from the same root as shalom, implying that it was related to the reestablishment of community peace. Along with restitution came the notion of vindication of the victim and the law itself. This concept was embodied in another word derived from the same root as shalom and shillum: *shillem*. Shillem can be translated as "retribution" or "recompense," not in the sense of revenge (that word derives from an entirely different root), but in the sense of satisfaction or vindication.[7] In short, a purpose of the justice process was, through vindication and reparation, to restore a community that had been sundered by crime.

This view of justice is not confined to the distant past. Pre-colonial African societies were apparently willing to forgo punishment of criminal offenders in order to resolve the consequences to their victims and the community. Many sanctions were compensatory rather than punitive, intended to restore victims to their previous position. Contemporary Japanese culture exhibits a similar emphasis on compensation to the victim and restoration of community peace. The approach (as we will discuss later) involves a process that has been referred to as "confession, repentance, and absolution." Indigenous populations in North America, New Zealand, Australia, and elsewhere are finding ways their traditional approaches to crime, which have similarities to restorative justice, might exist in the context of the dominant Western legal system.

A Shift in Thinking

■ ■ ■ ────────────────────────────────────

As tribal societies in Europe were united into kingdoms, the interests of victims began to be replaced by the interests of the king. Fines replaced restitution as the financial sanction of choice.

──────────────────────────────────── ■ ■ ■

For all of its tradition, this approach to criminal justice is unfamiliar to most of us today. As tribal societies in Europe were united into kingdoms under feudal lords, rulers took an increased interest in reducing sources of conflict, and the interests of victims began to be replaced by the interests of the state in the resolution of those conflicts. By the middle of the ninth century, fines paid to the state had replaced restitution as the financial sanction of choice. For common law jurisdictions, the Norman invasion of Britain marked the turning point in this changing understanding of crime. William the Conqueror and his successors found the legal process an effective tool for establishing the preeminence of the king over the Church in secular matters and in replacing local systems of dispute resolution. The *Leges Henrici Primi*, written early in the twelfth century, asserted royal jurisdiction over offenses such as theft punishable by death, counterfeiting, arson, premeditated assault, robbery, rape, abduction, and "breach of the king's peace given by his hand or writ."[8] Breach of the king's peace gave the royal house an extensive claim to jurisdiction:

[N]owadays we do not easily conceive how the peace which lawful men ought to keep can be any other than the Queen's or the commonwealth's. But the King's justice ... was

at first not ordinary but exceptional, and his power was called to aid only when other means had failed.… Gradually the privileges of the King's house were extended to the precincts of his court, to the army, to the regular meetings of the shire and hundred, and to the great roads. Also the King might grant special personal protection to his officers and followers; and these two kinds of privilege spread until they coalesced and covered the whole ground.[9]

Thus, the king became the paramount crime victim, sustaining legally acknowledged (although symbolic) injuries. The actual victim was ousted from any meaningful place in the justice process, illustrated by the redirection of reparation from the victim in the form of restitution to the king in the form of fines. With the new political structure, a new model of crime emerged, one in which the government and the offender were the sole parties. This model brought with it a new purpose as well: Rather than making the victim whole, the system focused on upholding the authority of the state. Instead of repairing past harm, criminal justice became future-oriented, attempting to make offenders and potential offenders law-abiding. It is not surprising, then, that restitution, which is both past-oriented and victim-centered, was eventually abandoned, with fines, corporal punishment, and the death sentence taking its place as the central responses to wrongdoing. Whipping, the stocks, branding, and other forms of public retribution not only inflicted physical pain on offenders but also served to humiliate them and, it was hoped, to dissuade them and others from engaging in similar behavior in the future.

Partially in reaction to this increasingly brutal treatment of offenders, reformers began to call for a different approach to the punishment of offenders. In the eighteenth century, progressive thinkers in England, such as Henry Fielding, John Howard, and Jeremy Bentham, called for segregation of offenders from their criminogenic environments, much as doctors would quarantine persons with a contagious disease. Like good doctors, they proposed a treatment for those offenders that would focus on "correction of the mind."[10] In the United States, like-minded reformers convinced policymakers to implement this rehabilitative model of sentencing. With that model emerged an institution that, although novel at that time, has become a symbol of the criminal justice system itself: the prison. Prior to 1790, prisons were used almost exclusively to hold offenders until trial or sentencing, or to enforce labor while a person worked off debts.[11] Reformers in Philadelphia, aghast at the cruelty of contemporary punishments and jail conditions, and stirred by the belief that criminals were the products of bad moral environments, succeeded in persuading local officials to turn the Walnut Street Jail into what they called a "penitentiary," or place of penitence.

How did they arrive at the idea of imprisonment as the vehicle for reform? It appears they drew from the use of confinement in monasteries beginning as early as the fourth century. Initially, confinement was to the monk's room, but over time special rooms were built to hold those who needed time for reflection and change.[12]

The 1787 preamble to the constitution of the Philadelphia Society for Alleviating the Miseries of Public Prisons clearly stated their intention not only to save offenders from dehumanizing punishment but also to rehabilitate them:

> *When we consider that the obligations of benevolence, which are founded on the precepts of the example of the author of Christianity, are not canceled by the follies or crimes of our fellow creatures ... it becomes us to extend our compassion to that part of mankind, who are the subjects of these miseries. By the aids of humanity, their undue and illegal sufferings may be prevented ... and such degrees and modes of punishment may be discovered and suggested, as may, instead of continuing habits of vice, become the means of restoring our fellow creatures to virtue and happiness.*[13]

■ ■ ■ ▬▬▬▬▬▬▬▬▬▬▬▬▬▬▬▬▬▬▬▬▬▬▬▬▬▬▬▬▬

Prison reformers moved from theories of repentance to hard work, then to discipline and training, and finally to medical and psychological treatment. Each generation of reformers was disappointed.

▬▬▬▬▬▬▬▬▬▬▬▬▬▬▬▬▬▬▬▬▬▬▬▬▬▬▬▬▬ ■ ■ ■

Prisoners at this penitentiary were isolated in individual cells, away from the immoral elements of society. They were given a Bible and time to contemplate it. Yet, by the early 1800s, prisons were already being denounced. "Our state prisons as presently constituted are grand demoralizers of our people," concluded a New York lawyer.[14] This, however, did not discourage prison advocates; if isolation did not achieve the goals of repentance and rehabilitation, then perhaps other measures would work. Succeeding generations of prison reformers moved from theories of repentance to those of hard work, then of discipline and training, and eventually of medical and psychological treatment. Each generation of reformers was disappointed as prisoners proved to be unchanged by their particular model of rehabilitation. As a result of this history, since the mid-1970s many criminal justice policymakers have concluded that rehabilitation is simply an impossible goal, and that pursuing it is a failed policy.

Commentators have offered a variety of practical and conceptual explanations for why rehabilitative programs have not met the expectations of their advocates. The practical explanations have ranged from inadequate funding to improper screening of participants. A challenge to the conceptual underpinnings of the model has been that it reflected an overly optimistic view of human nature—that people are morally good and make bad choices only because of their circumstances. The rehabilitation model was predicated on the assumption that if an individual's social environment improves, or his or her psyche becomes healthy, that person will naturally make the right choices. Furthermore, it assumed that the state could identify those deficiencies and force the individual to receive treatment that would be effective even though compelled.

Unfortunately, contemporary dissatisfaction with the rehabilitation model of sentencing has not led to rethinking the idea that crime is simply an offense against the state. Instead, it has prompted states to impose increasingly repressive and punitive sanctions against those who commit crimes, with the claimed goals of punishing and incapacitating criminals. This wave of "get tough" measures has been no more successful than the rehabilitation model in controlling crime, and by increasing prison crowding it contributes to the inefficiency and ineffectiveness of the criminal justice system.

The Declining Role of the Crime Victim

Even after Henry I succeeded in redefining crime as an offense against the king instead of the victim, the victim was assured a significant procedural role in the criminal process through the mechanism of private prosecution.

Private prosecution had its roots in medieval England, preceding the Norman Conquest. A private prosecutor managed the entire case (from apprehension through trial) as though it were a civil matter. Although the private citizen (usually the victim) was required to bear the financial costs of the prosecution, there were also financial incentives for the successful victim, as much as threefold restitution.[15]

However, during the nineteenth century, British reform advocates such as Jeremy Bentham and Sir Robert Peel began campaigning for the establishment of a public prosecutor. They did not argue for the abolition of private prosecution; in fact, Bentham argued for a system with both public and private prosecution. Private prosecution alone, he believed, was inadequate for crimes that were essentially public in nature. At the same time, he opposed giving the state a monopoly on prosecution because this put too much power in the hands of the government.

There were other complaints as well: that at times of high crime, when so much depended on the deterrent ability of the legal system, it was unwise to rely heavily on the willingness of victims to prosecute; that private prosecution might be ineptly conducted and result in unnecessary acquittals; that it might be motivated by revenge or greed; and that the victim and offender might settle privately.

■ ■ ■ ▬▬▬▬▬▬▬▬▬▬▬▬▬▬▬▬▬▬▬▬▬▬▬▬▬▬▬▬▬▬▬▬▬▬

Private prosecution could be burdensome for victims.

▬▬▬▬▬▬▬▬▬▬▬▬▬▬▬▬▬▬▬▬▬▬▬▬▬▬▬▬▬▬▬ ■ ■ ■

This debate culminated in the passage of the Prosecution of Offenses Act in 1879, which established the office of the public prosecutor, charged with supervising prosecutions of a limited range of offenses in which the ordinary form of prosecution was seen as insufficient. The remainder of the cases was left to private prosecutors, and the overwhelming numbers of those prosecutions (some report 80%) were initiated by police officers.[16]

It was the rise of professionalized justice that finally relegated victims to their current, passive role as witnesses for the prosecution. By the end of the nineteenth century, police dominated the investigation of crime, public prosecutors dominated prosecution, and correctional officials dominated the sentencing process.

The United States is an instructive example. Between 1815 and 1900, the United States created its modern criminal justice system. In 1815, key institutions—the police, the prison, probation, and parole—did not yet exist in their modern form. By 1900, they were parts of a new apparatus of social control. To be sure, not every state had adopted all of the new institutions by 1900, but the idea of a criminal justice system was firmly established. This system involved a set of interrelated bureaucratic agencies performing specialized tasks for the purpose of controlling crime, deviance, and disorder. The victim's role was to serve as little more than a witness.

For years, historians equated adoption of public prosecution with the elimination of private prosecution, and they concluded that private actions fell into disuse in the United States after the Revolution. It was historian Allen Steinberg's research into the magistrate's courts in Philadelphia that shed new light on the operation of a hybrid public–private prosecution process to late in the nineteenth century. In his book, *The Transformation of Criminal Justice: Philadelphia, 1800–1880*,[17] Steinberg makes a convincing case for the dominance of private prosecution until the 1880s (at least in dealing with the largest numbers of prosecutions—those for relatively minor offenses). The reason for this dominance was the popularity of the magistrate courts, operated in Philadelphia by elected officials known as aldermen who conducted administrative as well as judicial functions.

Although these courts were highly informal in operation, the aldermen/justices had the power to hold defendants in jail pending trial by a court of record, to dispose of certain minor cases, and to require the posting of a peace bond. The aldermen were for the most part unschooled in the law, and they were even willing to create new offenses on the spot if it seemed necessary. Poor people in particular frequently resorted to aldermen for justice.

It is the popularity of the magistrate's courts that Steinberg finds intriguing, particularly in light of what appear to twentieth-century lawyers to be significant flaws in how these courts operated. They were crowded, unruly, and undignified. Because the aldermen were "unencumbered" by the law, the decisions were often arbitrary. They created new offenses and made them effective retroactively. Private prosecutors were occasionally motivated by spite; others failed to pursue their cases to completion (sometimes leaving impoverished defendants languishing in jail). Finally, because the aldermens' fees came from the litigants, there was little incentive for them to refuse a prosecution—and ample opportunity for corruption.

Steinberg concludes that these courts were a form of popular, local, and informal justice. They offered a forum in which disputes could be readily resolved. More important, they offered a forum in which the disputants controlled what happened. Although there were regular outcries against the courts' abuses, these were raised by reformers who did not use the courts.

Eventually, the development of the public police force (combined with the long-standing complaints about abuses of informality) led to a reorganization of the magistrate courts, which effectively ended private prosecution. Philadelphia did not have a police department until 1854. Prior to that time, it relied on a night watch system with only limited police coverage during the day, and the patrol was much more passive than it was proactive. This is why the police force was such an innovation.

■ ■ ■ ▬▬▬▬▬▬▬▬▬▬▬▬▬▬▬▬▬▬▬▬▬▬▬▬▬▬

The development of professional police led to the creation of public prosecutors.

▬▬▬▬▬▬▬▬▬▬▬▬▬▬▬▬▬▬▬▬▬▬▬▬▬▬ ■ ■ ■

With the advent of the police force, a new possibility emerged for initiating criminal cases, one that was believed would bring greater efficiency to crime fighting: to require that all cases be initiated by the public prosecutor based on investigative work performed by the police.

The principal reason for this development (the transformation to which Steinberg refers in the title of his book) is that other parts of criminal justice had become professionalized. The police and the prison agency were deemed more effective in dealing with lawbreakers than were the victims and community. Salaried magistrates were more likely to administer even-handed justice than were those who were paid for each case they accepted. Nevertheless, Steinberg mourns the demise of the courts and of private prosecution, because in a real sense those courts were "people's courts." Although that was ultimately their downfall, it was also their strength:

> The central point is that, at bottom, the criminal court was dominated by the very people the criminal law was supposed to control.... The ordinary people of Philadelphia extensively used a system that could also be so oppressive to them because its oppressive features were balanced by the peoples' ability to control much of the course of the criminal justice process. Popular initiation and discretion were the distinctive features of private prosecution, rooted in the offices of the minor judiciary where it began, and remained the most important aspect of the process even in the courts of record. Whether it be to intimidate a friend or neighbor, resolve a private dispute, extort money or other favors, prevent a prosecution against oneself, express feelings of outrage and revenge, protect oneself from another, or simply to pursue and attain a measure of legal justice, an enormous number of nineteenth-century Philadelphians used the criminal courts.[18]

Critiques Pointing to a New Pattern

Pre-Copernican astronomers were right that the sun and planets move through the heavens, but they were wrong about one fundamental premise: The Earth is not the stationary center of creation; it too swirls through the universe. Likewise, current criminal justice policy is built on the partial truth that crime involves lawbreaking. The flaw is that it ignores another critical dimension of crime—that it causes injuries to victims, the community, and even to offenders. As a consequence, criminal justice policy is preoccupied with maintaining security—public order—while trying to balance the offender's rights and the government's power. These are, of course, important concerns, but order and fairness would be only part of society's response to crime if its overall purpose were to heal the injuries caused by crime.

What other responses might there be? During the past decades, a variety of candidates have emerged. Some grew out of critiques of the current system; others out of political, philosophical, and theological foundations at odds with those of criminal justice. While there was diversity in their underlying premises as well as in their conclusions, they pointed toward certain fundamental principles that have contributed to the development of a new pattern of thinking.

Any history of restorative justice must begin with a brief description of certain antecedents as well as the individuals and organizations that contributed to their development. So we begin by describing critiques and competing views of justice whose contributions have been key to the development of the restorative justice movement. In Chapter 2, we trace key international developments, individuals, and organizations that contributed to the emerging understanding of restorative vision, policies, and programs.

Critiques of Contemporary Criminal Justice

Some of the impetus for restorative justice grew out of complaints about how contemporary criminal justice operated. Two important critiques were those made by and on behalf of victims and of prisoners.

Victims' Rights and Assistance

As we have seen, until recent years, the interests and needs of victims were ignored by criminal justice systems. The contemporary rediscovery of crime victims was the product of an accumulation of criticisms and reforms by individuals and groups who were frustrated and angry that victims' interests were disregarded by a system preoccupied with the criminal suspect. The reform efforts have focused on three broad thrusts: (1) increasing services to victims in the aftermath of the crime, (2) increasing the likelihood of financial reimbursement for the harm done, and (3) asserting victims' rights to information and intervention during the course of the criminal justice process.

In *The Crime Victim's Book*,[19] Morton Bard and Dawn Sangrey addressed the range of needs that crime victims may confront, and they gave practical suggestions for how those might be met. They offered advice not only for crime victims but also for their families and for those who might assist them. Albert Roberts subsequently surveyed victim services programs in the United States; these were often affiliated with parts of the law enforcement system and funded by state or federal grants. He described and evaluated these programs in his book *Helping Crime Victims*.[20]

■ ■ ■ ━━━

The harm resulting from crime can be extensive: financial losses, physical injury, fear, trauma, and feelings of guilt.

━━━ ■ ■ ■

The harm resulting from victimization can be extensive. There may be direct and indirect financial losses; physical injury; and psychological harms such as fear, trauma, and feelings of guilt. Added to these may be costs for increased insurance and security measures, as well as psychological and behavioral costs in the form of changed patterns, increased precautions, avoidance, and protection. Victim compensation programs, through which governments provide financial assistance to crime victims, do not address many of these losses.

The third major reform effort has been to increase the availability of information and opportunities for participation in the criminal justice process. William McDonald's edited collection of articles, *Criminal Justice and the Victim*,[21] provided a comprehensive survey of the opportunities for, and the barriers to, victim participation in the prosecution and sentencing of the suspect. Beginning with the victim's decision to call the police and concluding with issues related to the victim and correctional policy, McDonald and colleagues described the alienating effects on victims of an essentially offender-oriented system.

Prison Abolition

Quakers (The Society of Friends) were among those who developed the penitentiary at the Walnut Street Jail in the late 1700s. Nearly two centuries later, during the 1960s and 1970s, members of this Society began urging that the use of prisons be significantly curtailed or abolished, and that other responses to crime be substituted. In part, this was due to prison abuses—abuses that seemed to be inherent in the institution of prison itself and consequently not amenable to reform. This skepticism was increased by the conviction that criminal *justice* could not be achieved in an unjust society. One influential expression of this concern was *Struggle for Justice*,[22] a report presented to the American Friends Service Committee and published in 1971.

During the late 1960s and into the 1970s, an informal reform initiative emerged in Europe and North America calling for the abolition of prisons. Attracting support from a number of political and philosophical perspectives, the critique's common theme was that prisons were not only a failure at rehabilitation but also in fact places of acute suffering by prisoners.

Some proponents of abolition called for prisons to be done away with completely. Others sought to decrease the use of prisons dramatically. Still others campaigned for a moratorium on construction of new prisons. In place of prisons, they suggested that restitution, compensation, and reconciliation programs be established in local communities so that the response to crime could be decentralized. They took inspiration from Jerome Miller, who became head of the Massachusetts Department of Youth Services in 1969. He promptly began shutting down the state's youth facilities, replacing them with community-based programs. By the time he left his position 3 years later, there were essentially no custodial facilities remaining for young people in the state.

Some of the leading personalities in this critique included a small group of scholars who became known as the "Utrecht School" because of their affiliation with Utrecht University in The Netherlands: Herman Bianchi and Louk Hulsman, also Dutch; Thomas Mathiesen of Norway; Fay Honey Knopp of the United States; and Ruth Morris of Canada. Key organizations offered leadership for periods of time before being succeeded by others. An early example was the Unitarian Universalist Service Committee's National Moratorium on Prison Construction, which was active during the 1970s and into the 1980s. Ruth Morris and others organized the first International Conference on Prison Abolition in 1983, a conference that has been repeated every 2 years since then. A new generation of abolitionists organized the Prison Moratorium Project in New York in 1995, and others subsequently formed the California Prison Moratorium Project.

Competing Views of Justice

In addition to, and perhaps in response to, complaints about how contemporary criminal justice was adversely affecting victims and prisoners, several movements arose to challenge its very conception of justice. These were the informal justice, indigenous justice, reparative justice, and social justice movements.

Informal Justice

■ ■ ■ ━━━

> Conflict is not something to be solved, but something to be owned. The criminal justice system represents a theft by the state of the victim and offender's conflict.

━━━ ■ ■ ■

The informal justice critique developed in the 1970s with the recognition by legal anthropologists that legal structures and ways of thinking about law are specific to particular times and places, and that in virtually all societies, justice is pursued using both formal and informal proceedings. Because the legal system confronted a growing crisis of confidence in the legitimacy of its formal structures, a series of proposals followed for informal alternatives, with "an emphasis on (a) increased participation, (b) more access to law, (c) deprofessionalization, decentralization, and delegalization, and (d) the minimization of stigmatization and coercion."[23] Two of the leading proponents of informal justice were Jerold S. Auerbach (whose *Justice without Law?*[24] argued forcefully for the need to deprofessionalize the justice system) and Nils Christie. Christie has been frequently cited in restorative justice literature because of several key themes in his work.

Christie, a Norwegian, suggested in the 1977 article, "Conflict as Property," that conflict is not in fact something to be "solved" but something to be possessed. The criminal justice system, from this perspective, reflects a theft by the state of the victim and offender's conflict. This represents a real and a serious loss:

> *This loss is first and foremost a loss in opportunities for norm-clarification. It is a loss of pedagogical possibilities. It is a loss of opportunities for a continuous discussion of what represents the law of the land. How wrong was the thief, how right was the victim? Lawyers are, as we say, trained into agreement on what is relevant in a case. But that means a trained incapacity in letting the parties decide what they think is relevant. It means that it is difficult to stage what we might call a political debate in the court.*[25]

In his subsequent book on punishment, *Limits to Pain*, Christie drew a connection between this "theft" and the use of punishment. In criminal law, values are clarified by graduated punishment. "The state establishes its scale, the rank-order of values, through variation in the number of blows administered to the criminal, or through the number of months or years taken away from him."[26] Rather than being made clear through conversation among the participants—the rightful "owners" of the conflict—values are communicated by the state through the infliction of pain. He proposed participatory justice as a better response to crime, a response characterized by direct communication between the owners of the conflict leading to compensation.

Indigenous Justice

Related to informal justice have been studies and reflections on what are called customary, traditional, or indigenous approaches to justice. These are the approaches used by people prior to, or alongside of, the Western concepts of justice introduced by colonizers. Indigenous practices have contributed to restorative justice in at least three ways. First, they have demonstrated that justice practices may reflect an intention to repair harm rather than simply to inflict equivalent harm. Second, as we discuss in Chapter 2, several restorative processes (conferencing and circles) have their roots in indigenous practices: Conferencing was adapted from practices of the Maori people in New Zealand and circles from the traditions of First Nations people in Canada. Third, in many non-Western countries, the memories of indigenous practices have contributed to acceptance of restorative justice theory and practice.

Reparative Justice

Restitution as a reform initiative developed from the rediscovery in the 1960s that paying back the victim could be a sensible criminal justice sanction. Several rationales were offered for restitution: (1) The victim is the party harmed by criminal behavior, (2) alternatives to restrictive or intrusive sanctions such as imprisonment are needed, (3) there may be rehabilitative value in requiring the offender to pay the victim, (4) restitution is relatively easy to implement, and (5) this might lead to a reduction in retributive sanctions when the public observes the offender actively repairing the harm done. Evaluations conducted in the 1970s and 1980s raised questions about whether restitution programs had lived up to those expectations,[27] but restitution has been increasingly ordered (and less frequently collected) in many countries nonetheless.

■ ■ ■ ──────────────────────────────────────

> Criminal justice policy is based on the partial truth that crime is lawbreaking. Its flaw is that it ignores another critical dimension of crime.

────────────────────────────────────── ■ ■ ■

One of the earliest proponents of restitution was Stephen Schafer,[28] who made a comprehensive and influential case for reinstating the historic role of restitutionary sanctions. In his writings, he described the era of compensatory justice prior to the development of centralized governments in Europe as the "golden age of the victim" because it was a time in which the victim's interests and freedom of action were given greatest deference. He proposed that compensation could once again become a means of sanctioning offenders, either in conjunction with or as an alternative to imprisonment.

Charles F. Abel and Frank A. Marsh, in their 1984 book *Punishment and Restitution*,[29] argued that restitution offers an approach to punishment that is ethically, conceptually, and practically superior to contemporary criminal justice. In their model, imprisonment should be used only as a last resort for offenders who pose a danger to the community, and those who are imprisoned should be given the opportunity and obligation to earn wages and compensate the victim (and the state for the cost of their incarceration). Most offenders, however, would live outside prison under varying degrees of supervision as necessary, working and paying restitution.

Randy Barnett and John Hagel argued in *Assessing the Criminal*[30] that criminal law should be abolished and replaced with the civil law of torts. They suggested that restitution constitutes a new paradigm of justice, one that is preferable to criminal justice. Crime should be defined by exploring the rights of the victim, not the behavior of the offender. The rights of society are satisfied, they contended, when the rights of individual victims within it are vindicated through restitution.

Social Justice

Gerald Austin McHugh's *Christian Faith and Criminal Justice*[31] argued that penal models in America grew out of a medieval Christian view of sin and punishment, but that this was not the only relevant motif inherent in the Christian faith, which also affirms values of mercy, relationship, restoration, forgiveness, reconciliation, and hope. He suggested that such values, if applied to criminal justice policy, would result in very different structures and processes from those now in place. Similar biblical reflection has been offered by members of the Mennonite tradition in North America, resulting in a wealth of literature and programs on alternatives to current approaches.

■ ■ ■ ▬▬▬▬▬▬▬▬▬▬▬▬▬▬▬▬▬▬▬▬▬▬▬▬▬▬▬▬▬▬▬▬▬▬▬

> The Christian faith not only speaks of sin and punishment but also affirms mercy, relationship, restoration, forgiveness, reconciliation, and hope.

▬▬▬▬▬▬▬▬▬▬▬▬▬▬▬▬▬▬▬▬▬▬▬▬▬▬▬▬▬▬▬▬ ■ ■ ■

Drawing from his experience as a prisoner and then as an advocate of volunteer involvement within the correctional environment, Charles Colson offered a critique from a different theological perspective. He argued that criminal justice must underscore personal responsibility, and that consequently restitution should be used instead of imprisonment for offenders who do not pose a danger to society.[32] His colleague, Daniel W. Van Ness, contended in *Crime and Its Victims*[33] that biblical justice is highly concerned with the needs and rights of victims, as well as with the worth of offenders. He proposed a series of public policy implications growing out of this premise.

Feminist scholar M. Kay Harris called for a fundamental restructuring of criminal justice to reflect feminist values—"that all people have equal value as human beings, that harmony and felicity are more important than power and possession, and that the personal is the political"[34]—in place of the values of control and punishment. She suggested that preoccupation with rights blinds parties to the need for a caring and interdependent response.

Recognition of the broader dimensions of justice would increase awareness of the need and opportunity for participation by all parties in order to address the needs of all.

In 1991, criminologists Hal Pepinsky and Richard Quinney edited a book titled *Criminology as Peacemaking*.[35] Rather than adopting a negative focus, as does criminology ("What causes deviance and criminal behavior?") and criminal justice policy ("How do we win the war on crime and violence?"), this book examined the factors that positively contribute to peace and safety. Pepinsky explained elsewhere, "I seek to understand how we become safer in the face of violence. I want to find out what safety is and how we get more of it with one another."[36]

John Fuller identified the focus of peacemaking as social justice, conflict resolution, rehabilitation, and cooperation. Meaningful communities, he wrote, emerge from democratic institutions and practices in which crime is not excused but in which both individual responsibility and society's contribution are considered. It is only by transforming both the criminal and society that a community can develop effective, fair, and humane responses to crime.[37]

Conclusion

None of these critiques or reform efforts alone has led to restorative justice theory, but all have influenced its development. Although there is significant common ground—and also notable differences—among them, much in restorative justice theory and practice has been drawn from these predecessors, as we shall see in Chapter 2.

Review Questions

1. Why are patterns of thinking relevant to the discussion of criminal justice?
2. The ancient pattern of thinking was that offenders and their families should help restore community peace by making amends. The contemporary pattern is that crime is lawbreaking and society's goal in responding to the offender should be to reduce future crime. What changes did the shift from the ancient to the contemporary approach bring about for crime victims? For offenders?
3. In what ways are the critiques of contemporary criminal justice made by the victim rights and prison abolition movements similar? In what ways are they different?
4. Which of the competing views of justice described in Chapter 1 seems most compelling to you? Why?

Endnotes

1. Peter C. Hart Research Associates, Inc., "Changing Public Attitudes Toward the Criminal Justice System" (Open Society Institute, February 2002). Text available online at http://www.opensocietyfoundations. org/reports/changing-public-attitudes-toward-criminal-justice-system as of August 1, 2013. A more in-depth resource on victims' attitudes is Mark Umbreit *et al.*, *Victim Meets Offender: The Impact of Restorative Justice and Mediation* (Monsey, NY: Criminal Justice Press, 1994).

2. Howard Zehr, *Changing Lenses: A New Focus for Crime and Justice* (Scottdale, PA: Herald Press, 1990), 86–87.

3. Edward de Bono, *Conflicts: A Better Way to Resolve Them* (New York: Penguin, 1991).

4. Some commentators have argued that restorative justice proponents use history selectively, offering a partial and misleading account of the past in an effort to legitimize restorative justice. (See, for example, Douglas J. Sylvester, "Myth in Restorative Justice History," *Utah Law Review* (2003): 1445–1496, and Kelly Richards, "Exploring the History of the Restorative Justice Movement," paper presented at the 5th International Conference on Conferencing & Circles, organized by the International Institute for Restorative Practices, August 5–7, 2004, Vancouver, Canada). We are not historians, and our purpose here is not to offer a complete view of criminal justice in the past. The systems that included restitution, that gave an important status to the needs of victims, and that sought to repair broken relationships within communities also had other elements that were nothing like restorative justice. Furthermore, powerful victims received different treatment than those who were poor and powerless. We agree that it is important not to view the past with rose-tinted glasses.

   This short historical review is provided for two reasons. The first reason is to demonstrate that at one time, societal responses to crime included elements that until recently were entirely omitted from contemporary criminal justice. The second reason is strategic. Restorative justice is sometimes discounted on first hearing as an outlandish, naive attempt to accomplish something impossible. Anecdotes are somewhat useful in countering this, but they can be discarded as exceptional cases. So the appeal to those elements of legal history that are similar to restorative justice themes is an appeal to suspend any immediate judgment that these themes are strange, untested, and never-before-conceived-of. The argument we make in this chapter is that a reason we may discount the ideas behind restorative justice is because we unknowingly operate within a pattern of thinking that leads us to this conclusion. There are in fact other possible patterns of thought.

5. See, for example, Exodus 22 and Leviticus 6. Restitution did not necessarily mean that justice was done. A Psalm attributed to King David complained that he was forced to restore what he had not stolen (Psalm 69:4). But the idea of restitution was so well accepted that it forms the backdrop of a New Testament story about a corrupt tax collector (Luke 19) and another about a runaway slave (Philemon).

6. We distinguish *shalom* from the irrational belief that the world is basically a safe and just place in which to live. Psychologist Melvin Lerner has concluded that humans need to believe that people basically get what they deserve, that the world is just and safe even when events suggest otherwise. This self-delusion, Lerner argues, is necessary in order for people to function in their daily lives. Melvin J. Lerner, *The Belief in a Just World: A Fundamental Delusion* (New York: Plenum, 1980), 11–15. But the Hebrew word *shalom* does not imply a delusional belief that all is well. To hold healing and shalom as goals for society's response to crime is to recognize that hurt and injustice do exist, and that they must be healed and rectified.

7. How is it that a root word meaning "wholeness and unity, a restored relationship" could produce derivatives with such varied meanings in the Hebrew Scriptures? "The apparent diversity of meanings ... can be accounted for in terms of the concept of peace being restored through payment (of tribute to a conqueror, Joshua 10:1), restitution (to one wronged, Exodus 21:36), or simple payment and completion (of a business transaction, II Kings 4:7). The payment of a vow (Psalm 50:14) completes an agreement so that both parties are in a state of shalom. Closely linked with this concept is the eschatological motif in some uses of the term. Recompense for sin, either national or personal, must be given. Once that obligation has been met, wholeness is restored (Isaiah 60:20, Joel 2:25)." G. Lloyd Carr, "Shalom," in R. L. Harris *et al.*, eds., *Theological Wordbook of the Old Testament* (Chicago: Moody Press, 1980), 931.

8. *Leges Henrici Primi* 109 (L. J. Downer, ed. & trans., 1972).

9. Frederick Pollock, "English Law before the Norman Conquest," *The Law Quarterly Review* 14 (1898): 291, 301.

10. Vivien Stern, *A Sin against the Future: Imprisonment in the World* (London: Penguin, 1998), 16–17.

11. Norval Morris and David Rothman, eds., *The Oxford History of the Prison: The Practice of Punishment in Western Society* (New York: Oxford University Press, 1995).

12. Andrew Skotnicki, *Criminal Justice and the Catholic Church* (Lanham, MD: Sheed & Ward, 2008), 73–103.

13. Quoted in Blake McKelvey, *American Prisons: A History of Good Intentions* (Montclair, NJ: Patterson Smith, 1977), 7.

14. Morris and Rothman, supra note 11, at 115.

15. Juan Cardenas, "The Crime Victim in the Prosecutorial Process," *Harvard Journal of Law and Public Policy* 9 (1986): 359, 360, 367.

16. Douglas Hay and Francis Snyder, eds., "Using the Criminal Law, 1750–1850: Policing, Private Prosecution, and the State," in *Policing and Prosecution in Britain 1750–1850* (Oxford: Clarendon, 1989), 3.

17. Allen Steinberg, *The Transformation of Criminal Justice: Philadelphia, 1800–1880* (Chapel Hill: University of North Carolina Press, 1989).

18. Ibid., 78.

19. Subsequently reissued as Morton Bard and Dawn Sangrey, *The Crime Victim's Book*, 2nd ed. (Secaucus, NJ: Citadel Press, 1986).

20. Albert R. Roberts, *Helping Crime Victims: Research, Policy, and Practice* (Newbury Park, CA: Sage, 1990).

21. William F. McDonald, ed., *Criminal Justice and the Victim* (Beverly Hills, CA: Sage, 1976).

22. G. Richard Bacon, *et al.*, *Struggle for Justice: A Report on Crime and Punishment in America* (New York: Hill & Wang, 1971).

23. Roger Matthews, "Reassessing Informal Justice," in Roger Matthews, ed., *Informal Justice?* (Newbury Park, CA: Sage, 1988).

24. Jerold S. Auerbach, *Justice without Law?* (New York: Oxford University Press, 1983).

25. Nils Christie, "Conflict as Property," *British Journal of Criminology* 17(2) (1977): 1, 8.

26. Nils Christie, *Limits to Pain* (Oslo-Bergen-Tromsø: Universitetsforlaget, 1981), 94.

27. See, for example, Joe Hudson and Burt Galaway, "Financial Restitution: Toward an Evaluable Program Model," *Canadian Journal of Criminology* 31 (1989): 1–8.

28. Stephen Schafer, *Victimology: The Victim and His Criminal* (Reston, VA: Reston, 1968). See also Stephen Schafer, *Compensation and Restitution to Victims of Crime* (Montclair, NJ: Patterson Smith, 1970); Stephen Schafer, "Victim Compensation and Responsibility," *Southern California Law Review* 43 (1970): 55; and Stephen Schafer, "The Restitutive Concept of Punishment," in Joe Hudson and Burt Galaway, eds., *Considering the Victim* (Springfield, IL: Charles C Thomas, 1975).

29. Charles F. Abel and Frank A. Marsh, *Punishment and Restitution: A Restitutionary Approach to Crime and the Criminal* (Westport, CT: Greenwood Press, 1984).

30. Randy E. Barnett and John Hagel, eds., *Assessing the Criminal: Restitution, Retribution, and the Legal Process* (Cambridge, MA: Ballinger, 1977), 1, 15. See Chapter 8 for a critique of this position.

31. Gerald A. McHugh, *Christian Faith and Criminal Justice: Toward A Christian Response to Crime and Punishment* (New York: Paulist Press, 1978).

32. Charles W. Colson, "Towards an Understanding of the Origins of Crime" and "Towards an Understanding of Imprisonment and Rehabilitation," in John Stott and Nick Miller, eds., *Crime and the Responsible Community: A Christian Contribution to the Debate about Criminal Justice* (London: Hodder & Stoughton, 1980).

33. Daniel W. Van Ness, *Crime and Its Victims: What We Can Do* (Downers Grove, IL: InterVarsity Press, 1986).

34. M. Kay Harris, "Moving into the New Millennium: Toward a Feminist Vision of Justice," *The Prison Journal* 67(2) (1987): 27–38. Kathleen Daly and Julie Stubbs observe that feminist thought concerning alternative justice approaches has changed over time. Kathleen Daly and Julie Stubbs, "Feminist Theory, Feminist and Anti-Racist Politics, and Restorative Justice" in Gerry Johnstone and Daniel W. Van Ness, eds., *Handbook of Restorative Justice*. (Cullompton, UK: Willan, 2007), 152–55.

35. Harold E. Pepinsky and Richard Quinney, eds., *Criminology as Peacemaking* (Bloomington: Indiana University Press, 1991).

36. Hal Pepinsky, "Empathy Works, Obedience Doesn't," *Contemporary Justice Review* 3(2) (2000): 175–186. (Also available online at http://cdn.umb.edu/images/bcvi/Empathy_Works,_Obedience_Doesnt_Pepinsky.pdf as of August 1, 2013.)

37. John R. Fuller, *Criminal Justice: A Peacemaking Perspective* (Needham Heights, MA: Allyn & Bacon, 1997).

A Brief History of Restorative Justice
The Development of a New Pattern of Thinking

KEY CONCEPTS

- Restorative justice terminology
- Developers of restorative justice ideas and processes
- Restorative programs
- Restorative justice and criminal justice policy
- Significant milestones

To date, there has been no serious effort to record the history of the modern development of restorative justice. This is a project that needs to be done as the field moves into its fourth decade; before long, people, documents, and memories will be gone, and it will be much more difficult not only to collect information but also to understand how the pieces fit together. In some places, restorative thinking and practices developed internally and it was only later that connections were made with others from other countries or continents. Elsewhere, restorative programs and ideas were imported from outside and adapted to the local context.

We will not attempt such a thorough history in this chapter but instead will offer a kind of "patchwork history" by focusing on particular topics. First, we consider how the term *restorative justice* came to be used. Next, we examine some of the early attempts to articulate the vision and theory of restorative justice. Then we consider the development of three prototypical restorative processes: victim–offender mediation, conferencing, and circles. We follow this by reviewing the steady incorporation of restorative principles and practices into the criminal justice system. Finally, we present a time line outlining key events in the development and expansion of restorative justice worldwide.

The Term *Restorative Justice*

To the best of our knowledge, the first use of the term *restorative justice* in the context of criminal justice was by Albert Eglash in several 1958 articles in which he suggested that there are three types of criminal justice: (1) retributive justice, based on punishment; (2) distributive justice, based on therapeutic treatment of offenders; and (3) restorative justice, based on restitution.[1] Both punishment and treatment models, he noted, focus on the actions of offenders, deny victim participation in the justice process, and require merely passive participation by the offender. Restorative justice, on the other hand, focuses on the harmful effects of offenders' actions and actively involves victims and offenders in the process of reparation and rehabilitation.

As discussed in Chapter 3, people do not necessarily mean the same thing when they speak of restorative justice or describe particular programs or interventions as restorative. In his highly influential book, *Changing Lenses*, Howard Zehr described restorative justice as follows: "Crime is a violation of people and relationships. It creates obligations to make things right. Justice involves the victim, the offender, and the community in a search for solutions which promote repair, reconciliation, and reassurance."[2]

Tony Marshall described it as "a process whereby all the parties with a stake in a particular offense come together to resolve collectively how to deal with the aftermath of the offense and its implications for the future."[3] Martin Wright has argued that the new model should be one in which

> *the response to crime would be, not to add to the harm caused by imposing further harm on the offender, but to do as much as possible to restore the situation. The community offers aid to the victim; the offender is held accountable and required to make reparation. Attention would be given not only to the outcome, but also to evolving a process that respected the feelings and humanity of both the victim and the offender.[4]*

The differences may be due in part to the diverse critiques and reform efforts that contributed to restorative justice theory. It may also be that each description is partial, like those of blindfolded people explaining what elephants are like based on the part they happen to be touching—the trunk, the leg, the tail. Adding to the confusion, some have chosen to use alternative names to describe what others call restorative justice. Ruth Morris spoke of "transformative justice," emphasizing that crime is not simply a violation of people and relationships but that it also offers an opportunity for a transformation of those people and relationships; such a transformation would deal with the causes of crime and increase safety in the community.[5] Jonathan Burnside and Nicola Baker used the term *relational justice*, highlighting the importance of crime's relational (and not simply its legal) dimensions.[6] Marlene Young proposed *restorative community justice* to stress both the importance of community involvement and the value and potency of community action in crime prevention.[7]

■ ■ ■ ▬▬▬▬▬▬▬▬▬▬▬▬▬▬▬▬▬▬▬▬▬▬▬▬▬▬▬▬▬▬▬▬▬▬▬▬▬▬

Victim-offender mediation, conferencing, and circles began independently of restorative thinking. They have been embraced as restorative, and they have influenced restorative theory.

▬▬▬▬▬▬▬▬▬▬▬▬▬▬▬▬▬▬▬▬▬▬▬▬▬▬▬▬▬▬▬▬▬▬▬▬ ■ ■ ■

There is no authoritative body with the responsibility or credibility to make final determinations concerning what is or is not restorative. Furthermore, the field has developed in piecemeal fashion, over a period of time, and in different areas of the world. Processes now considered core to restorative justice developed independently of restorative thinking. They have been embraced as restorative, and they have influenced and been influenced by efforts to conceptualize restorative theory. Furthermore, innovations coming from outside restorative justice, such as victim assistance, community policing, and problem-solving courts, appear to reflect elements of restorative thinking. Thus, before considering the definition of restorative justice, it might be useful to sketch out a history of its development and growth. We begin by looking at the writings of people who influenced early restorative justice theory.

Explorers of Restorative Justice Theory

To many, Howard Zehr is the "grandfather" of restorative justice; he was certainly one of the first articulators of restorative justice theory. His interest grew out of work with victim–offender reconciliation programs, and his articles, speeches, books, and teaching have profoundly influenced the field. In his 1990 book, *Changing Lenses,*[8] he consolidated and advanced his critique of criminal justice as failing to meet the needs of victims or offenders. He suggested that the current criminal justice "lens" views crime as lawbreaking and justice as allocating blame and punishment. He contrasted that with restorative justice, which views crime as a violation of people and relationships, which in turn leads to obligations to "make things right" and views justice as a process in which all parties search for reparative, reconciling, and reassuring solutions.[9]

Martin Wright's prolific and important work has contributed to the development of restorative justice thinking and practice, particularly in Europe. In his 1991 book, *Justice for Victims and Offenders,*[10] he drew from his experiences as an advocate for victims and as an advocate for prison reform in arguing that criminal justice should be restorative rather than retributive. He argued that the present exclusion of victims from the system could be remedied by expanding compensation, restitution, and mediation processes to permit greater participation by both victims and offenders. He suggested that such a model might be constructed by creating two governmental departments. The first, responsible for crime prevention, would emphasize deterrence through enforcement rather than deterrence through punishment. The second department would be responsible for a just response to crimes when they do occur. This would include victim support, mediation, and reparation, as well as courts that emphasize restitution.[11]

In 1992, Virginia Mackey wrote an evocative "discussion paper" on restorative justice for the Criminal Justice Program of the Presbyterian Church (USA).[12] This document was intended to facilitate conversation within that faith community on the problems of current approaches to crime and on biblically reflective alternatives. Using Fay Honey Knopp's terminology, she proposed a "Community Safety/Restorative Model"[13] predicated on six principles: (1) that safety should be the primary consideration for the community, (2) that offenders should be held responsible and accountable for their behavior and the resulting harm, (3) that victims and communities harmed by crime need restoration, (4) that the underlying conflicts that led to the harm should be resolved if possible, (5) that there must be a continuum of service or treatment options available, and (6) that there must be a coordinated and cooperative system in place that incorporates both public and private resources.

With the publication of Wesley Cragg's *The Practice of Punishment*[14] that same year, the discussion of restorative justice took a more conceptual turn. Cragg, a philosopher and a long-time volunteer with a prisoner advocacy and prison reform organization, revisited foundational theoretical positions on the role and use of punishment. He criticized traditional justifications but insisted on the importance of formal processes in which conflict can be resolved. These formal processes, however, should provide within their frameworks the opportunity for informal resolution and offender acceptance of responsibility. Formal justice, in his view, need not be antithetical to virtues such as forgiveness, compassion, mercy, and understanding; what was antithetical in his view was an insistence on punishment, the sole justification of which is to cause suffering.[15]

Others have also attempted to find theoretical frameworks within which to understand and analyze restorative justice. *Reintegrative shaming* is the term John Braithwaite used in 1989 for his theories concerning the causes and consequences of crime,[16] but it was not until a family group conferencing program was being organized in Wagga Wagga, New South Wales, Australia, that reintegrative shaming and restorative justice were intentionally linked. In 1993, David Moore proposed that the work of Silvan Tomkins and Donald Nathanson may offer a "psychology of reintegrative shaming"[17] and reflected on this approach to crime and reintegration from the perspective of moral psychology, moral philosophy, and political theory.[18] He concluded that reintegrative shaming offered a framework for theoretical analysis and evaluation of conferencing programs.

In a 1993 exchange in the journal *Criminal Law Forum*, Daniel Van Ness and Andrew Ashworth debated the case for restorative justice and the role of victims in the criminal justice process. In his article, Van Ness suggested that there was a historical basis for questioning the criminal–civil separation in Western legal systems and for establishing criminal justice objectives that aimed at addressing the harms experienced by all stakeholders. Ashworth warned that it is important to distinguish between the needs of victims for assistance and any rights that they might have in criminal courts. He also cautioned about attempting to accomplish larger criminal justice goals through sentencing policy.

An attempt to root restorative concepts within a larger conceptual framework was offered in a 1994 book edited by Jonathan Burnside and Nicola Baker titled *Relational Justice*.[19] Noting the decline in the quality of relationships in Western cultures, these authors considered whether "relationalism" might offer an antidote to problems plaguing criminal justice. Although not specifically referring to restorative justice theory, contributors presented victim–offender mediation and family group conferences as examples of relational justice, and they suggested ways the activities of police, probation, and prison authorities might be evaluated by their capacity to strengthen relationships.

Although a number of writers have noted in passing that restorative justice principles may have relevance to crime prevention, one of the more comprehensive proposals on that aspect of criminal justice policy was offered by Marlene A. Young, then Executive Director of the U.S.-based National Organization for Victim Assistance, in her 1995 paper *Restorative Community Justice: A Call to Action*.[20] After defining restorative community justice, she reviewed a series of program elements that might constitute a model of such a system, including community policing, community prosecution, community courts, and community corrections. The first, community policing, involves police officers actively building strong community bonds within the neighborhoods in which they function. The other three are similar: Community prosecution involves a shift from reactive prosecution to proactive problem solving within the community; community courts increase the level of victim and community participation during adjudication; and community corrections offers communities and victims meaningful ways of participating in the correctional process.

Programs Offering Restorative Processes

Victim–Offender Mediation

Three key programs have influenced the development of restorative justice. The first is victim–offender mediation. Although there were attempts during the 1960s and 1970s to bring victims and offenders together in restitution programs,[21] the origin of the modern restorative justice movement is generally located in Elmira, Ontario, Canada, in 1974. Two intoxicated young men, ages 18 and 19 years, had vandalized the houses and cars of 22 people. They pleaded guilty, and while the probation officer, Mark Yantzi, was preparing a report to the judge, he had a conversation with Dave Worth, a volunteer from the Mennonite Central Committee. In the course of the conversation, they agreed that prison or probation would probably not have the kind of effect on the defendants that meeting the victims, listening to their stories, apologizing, and paying restitution would have. Although the judge was initially resistant to the idea, he ended up ordering that the young men do this as a condition of probation. The results of the meeting were sufficiently positive that judges continued to order this process from time to time. In 1976, the probation officer formed a nonprofit organization to provide and promote these meetings.

The program attracted interest from Canada and the United States, largely through publicity by the Mennonite Central Committee. Three of the earliest practitioners and writers on mediation in the United States were Howard Zehr, Ron Claassen, and Mark Umbreit. Umbreit has produced a series of articles and books explaining and evaluating victim–offender mediation, including the use of such programs in cases of violent crime.[22] Zehr and Claassen, who themselves are members of the Mennonite Christian tradition, have maintained that church-based—or at least, community-based—programs offer greater potential than state-run programs for helping the parties move toward genuine healing. The community base strengthens the vitality of victim–offender mediation, and it is preferable (even though it may be more work) to organize programs in this way rather than as a part of, or funded by, the criminal justice system.[23]

■ ■ ■ ▬▬▬▬▬▬▬▬▬▬▬▬▬▬▬▬▬▬▬▬▬▬▬▬▬▬▬▬▬▬▬▬▬▬▬▬▬▬

Early victim–offender mediation began as a program to impact offenders and to help them understand the harm they caused to victims.

▬▬▬▬▬▬▬▬▬▬▬▬▬▬▬▬▬▬▬▬▬▬▬▬▬▬▬▬▬▬▬▬▬▬▬▬▬ ■ ■ ■

Thus, early victim–offender mediation began as a program to impact offenders and to help them understand the harm they caused to victims. It also began as a community-based program rather than one carried out by the criminal justice system. Early programs called themselves victim–offender *reconciliation* programs, wanting to emphasize the relational impact that the process could have.

However, as the programs expanded throughout North America and then throughout the world, they began to be used by probation offices and other governmental agencies as well as by community-based groups. Many began using the terms *mediation* or *dialogue* instead of *reconciliation* because of concern that the latter term sounded too religious. Eventually, victim–offender meetings began taking place even when there was no expectation that they would influence the sentence of the offender in any way. For example, in 1991, the Texas prison system began allowing victims and survivors of serious violent crimes the opportunity to meet with their offender (after careful screening, if they request it). The purpose of the meeting is for the victim and offender to achieve some level of healing.

Apparently, independently of what was happening in North America, victim–offender mediation programs began to be tested in Scandinavian countries. This was in response to Norwegian scholar Nils Christie's thesis that criminal justice is a process through which the government has "stolen" a conflict that ought to be owned by victims and offenders. The initial pilots were attempts to explore how victims and offenders might be given a role as primary participants. The first pilot began in 1981 in Norway and was sufficiently successful that by the end of the decade, approximately 20% of the country's municipalities offered mediation. These programs tended to be settlement-driven (as opposed to dialogue-driven). Two years later, similar programs began in Finland and England, although it is fairly clear that some of the influences in England came from North America. From these beginning points, it spread throughout Europe and beyond. Some of the key individuals in introducing mediation to Europe were Juhani Ilivari of Finland, John Harding and Martin Wright of England, and Frieder Dünkel and Dieter Rössner of Germany.[24]

Conferencing

In 1989, the government of New Zealand adopted a new approach to dealing with young offenders. The Children, Young Persons and Their Families Act created the family group conference and used it to replace Youth Court for most young offenders (between 14 and 16 years of age, inclusive). This dramatic reform was the result of increasing concern about the juvenile justice system, following 5 years of monitoring and studying the impact of that system on Maori communities. It became evident that the Maori were very concerned about the increasing numbers of their children who were being removed from their families to state facilities by courts. Maori culture is communitarian rather than individualistic, but each individual is a critically important part of the family. Removing a child is destructive of Maori culture because it impairs the family and because children are considered to be the future of the Maori people. The Maori have processes to deal with conflict, but those essentially involve the family in a process of conversation to understand the problem and to find a solution. The solution is generally collective rather than individualistic—the family of the offender assumes responsibility for making things right with the victim and the victim's family.

Family group conferencing, as created in the legislation, has some similarities with the Maori processes; it also is different in important respects. However, conferencing did take the power to decide what should happen from the judge and place it in the hands of the conference. The community people required to be at the conference are the offenders and members of their family or support group; victims are invited, but if the victims cannot or will not come, the conference can proceed nonetheless.

The New Zealand approach is based in social welfare, not the criminal justice system. An Australian police officer, Terry O'Connell, learned about the New Zealand model and adapted it for use by police as an alternative to charging young offenders with juvenile offenses. He and some colleagues developed a script for police officers to use in facilitating the conferences. In other respects, the New Zealand model and the "Wagga Wagga" model of conferencing are similar. Both have been adapted to address adult offenders and are being increasingly used throughout the world.

Conferencing differs from victim–offender mediation in several ways, but one of the most notable is that more people are included in the meetings: In addition to the victim and offender are family members, supporters, and government representatives. Gale Burford, Joan Pennell, Paul McCold, Gabrielle Maxwell, and Allison Morris are some of the leading researchers and expositors of this model.[25]

Circles

A third method of restorative encounter emerged at approximately the same time as conferencing, this one also having indigenous roots. Known variously as sentencing circles, community circles, and healing circles, these processes drew on aboriginal understandings of justice among the First Nations people of Canada. The first known instance of applying the circle process to a sentencing hearing took place in the town of Mayo in the Yukon Territory of Canada and is reported in a 1992 opinion by the trial judge, Barry Stuart.[26] The case involved a 26-year-old offender with a long history of alcohol abuse and 43 criminal convictions. He had been in and out of jails and other state institutions; each time, the assessments stated that he needed long-term counseling and substance abuse treatment, among other interventions. These were never provided.

Concerned that this cycle could not be broken by ordering standard criminal justice processes, the judge, probation officer, and Crown counsel began to explore whether there were ways that the sentencing determination could include his family, leadership of his Nation, the victim, and other members of the community. After conversations with the Chief and other First Nations members, the judge modified the physical setting of the courtroom by creating a circle with 30 chairs in which the judge, lawyers, police, First Nations officials and members, probation officer, victim, and others could sit. After opening remarks by the judge and the Crown and defense counsel, the hearing became an informal conversation as discussion moved around the circle. In the end, the First Nations community agreed to help the offender and his family as he dealt with his substance abuse, the offender agreed to a three-part program of treatment, and his family agreed to support him in his change process in tangible ways.

The judge identified a number of advantages to using a circle process as opposed to a traditional sentencing hearing. It challenged the monopoly of the professionals, encouraged lay participation, enhanced the amount and quality of information available, led to a creative search for new options, promoted a sense of shared responsibility, encouraged the offender to participate, involved the victim in sentencing, created a constructive environment, provided everyone with a greater understanding of the limitations of the justice system, extended the focus of the criminal justice system beyond blame to the underlying causes, helped mobilize community resources, and helped merge the values of the First Nation with those of the Canadian government.

Circles have expanded into many areas of North America and are beginning to appear on other continents as well. They are the most inclusive of the three processes, with interested members of the community allowed to participate even if they have no relationship with the victim or offender. Aboriginal leaders have included Berma Bushie of the Hollow Water Community Holistic Circle Healing Program. In addition, non-aboriginals such as Barry Stuart, Bria Huculak, and Kay Pranis have helped adapt circles to non-aboriginal contexts.[27]

Incorporation of Restorative Justice into Criminal Justice Systems

In an increasing number of countries, restorative justice is one of several competing approaches to crime and justice regularly considered by courts and legislatures. As a result, governments are supporting the development or expansion of restorative programs, and many are modifying legislation to provide for restorative interventions.

Some governments have invested substantial resources into restorative programs. Agencies within the U.S. Department of Justice, for example, sponsored a number of initiatives during the 1990s, such as the Office of Juvenile Justice and Delinquency Prevention's Balanced and Restorative Justice Project (BARJ), administered by Gordon Bazemore and colleagues at Florida Atlantic University. Beginning in 1994, BARJ offered training, technical support, and consultation to state and local officials establishing restorative justice programs. From 1997, the National Institute of Corrections established demonstration projects and provided leader-led and videoconferencing training on restorative justice for criminal justice officials and policymakers through its Academy Division.

■ ■ ■ ▬▬▬▬▬▬▬▬▬▬▬▬▬▬▬▬▬▬▬▬▬▬▬▬▬▬▬▬▬▬▬▬▬▬▬▬▬

Increasingly, restorative justice is being considered by courts and legislatures. Governments are funding the development of restorative programs, and many are modifying their laws to allow restorative interventions.

▬▬▬▬▬▬▬▬▬▬▬▬▬▬▬▬▬▬▬▬▬▬▬▬▬▬▬▬▬▬▬▬▬▬▬▬▬ ■ ■ ■

The Canadian government has similarly invested resources in training and development of restorative justice programs at the provincial and federal levels. In addition, the federal government adopted sentencing reform legislation in 1995 that incorporated restorative justice in its sentencing principles, legislation that the Supreme Court of Canada stated has marked a "reorientation" in sentencing policy. Even more extensive reforms were contained in its Youth Criminal Justice Act.

New Zealand's Children, Young Persons and Their Families Act, discussed in the previous section, has now been joined by legislation providing restorative processes for adult offenders. A number of states in Australia have adopted juvenile justice bills that are variations on the theme sounded by New Zealand. Similarly, Uganda, South Africa, and other African nations have enacted legislation providing for the use of various restorative practices. Many European countries have adopted restorative approaches to juvenile and adult offending; of particular interest is how former Soviet bloc countries have made mediation and other restorative processes part of their post-Communist codes concerning criminal and juvenile justice. Some Asian and Latin American countries have begun to provide legislative support and openings for restorative processes.

Restorative processes have been used to resolve conflict between citizens and their governments. Bishop Desmond Tutu has described the Truth and Reconciliation Commission in South Africa as an expression of restorative justice. New Zealand appointed a tribunal to provide redress for violations of the Treaty of Waitangi in 1840 between the Queen and the (indigenous) Maori chiefs. This process, which resulted in several very large financial settlements from the government to particular tribes, has been characterized by steps that go far beyond negotiation of restitution to attempts at cultural reconciliation. In the United Kingdom, the Thames Valley police force has used conferencing to resolve citizen complaints against the police.

Intergovernmental bodies have taken note of restorative justice. In 1999, the Committee of Ministers of the Council of Europe adopted a recommendation on the use of mediation in penal matters. That same year, the European Union (EU) funded creation of the European Forum for Victim–Offender Mediation and Restorative Justice. The EU subsequently adopted legislation to encourage use of restorative justice by its members. In 2002, the United Nations Economic and Social Council (ECOSOC) endorsed a *Declaration of Basic Principles on the Use of Restorative Justice Programmes in Criminal Matters*, designed not only to encourage global use of restorative justice but also to provide guidelines for incorporating restorative approaches into criminal justice without violating the human rights of victims and offenders.

Time Line of Significant Developments Related to Restorative Processes

On the following pages is a time line identifying some of the significant developments related to restorative processes. For reasons of space, it certainly does not record *all* significant developments. In deciding what to include, we looked for (1) initial use of restorative processes in a country, (2) initial recognition of restorative processes in legislation, and (3) events that seem in retrospect to have been very important in the subsequent development and use of restorative processes. Examples of the last criterion include significant conferences, pivotal studies, and the creation of organizations that have played or are playing key roles. We have focused more on beginnings than on later developments; for example, we have noted early legislation in some countries but not included subsequent, far more substantial legislative changes.*

What does this brief summary tell us? First, restorative justice is global. Not only has it been influenced by people and developments in many areas of the world but also it has been adopted in diverse cultures, economies, political systems, and legal systems. In fact, one of the remarkable features of restorative justice is that elements of it emerged virtually simultaneously in diverse regions of the world. In some cases, the program or theory was developed prior to contact with the ideas of restorative justice.

■ ■ ■ ▬▬▬▬▬▬▬▬▬▬▬▬▬▬▬▬▬▬▬▬▬▬▬▬▬▬▬▬▬

One of the remarkable features of restorative justice is that elements of it emerged almost simultaneously in different regions of the world.

▬▬▬▬▬▬▬▬▬▬▬▬▬▬▬▬▬▬▬▬▬▬▬▬▬▬▬▬▬ ■ ■ ■

Second, there have been stages of growth in the understanding of restorative processes and their impact on the criminal justice system. These might be described as stages in a developing awareness of the potential of restorative justice as a reform dynamic.

- *Restorative justice as a community-based alternative to the criminal justice system.* During the first decade or so, particularly in common law countries, restorative processes were viewed as an alternative, community-based approach to crime. That was certainly true of the first victim–offender reconciliation programs in Canada, the United States, and England. In countries in continental Europe, where the legality principle limits the discretion of police and prosecutors to divert cases out of the justice system, some legislative changes were needed, but the purpose of the changes was to allow pilot projects for demonstration and research.
- *Restorative justice as a source of public policy.* In the latter half of the 1980s, countries and organizations began exploring the policy implications of what was being learned from restorative processes. Justice Fellowship in the United States embarked on a multiyear project to translate restorative vision into principles of public policy; Canada's Parliamentary Standing Committee (known as the Daubney Committee for its chairman) affirmed that sentencing law changes in that country should take into consideration what was being learned in restorative

---

*Of course, the most significant limitation is lack of information, either because we are not aware of all developments or because we were aware but simply forgot. To those whose energy and resources have brought about valuable contributions to the restorative justice field, and whose part is not recognized here, we apologize and ask that you contact us with information. You may reach us at dvanness@pfi.org.

processes. New Zealand incorporated elements of Maori practices in revising its juvenile justice laws.

- *Restorative justice as a viable part of the criminal justice system.* The 1990s were a decade of remarkable growth and expansion. New models, and variations on those models, were developed as conferencing and circles took their place with victim–offender mediation. Governments took steps to encourage the use of restorative processes through grants, research, legislative change, and, in some instances (e.g., the Thames Valley police and the Royal Canadian Mounted Police), through offering restorative processes themselves. Organizations dedicated to promoting and expanding restorative processes emerged. These organizations offered practitioners and researchers the opportunity to network with others and to learn from their experiences. This networking and information-sharing has expanded dramatically with the increasing availability of the Internet and the growing number of excellent sites dedicated to restorative justice.
- *Restorative justice as an international reform dynamic.* The past few years have seen multinational bodies such as the United Nations, the Council of Europe, and the European Union strongly endorse the potential of restorative justice and urge their member states to introduce and then expand their use of restorative processes. Where early work with restorative processes was done by grassroots organizations, now they have been joined by multinational organizations in calling on governments to use these dramatic new approaches to criminal justice.

Time Line of Significant Advances Concerning Restorative Processes

1974	**Canada**
	Victim–Offender Reconciliation (VORP) used for first time in a sentencing hearing in Elmira, Ontario.
1976	**Canada**
	Community Justice Initiatives is formed in Kitchener, Ontario, to provide and to promote VORPs.
1978	**United States**
	First U.S. VORP program started in Elkhart, Indiana.
1981	**Norway**
	Diversionary mediation project started for young offenders; by 1989, the project was in 20% of municipalities.
	United States
	"Genesee Justice" developed as a sheriff's department program in Batavia, New York. The program offers community service sentencing, victim assistance and support, and victim–offender mediation sessions.
1983	**Finland**
	Pilot diversionary mediation program started.
	England
	First mediation pilot program established in South Yorkshire.

Continued

Time Line of Significant Advances Concerning Restorative Processes—cont'd

1984	**Austria**
	Pilot diversionary mediation program started.

1985	**England**
	Home Office funds four mediation pilot projects in order to research effectiveness.

1986	**United States**
	Justice Fellowship, a criminal justice reform advocacy group, begins multiyear research project to identify core principles of restorative justice and their public policy implications.

1988	**Canada**
	Parliamentary Standing Committee releases "Taking Responsibility" report recommending national expansion of VORP and modification of Canadian sentencing laws to add the purposes of victim and community reparation.
	United States
	U.S. Association for Victim Offender Mediation formed.

1989	**New Zealand**
	Adopts the Children, Young Persons and Their Families Act, which establishes family group conferences as the preferred means of dealing with juveniles as opposed to courts, except in cases of serious violence.

1990	**Italy**
	NATO Advanced Research Workshop on Conflict, Crime and Reconciliation convenes to examine the current status of restorative justice in Western countries.

1991	**Norway**
	Municipal Mediation Act adopted, expanding diversionary mediation to adults.
	Australia
	Wagga Wagga, New South Wales, pilot test of family group conferences begins; uses police officers rather than social workers.

1992	**Canada**
	Sentencing in *R. v. Moses*, a Yukon criminal case, is decided on in a sentencing circle; believed to be the first official use of circles.
	Zimbabwe
	Community service project initiated to reduce jail populations; incorporated meetings between offenders and communities.
	Australia
	South Australia adopts family group conferencing legislation for juveniles; by 2005, all states but Victoria had adopted similar measures.
	South Africa
	National Institute for Crime Prevention and Reintegration of Offenders starts pilot victim–offender mediation project.

Time Line of Significant Advances Concerning Restorative Processes—cont'd

1993	**United States** U.S. Association for Victim–Offender Mediation goes international and becomes Victim–Offender Mediation Association (VOMA).
	South Africa Truth and Reconciliation Commission established to apply restorative justice to crimes committed during the apartheid era.
1994	**United States** Real Justice founded to promote family group conferencing.
	England Retail Theft Initiative at the Milton Keynes Shopping Centre in Thames Valley leads to Thames Valley Police adopting conferencing as a way of dealing with offenders.
	Canada Circles of Support and Accountability developed as means of reintegrating high-risk sexual offenders into community.
	United States Minnesota Department of Corrections creates position of "Restorative Justice Planner" and appoints Kay Pranis to the position.
	United States U.S. Office of Juvenile Justice and Delinquency Prevention funds a multiyear training and technical assistance program called the Balanced and Restorative Justice Project.
	Jamaica Dispute Resolution Foundation created to increase use of mediation in criminal matters, among other things.
1995	**Mexico** Fundación Centro de Atención para Victimas del delito (Foundation Center for Attention to Victims of Crime) established to promote mediation; begins to offer conciliation in criminal cases.
	New Zealand Three community-based conferencing pilots for adults established; by 2005, these had grown to 19.
	Colombia Casa Justicia (Houses of Justice) created to offer penal mediation, among other things.
	Canada Royal Canadian Mounted Police adapt family group conferences into Community Justice Forums for less serious crimes where offenders admit responsibility.
	Canada Sentencing reform legislation introduces restorative justice principles into the federal criminal code.

Continued

Time Line of Significant Advances Concerning Restorative Processes—cont'd

1996	**Uganda** Child Justice Act allows certain juvenile cases to be addressed by informal Local Council Courts.
	South Africa Family group conferencing projects piloted.
	Canada Correctional Service of Canada's first restorative justice week.
	Poland Pilot mediation programs initiated.
	Costa Rica Ley de Justicia Penal Juvenil (Juvenile Penal Justice Act) adopted; includes provision for penal conciliation.
	United States Prison Fellowship International inaugurates Restorative Justice Online (http://www.restorativejustice.org).
1997	**United States** Federal Department of Justice conducts national conference on restorative justice.
	Belgium First international conference sponsored by the International Network for Research on Restorative Justice for juveniles.
	Canada National conference on restorative justice, "Satisfying Justice," held in Vancouver.
1998	**Argentina** First penal mediation pilot project started.
	Chile Proyecto CREA (Center for Alternative Dispute Resolution) created to promote penal mediation, among other things.
	Brazil Community-based restorative conferencing piloted for juveniles at schools in São Paulo.
	Europe Survey finds more than 900 mediation programs in existence.
	England Crime and Disorder Act and 1999 Youth Justice and Criminal Evidence Act effectively diverts all first-time young offenders to restorative justice projects.
	Philippines Government establishes the Barangay Justice System (local dispute resolution programs) to give legal status to existing traditional processes.
1999	**Bulgaria** Institute for Conflict Resolution created in Sofia to provide and promote VOM.
	Hong Kong Family group conferencing pilot programs started.
	Europe Council of Ministers of Council of Europe adopts Recommendation No. R(99)19 concerning mediation in penal matters.

Time Line of Significant Advances Concerning Restorative Processes—cont'd

2000	**Rwanda**
	Gacaca (traditional) courts established to deal with all genocide defendants except ringleaders.
	Europe
	European Forum on Victim–Offender Mediation and Restorative Justice formed.
	United States
	International Institute for Restorative Practices created to promote restorative practices in a variety of social disciplines.
2001	**Romania**
	Community Mediation and Safety Center created to conduct first mediation programs.
	Czech Republic
	Probation and Mediation Services Act enacted.
	Brazil
	Câmaras restaurativas (restorative conferences) piloted in Porto Allegre.
2001	**New Zealand**
	Court-referred restorative justice conference pilot projects start.
	Europe
	European Union issues framework decision on the standing of victims in criminal proceedings, which obligates each member state to promote mediation in those criminal matters for which it is appropriate.
2002	**United Nations**
	Endorses *Declaration of Basic Principles on the Use of Restorative Justice Programmes in Criminal Matters.*
	Colombia
	Constitutional amendment adopted that requires prosecutors to offer restorative justice to victims.
2003	**China**
	Research Institute of Crime Prevention and Control at Nanjing University conducts first national conference on restorative justice.
	Thailand
	Family group conferencing pilot programs started.
2004	**China**
	Centre for Restorative Justice established at China University of Political Science and Law in Beijing.
2005	**Costa Rica**
	First all-Latin America symposium on restorative justice.
	United States
	Fresno Pacific University adopts restorative disciplinary system.
	Belgium
	Adopts a law allowing mediation in any criminal case at the request of victims or offenders.
2006	**Philippines**
	Juvenile Justice and Welfare Act introduces restorative justice.
	United Nations
	Publishes *Handbook on Restorative Justice Programmes.*

Continued

Time Line of Significant Advances Concerning Restorative Processes—cont'd

2007	**England**
	Restorative Justice: The Evidence demonstrates benefits of restorative approaches over traditional criminal justice.
	Europe
	European Commission for the Efficiency of Justice (CEPEJ) issues new guidelines for implementing mediation in penal matters.
	Portugal
	Law enacted regulating the use of victim–offender mediation.
2008	**England**
	Why Me?, a nongovernmental organization (NGO), formed to promote the right of crime victims to access to restorative justice.
2009	**South Africa**
	New Child Justice Act enacted with provisions to "entrench the notion of restorative justice."
	El Salvador
	Tribunal of Restorative Justice begins hearing testimony from victims of the civil war.
	Jamaica
	Restorative and Community Justice Programme piloted in violence-prone areas.
2010	**United States**
	State of Virginia adopts legislation giving crime victims the right to meet with their offenders in prison where they are incarcerated.
2011	**United States**
	Miami-Dade County Public Schools adopts restorative justice as an alternative to "zero tolerance"
	England & Wales
	Restorative Justice Council launches a restorative justice Practitioner Register.
2012	**Europe**
	Directive Establishing Minimum Standards on the Rights, Support and Protection of Victims of Crime adopted giving victims (among other things) the right to review a decision not to prosecute as well as safeguards when choosing restorative justice.
	El Salvador
	Mediators negotiate a truce between the country's two main gangs; results in a substantial reduction of the homicide rate.
	Canada
	Nova Scotia Human Rights Commission adopts a restorative justice approach to human rights disputes.
2013	**England**
	First scheme established in Europe to allow victims to request face-to-face meetings with their offender without the offender having already requested it.
	United States
	Colorado adopts legislation requiring judges to offer restorative justice options to every victim and defendant.

Conclusion

Dissatisfaction with modern criminal justice has led to a number of reform movements. Some can be relatively easily incorporated into the criminal justice system, whereas others are more difficult to reconcile. The intersection of these movements created an environment of discontent, and creativity. Out of it has emerged a new pattern of thinking—restorative justice—one that has been increasingly influential in governmental policy.

Review Questions

1. Where did the term *restorative justice* come from?
2. Who were early "explorers" of restorative justice, and what did they contribute?
3. What programs emerged to offer restorative processes?
4. How has restorative justice grown across the globe since its early beginnings?

Endnotes

1. In previous editions, we cited Eglash's chapter, "Beyond Restitution: Creative Restitution, " in Joe Hudson and Burt Galaway, eds., *Restitution in Criminal Justice* (Lexington, MA: D.C. Heath, 1977), 92. In fact, Eglash developed his ideas of creative restitution nearly 20 years earlier in a series of articles published in 1958 and 1959 (cf. our Select Bibliography entries, Eglash 1958a, 1958b, 1958c; Eglash 1959–60)—one of which was adapted for inclusion in the 1977 book. Ann Skelton (2005) has traced Eglash's source for the term *restorative justice* to a 1955 book, *The Biblical Doctrine of Justice and Law*, which was originally published in German and then translated and adapted into English. The pertinent section addresses the connection between justice and love, and reads in part:

   This aligning of justice and love is something which it is the peculiar task of Christian believers to promote, and in doing so they need to see beyond the secular conception of justice in its threefold form of distributive, commutative and retributive justice. Justice also has a restorative element. It is perhaps misleading to picture a fourth element which can be added at will to the other three. Walther Schönfeld (Ueber die Gerechtigkeit, 1952) has suggested an alternative picture in terms of dimensions. He maintains that justice as the world knows it in its public life is three-dimensional, in the way just indicated; but that a four-dimensional justice, or perhaps a fourth dimension of justice, is disclosed to the Church, but hidden from the world, in Jesus Christ. The effect of this four-dimensional vision is to produce an inner transformation of the three-dimensional structure; to provide a new total view of man in community; and to uncover possibilities which are simply not there in terms of three-dimensional vision.… Restorative justice alone can do what law as such can never do: It can heal the fundamental wound from which all mankind suffers and which turns the best human justice constantly into injustice, the wound of sin. Distributive justice can never take us beyond the norm of reparation; commutative justice can provide only due compensation; retributive justice has no means of repairing the damage save by punishment and expiation. Restorative justice, as it is revealed in the Bible, alone has positive power for overcoming sin. (Heinz-Horst Schrey, Hans Hermann Walz, and W. A. Whitehouse, *The Biblical Doctrine of Justice and Law* (London: SCM Press, 1955), 182–183).

2. Howard Zehr, *Changing Lenses: A New Focus for Crime and Justice* (Scottdale, PA: Herald Press, 1990), 181. As we will see in Chapter 3, he now contrasts restorative justice with contemporary criminal justice, rather than with retributive justice.

3. Tony Marshall, *Restorative Justice: An Overview* (London: Home Office Research Development and Statistics Directorate, 1999), 5.

4. Martin Wright, *Justice for Victims and Offenders* (Philadelphia: Open University Press, 1991), 112.

5. Ruth Morris, *A Practical Path to Transformative Justice* (Toronto: Rittenhouse, 1994).

6. Jonathan Burnside and Nicola Baker, eds., *Relational Justice: Repairing the Breach* (Winchester, UK: Waterside Press, 1994). This name was drawn from the "Relational Movement, " defined in Michael Schluter and David Lee, *The R Factor* (London: Hodder & Stoughton, 1993).

7. Marlene A. Young, *Restorative Community Justice: A Call to Action* (Washington, DC: National Organization for Victim Assistance, 1995).

8. Zehr, supra note 2.

9. Ibid., 181.

10. Wright, supra note 4.

11. Ibid., 114–117.

12. Virginia Mackey, *Restorative Justice: Toward Nonviolence* (Louisville, KY: Presbyterian Justice Program, 1992).

13. Ibid., 41–42.

14. Wesley Cragg, *The Practice of Punishment: Towards a Theory of Restorative Justice* (New York: Rutledge, 1992).

15. Ibid., 213–216.

16. See, for example, John Braithwaite, *Crime, Shame and Reintegration* (New York: Cambridge University Press, 1989). See Chapter 6 for a more extensive discussion of his theory.

17. David Moore, "Evaluating Family Group Conferences, " in David Biles and Sandra McKillop, eds., *Criminal Justice Planning and Coordination: Proceedings of a Conference Held 19–21 April 1993* (Canberra: Australian Institute of Criminology, 1994).

18. David Moore, "Shame, Forgiveness, and Juvenile Justice, " *Criminal Justice Ethics* (Winter/Spring 1993): 3.

19. Burnside and Baker, eds. supra note 6.

20. Young, supra note 7.

21. See, for example, Joe Hudson's description of the victim–offender meetings in the Minnesota Restitution Center, which opened in 1972. Joe Hudson, "Contemporary Origins of Restorative Justice Programming: The Minnesota Restitution Center, " *Federal Probation* (2012) 76:82.

22. See, for example, Mark S. Umbreit, *The Handbook of Victim–Offender Mediation: An Essential Guide to Practice and Research* (San Francisco: Jossey-Bass, 2001).

23. Ron Claassen and Howard Zehr, *VORP Organizing: A Foundation in the Church* (Elkhart, IN: Mennonite Central Committee, U.S. Office of Criminal Justice, 1989).

24. See, for example, Juhani Ilivari, "Mediation in Finland, " in Tony Peters, ed., *Victim–Offender Mediation in Europe: Making Restorative Justice Work* (Leuven: Leuven University Press, 2000); John Harding, "Reconciling Mediation with Criminal Justice, " in Martin Wright and Burt Galaway, eds., *Mediation and Criminal Justice: Victims, Offenders and Community* (London: Sage, 1989); Wright, supra note 4; and Frieder Dünkel and Dieter Rössner, "Law and Practice of Victim/Offender Agreements, " in Martin Wright and Burt Galaway, eds., *Mediation and Criminal Justice: Victims, Offenders and Community* (London: Sage, 1989).

25. See, for example, Gale Burford and Joan Pennell, *Family Group Decision Making: New Roles for "Old" Partners in Resolving Family Violence: Implementation Report Summary* (St. Johns: Memorial University of Newfoundland, 1995); Joe Hudson, Allison Morris, Gabrielle Maxwell, and Burt Galaway, eds., *Family Group Conferences: Perspectives on Policy and Practice* (Annandale, Australia: Federation Press, 1996). Many of Paul McCold's articles and chapters are available through the database at http://www.iirp.org.

26. R. V. Moses, *Canadian Native Law Reporter* (Yukon Territory Court), 116 (1992).

27. See, for example, Berma Bushie, "Community Holistic Circle Healing: A Community Approach" (n.d.), posted at the International Institute for Restorative Practices website (available at http://www.iirp.or g/library/vt/vt_bushie.html#top as of October 10, 2009); Bria Huculak, "From the Power to Punish to the Power to Heal, " in Wanda D. McCaslin, ed., *Justice as Healing: Indigenous Ways* (St. Paul, MN: Living Justice Press, 2005); and Kay Pranis, Barry Stuart, and Mark Wedge, *Peacemaking Circles: From Crime to Community* (St. Paul, MN: Living Justice Press, 2005).

3 ∷

Restorative Justice

Justice That Promotes Healing

KEY CONCEPTS

- Conceptions used to define restorative justice
- Definition of restorative justice
- Principles of restorative justice
- Values of restorative justice
- Visual model of restorative justice

What is restorative justice? It can seem that there are as many answers as people asked. Some definitions focus on the elements of restorative processes. Others begin with the idea touched on in the first paragraphs of Chapter 1—that crime causes harm, and justice should promote healing. Others build on restorative values, such as respect for others. Still others suggest that restorative justice is a holistic approach to life and to relationships, one that has far-reaching effects beyond simply the issue of crime or rule-breaking.

Definition of Restorative Justice

Johnstone and Van Ness[1] suggested that one explanation for the difficulty in arriving at a single definition is that restorative justice is a *deeply contested concept*.[2] That is, it is a complex idea, the meaning of which continues to evolve with new discoveries. It is also a positive term, meaning that it is considered a good thing to have the name applied to a program or idea. In that sense, it is like the words "democracy" and "justice"; people generally understand what they mean, but they may not be able to agree on a precise definition.

It does seem possible, however, according to Johnstone and Van Ness, to identify three basic conceptions that proposed definitions of restorative justice typically center around. The first is the *encounter* conception. This focuses on the importance of stakeholder meetings and on the many benefits that come as stakeholders discuss the crime, what contributed to it, and its aftermath. It helps identify one of the key differences between restorative processes and criminal justice processes. In restorative processes, the victim, offender, and other interested parties are free to speak and to decide what to do in a relatively informal environment and through that come to terms with what happened. In court, on the other hand, the active participants are generally professionals who have only a professional connection to the crime and to those who were touched by it. Decisions are not made by the parties but, rather, by the judge. Whereas the defendant generally has a lawyer, the victim does not; instead, the victim's interests are considered to be identical with society's, which the prosecutor represents. The encounter conception would not consider something restorative if it did not involve the victim, offender, and other parties meeting together.

The second is the *reparative* conception. "Crime causes harm; justice must repair that harm." The harm is at many levels, as we will see, and it can often be addressed most fully when the parties meet in a restorative process to explore and respond to those. However, this conception is not limited by the inability or unwillingness of the parties to meet. In those circumstances, it would insist that court proceedings focus on identifying and taking steps to repair the harm caused by the crime. This conception would not describe something as restorative if it did not provide some sort of redress to direct victims and, perhaps, communities and offenders as well.

The third is the *transformation* conception. This is far more expansive than the other two because it has to do with broken relationships at multiple levels of society. It addresses not simply individual instances of harm but goes beyond to structural issues of injustice, such as racism, sexism, and classism. Each of these prevents people from living in whole, harmonious, and healthy relationships with others and with their social and physical environments. Restorative justice is therefore a way of life because it addresses all of our relationships, and it offers a way in which broken relationships can be repaired (often through challenging existing societal injustices). This conception would not describe something as restorative if it did not address structural impediments to wholesome, healthy relationships.

The three conceptions are closely related, and most proponents would find themselves at home in each of the three depending on the context of the conversation. However, most also will, when required to offer a precise definition, articulate something that draws primarily from one or that establishes a ranking of importance among them.

■ ■ ■ ▬▬▬▬▬▬▬▬▬▬▬▬▬▬▬▬▬▬▬▬▬▬▬

Restorative justice is a complex idea whose meaning continues to evolve with new discoveries.

▬▬▬▬▬▬▬▬▬▬▬▬▬▬▬▬▬▬▬▬▬▬▬ ■ ■ ■

As will be evident by the end of this book, our understanding of restorative justice falls within the reparative conception, with one important proviso: Repair is most fully accomplished when it results from an *encounter* of the parties. We suggest the following as our definition:

> *Restorative justice is a theory of justice that emphasizes repairing the harm caused or revealed by criminal behavior. It is best accomplished through cooperative processes that include all stakeholders.*

Although it will be apparent from our final chapter that we believe that those who work for restorative justice will be challenged to seek transformation of perspectives, structures, and people, when we approach the challenge of defining restorative justice we prefer the specificity of the reparative conception, modified by the encounter conception.

Principles of Restorative Justice

Three key principles govern implementation of restorative justice in processes and in systemic reform. First, justice requires that we work to heal victims, offenders, and communities that have been injured by crime. Second, victims, offenders, and communities should have the opportunity for active involvement in the justice process as early and as fully as they wish. Third, we must rethink the relative roles and responsibilities of government and community: In promoting justice, government is responsible for preserving a just order and the community for establishing a just peace. Let us consider each of these in turn.

Principle 1. Justice requires that we work to heal victims, offenders, and communities injured by crime.

Crime leaves injured victims, communities, and offenders in its wake, each harmed in different ways and experiencing correspondingly different needs. To promote healing, restorative justice must respond appropriately, considering the needs and responsibilities of each party.

Victims are those who have been harmed by the offender; this harm may be experienced either directly or secondarily. Primary victims, those against whom the crime was committed, may sustain physical injury, monetary loss, and emotional suffering. These may be only temporary, may last a lifetime, or may cause death. Secondary victims are indirectly harmed by the actions of offenders. These victims may include family members, neighbors, and friends of primary victims and offenders. Their injuries and needs may also be considered in constructing a restorative response to crime.

Because of the varying circumstances of victims, similar injuries may produce substantially different effects. In at least two respects, however, all victims have common needs: the need to regain control over their own lives and the need for vindication of their rights. Being victimized is by definition an experience of powerlessness—the victim was unable to prevent the crime from occurring. As a result, victims often need help regaining an appropriate sense of control over their lives. As described at the beginning of this book, Justice Kelly discovered that because victimization is also the experience of being wronged by another, it brings with it the need for vindication: an authoritative and decisive denunciation of the wrong and exoneration of the one who was wronged.

In order to consider the injuries and needs of the community—and, more important, to consider how the community and government may assume complementary roles in establishing safety (see Principle 3)—we need to be clear about what we mean by *community*. This term is used in different ways. Sometimes it refers to a geographic location—the neighborhood in which the victim or offender lives, for example, or in which the crime took place—a "local community." With increased mobility and transience, however, a more useful definition might be nongeographic, emphasizing the presence of connect-edness and relationships: a "community of care." Sometimes the word is used loosely in everyday conversation as a synonym for civil society as a whole.

■ ■ ■ ━━

Justice requires that we work to heal victims, offenders, and communities that have been injured by crime.

━━ ■ ■ ■

Each of these types of communities—the geographic community of the victim, offender, or crime; the community of care; and civil society—may be injured by crime in different ways and degrees, but all will be affected in common ways as well: The sense of safety and confidence of their members is threatened, order within the community is threatened, and (depending on the kind of crime) common values of the community are challenged and perhaps eroded. However, the injury to the first two communities is far more direct than the general injury to civil society. Furthermore, the local community and the com-munity of care share a characteristic of common interest. John Braithwaite suggested that the term *community of interest*[3] be used because the community is then defined by the willingness of its members to act according to interests larger than their own through a fundamental sense of duty, reciprocity, and belonging. This interest may be in the victim or the offender (and may or may not be motivated by compassion); it may be in reducing crime in the area in which the crime took place; and it may be in restorative justice and how that is applied. A particular community, then, is made up of people with sufficient interest to join it. Thus, when we speak of community in this book, we mean "community of interest."[4]

Finally, the injuries of offenders must also be addressed. These injuries can be thought of as either contributing to the crime or resulting from the crime. Contributing injuries are those that existed prior to the crime and that prompted in some way the criminal conduct of the offender. For example, it has been demonstrated that some victims of child abuse become abusers themselves and that some substance abusers commit crimes to support their addictions. Although these contributing injuries, or prior conditions, do not excuse the criminal choices of offenders, any attempt to bring healing to the parties touched by crime must address them. Resulting injuries are those caused by the crime itself or its aftermath. These may be physical (as when the offender is wounded during the crime or incarcerated as a result of it), emotional (as when the offender experiences shame[5]), or moral and spiritual (because the offender has chosen to harm another). Furthermore, offenders will likely be injured as a result of the criminal justice system's response, which further alienates them from the community, strains family relationships, may lead to long-term employment disadvantages, and may prevent them from making amends to their victims. We do not suggest that offenders are relieved of accountability by the recogni-tion of their "injuries." However, those injuries should be acknowledged and addressed in the response to crime. Unfortunately, there are no terms in the English language that appropriately describe this process. Consequently, we have adopted the admittedly awkward word "habilitation" to express this goal.

Principle 2. Victims, offenders, and communities should have the opportunity for active involvement in the justice process as early and as fully as they wish.

Virtually every facet of our criminal justice system works to reduce victims, offenders, and communities to passive participants. Because the government is considered to be the primary victim, its virtual monopoly over the apprehension, prosecution, and punishment of offenders seems logical and legitimate. Because of the legal presumption of innocence bestowed on all who are charged with crimes, as well as the panoply of due process rights that are afforded them, defendants have few incentives to assume responsibility for their actions and many incentives to remain passive while the government marshals its case and their lawyers attempt to dismantle it. Because victims are not parties of interest in criminal cases and rather are simply "piece[s] of evidence to be used by the state to obtain a conviction,"[6] they have very limited control over what occurs and no responsibility to initiate particular phases of the process. Finally, the direct participation of members of the community is also very limited, consisting almost exclusively of service on grand or petit juries or as witnesses.

■ ■ ■ ━━

Victims, offenders, and communities should have the opportunity for active involvement in the justice process as early and as fully as they wish.

━━ ■ ■ ■

Restorative justice, on the other hand, places a much higher value on direct involvement by the parties. For victims who have experienced powerlessness, the opportunity to participate restores an element of control. For an offender who has harmed another, the voluntary assumption of responsibility is an important step in not only helping those who were hurt by the crime but also building a prosocial value system. Likewise, the efforts of community members to repair the injuries to victims and offenders serve to strengthen the community and to reinforce community values of respect and compassion for others.

Principle 3. We must rethink the relative roles and responsibilities of government and community: In promoting justice, government is responsible for preserving a just order and the community for establishing a just peace.

The term *order* is sometimes used as though it were a synonym for public safety; politicians speak, for example, of the need for "law and order" as a means of ending "crime in our streets." Safety, however, is a broader, more inclusive concept than order. In other words, both order and peace are means of securing public safety. As ancient Jewish law incorporated notions of "shalom," so today we must think of "peace" as a cooperative dynamic fostered from within a community.

Peace requires a community's commitment to respect the rights of its members and to help resolve conflicts among them. It requires that those members respect community interests even when they conflict with their individual interests. It is in this context that communities and their members assume responsibility for addressing the underlying social, economic, and moral factors that contribute to conflict within the community. Order, on the other hand, is imposed on the community. It establishes and enforces external limits on individual behavior to minimize overt conflict and to control the resolution of conflict.[7] Like peace, a just order is important in preserving safety, and governments generally have both the power and the mandate to establish such an order.

■ ■ ■ ────────────────────────────────

Government should maintain a just order; the community should build a just peace.

──────────────────────────────── ■ ■ ■

Both order and peace are appropriate avenues for achieving safety. However, as imposed order increases, personal freedom decreases; hence, peace will be sought in a society that values freedom. Security built primarily on governmentally imposed order is detrimental to a free society, as conditions in police states throughout the world demonstrate. On the other hand, when the community fails to foster peace, it may be necessary for the government to intervene and impose order. The American civil rights movement is an example of that kind of action. Desegregation of public schools was met with violent resistance on the community level, and National Guard troops had to enforce order so that African-American children could enter the schools. The community, content with preserving the interests of the powerful by seeking to maintain the status quo, had failed in its role to seek peace for all members.

Describing peace as the community's responsibility and order as government's should not blind us to the difficult and important complexities involved. Each plays a role in achieving peace and order, as we see when community members form Neighborhood Watch programs to prevent crime, when law enforcement uses community policing strategies, or when government programs address economic and social injustices that inhibit peace. We emphasize a point that is often forgotten in the debate about crime and criminal justice: Safety comes as both government and community play their parts in upholding order and establishing peace.

Values of Restorative Justice

The processes identified with restorative justice—victim–offender mediation, conferencing, circles, and so forth—will not necessarily produce restoration if they are not used according to the principles and values of restorative justice. For example, a program that operates solely during the working day to accommodate the schedule of the paid facilitator is unlikely to be effective in engaging victims who work or have other responsibilities during the daytime. Similarly, a facilitator who does not have a good understanding of the cultural norms of one of the participants may fail to take steps to ensure that the person is able to participate effectively. A restorative process may be guided by values that are destructive rather than restorative, such as when the participants focus on excusing the wrongdoer or, at the other end of the spectrum, on humiliating that person. These problems may be confronted in a number of ways. One is to provide practice guidelines for practitioners. Another is to develop statements of best practices. A third is to create standards for use in accreditation processes. A final option is to focus on restorative values and to use those in designing and evaluating programs and in training and guiding practitioners.

Each of these approaches has advantages, and they are not mutually exclusive. Standards should reflect values; guidelines should be based on best practices. The first three are more specific to particular programs and justice systems, but values are less dependent on context. As a result, there has been growing interest in using them to measure and maintain the restorative character of particular interventions.

There may be almost as many lists of restorative values as there are definitions of restorative justice. John Braithwaite suggested that there are three kinds of values. The first keeps the restorative process from becoming abusive or indifferent to the participants. The second has to do with deciding whether the outcome of the process has been successful. The third is what he calls *emergent* values—those that may or may not result from a successful process (e.g., forgiveness, remorse, and reconciliation).[8]

■ ■ ■ ──

Restorative justice reflects both vision for the way the world should be and values guiding the way restorative programs should function.

────────────────────────────────────── ■ ■ ■

Another way of saying this might be to think in terms of a vision for the way the world ought to be while also being guided by particular values for the way restorative programs should function. Restorative justice envisions a world in which community life is actively peaceful and harmonious. When conflicts occur, they are addressed in ways that resolve the causes and care for the people involved. All people are worthy of respect and consideration, and they are empowered to participate in the process of community-building. Members of communities live in dynamic solidarity rooted in shared interests, purposes, sympathies, and responsibilities. They are connected, despite disagreements and dissimilarities. Also, they take active responsibility for their behavior, taking initiative to find solutions to problems and to make amends for harmful behaviors and their consequences.

The values that influence restorative justice programs and processes give practical guidance for how this vision of the world may be made real in the way a community and society respond to crimes when they occur. We have identified four that we call *cornerpost values.* If restorative justice were a building, we would expect to find these as key structural elements in its architecture. They are recurring and important dimensions in many programs and multiple places over time.

These cornerpost values are as follows:

1. *Inclusion*: All affected parties are invited to directly shape and engage in restorative processes in response to crime.
2. *Encounter*: Affected parties are given the opportunity to meet the other parties in a safe environment to discuss the offense, harms, and the appropriate responses.
3. *Amends*: Those responsible for the harm resulting from the offense also take responsibility for repairing it to the extent possible.
4. *Reintegration*: The parties are given the means and opportunity to rejoin their communities as whole, contributing members rather than continuing to bear the stigma of the harm and offense.

We consider each of these in detail in the next four chapters.

Restorative Justice or Restorative Practices?

As restorative processes have increasingly been applied in educational and business settings, some have suggested that the term *restorative justice* is inappropriate because it implies that they can only be used when the culpability of one party is clear and conceded. In fact, circles and other restorative encounters can be very useful in addressing many kinds of conflicts, whether or not they stem from misbehavior.

In other words, "justice" seems to narrow the use of restorative practices to situations that would ordinarily be handled by the justice system. This has practical consequences in advocacy: Should proponents promote restorative practices and encourage their application in multiple contexts, one of which would be in dealing with crime? Or is it better to focus attention on wrongdoing and, in particular, *criminal* wrongdoing?

This is being discussed as both a strategic and a principled question. Those who support use of the term *restorative justice* agree that restorative processes are effective in other settings and that increased use of them anywhere creates a "restorative-friendly" context that might increase their use in criminal matters. Thus, some organizations[9] have expanded their scope to all applications of restorative practices, not merely those that fall within the domain of criminal or juvenile justice.

That is the strategic issue. The question related to principles has to do with what is lost by using the term *restorative practices* rather than *restorative justice*. An obvious answer is that *justice* is lost when responding to crime or other rule violations. One of the needs of victims is to hear that this was not their fault (to the degree that is true). One can argue as well that offenders need to hear that they were wrong, and certainly society expects that there will be denunciation of certain kinds of behavior.

It is clear that there is a huge overlap between restorative practices and restorative justice in terms of worldview, values, principles, and methods.[10] However, the similarities are not complete, and it is there that the discussion is likely to continue.

Restorative Justice as Opposed to What?

In an early attempt to explain the uniqueness of the restorative vision, Howard Zehr offered a comparison between restorative justice and retributive justice. What he meant by the latter was criminal justice as we know it, a process focused on determining the guilt of an offender and then imposing a sentence.[11] Gordon Bazemore added to this distinction by contrasting restorative justice with both retributive justice and rehabilitation paradigm.[12] These differences are useful for purposes of description, but they suffer certain limitations as well.

■ ■ ■ ━━━

Restorative justice insists on accountability even when that is painful. This is consistent with the common understanding of punishment.

━━━ ■ ■ ■

One is that they do not serve restorative justice well in public debate. Restorative justice includes principles of accountability and acknowledges that accountability may be painful. This is a common understanding of retribution or punishment. The narrow definition given retribution by restorative justice proponents ("pain imposed for its own sake") may be helpful for analytical precision but misleading to a public that thinks less precisely.

Furthermore, the restorative–retributive dichotomy concedes too much. The retributive approach has traditionally justified imposing pain by arguing that crime creates an imbalance; the offender has benefited at the public's expense. The imbalance must be addressed by causing the offender to lose that benefit. However, as legal philosopher Conrad Brunk argues, this is what restorative justice also tries to achieve:

> *So, there is much in the retributivist theory that is very close to Restorative Justice. Restorative Justice is also concerned primarily with making the wrong right or restoring the justice of the situation. It is concerned with demanding that offenders take responsibility for their actions by actively making things right with the victims. It is also concerned that punishment not treat offenders unjustly. But, as we shall see, Restorative Justice gives a much more concrete and practical account of how the injustice done to victims can be redressed, and of how justice can be done to the offender as well.[13]*

Similarly, Kathleen Daly suggested that the distinction between restorative, retributive, and rehabilitative justice can be misleading:

> *In my view, restorative justice is best characterized as a practice that flexibly incorporates "both ways"—that is, it contains elements of retributive and rehabilitative justice—but*

at the same time, it contains several new elements that give it a unique restorative stamp. Specifically, restorative justice practices do focus on the offence and the offender; they are concerned with censuring past behaviour and with changing future behaviour; they are concerned with sanctions or outcomes that are proportionate and that also "make things right" in individual cases.[14]

Antony Duff proposes that retribution must be restorative and that restoration must have elements of retribution:

I will argue that restorative theorists are right to insist that our responses to crime should seek "restoration," whilst retributive theorists are right to argue that we should seek to bring offenders to suffer the punishments they deserve; but that both sides are wrong to suppose that these aims are incompatible. Restoration is not only compatible with retribution: It requires retribution, in that the kind of restoration that crime makes necessary can (given certain deep features of our social lives) be brought about only through retributive punishment.[15]

Interestingly, Zehr has moved away from drawing sharp distinctions between restorative justice and retributive justice, for reasons that are similar to those offered by Brunk and Daly. However, he cautions:

Retributive theory believes that pain will vindicate, but in practice that is often counterproductive for both victim and offender. Restorative justice theory, on the other hand, argues that what truly vindicates is acknowledgment of victims' harms and needs, combined with an active effort to encourage offenders to take responsibility, make right the wrongs, and address the causes of their behavior. By addressing this need for vindication in a positive way, restorative justice has the potential to affirm both victim and offender and to help them transform their lives.[16]

To try to capture these nuances, we two related terms to describe these alternative perspectives on punishment. *Retribution* means deserved punishment for wrong behavior. The active party is the government, and the purpose of retribution is for the government to inflict harm on the offender proportionate to the wrong done. *Recompense*, on the other hand, means the deserved obligation to pay for wrongfully causing an injury. The active party is the offender, and the purpose of recompense is for the offender to repair as fully as possible the injury caused by the wrong.

A second problem with the restorative-versus-retributive dichotomy is that in this context, "restorative justice" is presented as the better alternative. This is a questionable tactic strategically because it can inadvertently cause justice system people who might be supportive to focus instead on why the dichotomy is simplistic or unfair. An alternative approach when using dichotomies for teaching purposes is to contrast "restorative justice" with "nonrestorative justice."

■ ■ ■ ▬▬▬▬▬▬▬▬▬▬▬▬▬▬▬▬▬▬▬▬▬▬▬

Recompense means the deserved obligation to pay for wrongfully causing an injury. The active party is the offender, and the purpose is to repair as fully as possible the injury caused by the wrongdoer.

▬▬▬▬▬▬▬▬▬▬▬▬▬▬▬▬▬▬▬▬▬▬▬ ■ ■ ■

A third drawback to comparing restorative to retributive justice is that "retributive justice" is sometimes used in restorative justice literature to refer to the current criminal justice system. As a matter of fairness to retributivists, however, current criminal justice cannot accurately be called retributive because it is in fact a hybrid of several philosophies of justice (and sometimes, it appears, no philosophy of justice at all). What term should we use to describe current practice, then? Some have proposed *traditional justice*. Unfortunately, that is also used to refer to customary or indigenous practices. Another alternative is *criminal justice*, which emphasizes the offender orientation of current criminal justice practice. However, this usage would encounter the same problem as retributive justice: The common understanding of criminal justice is a societal response to crime and not the narrow definition of a response that focuses on the criminal.

We use the term *contemporary criminal justice* to describe the current justice system. It is possible that this term could be read narrowly to exclude the long history of offender orientation of the criminal justice system (i.e., contemporary as opposed to historical). We will not give it that narrow reading, and we assume that most readers will not as well.

Does Restorative Justice Work?

Frances Crook, director of the Howard League of Penal Reform, said that restorative justice is the most over-researched *and* the most under-used criminal justice innovation.[17] So, is it underutilized because of the research?

Apparently not. Lawrence Sherman and Heather Strang analyzed research conducted throughout the world that matched restorative justice with contemporary criminal justice.[18] They found 36 studies whose direct comparisons were between two reasonably similar groups, one of which received a restorative justice intervention while the other did not. Among their conclusions were the following:

- Crime victims who receive restorative justice do better, on average, than victims who do not, across a wide range of outcomes, including post-traumatic stress.
- In many tests, offenders who receive restorative justice commit fewer repeat crimes than offenders who do not.[19]
- In no large-sample test has restorative justice increased repeat offending compared with criminal justice.
- Restorative justice reduces repeat offending more consistently with violent crimes than with less serious crimes.
- Diversion from prosecution to restorative justice substantially increases the odds of an offender being brought to justice.

- Restorative justice does not conflict with the rule of law, nor does it depart from the basic paradigm of the common law of crime.
- Restorative justice can do as well as, or better than, short prison sentences, as measured by repeat offending.
- Restorative justice reduces stated victim desire for violent revenge against offenders.

The report was prepared for a United Kingdom charitable trust. On the basis of their highly favorable evidence, Sherman and Strang recommended that restorative justice "could be rolled out across the country with a high probability of substantial benefits to victims and crime reductions for many kinds of offenders."[20] Furthermore, restorative justice "as a diversion could provide the basis for far more general use of restorative justice, with possibly substantial crime reductions, less victim post-traumatic stress, and more offences brought to justice."[21]

Restorative Justice: A Visual Model

A series of figures illustrates some of the key features of restorative justice theory. Figure 3.1 illustrates how contemporary criminal justice focuses exclusively on the offender and the government. The government seeks to establish order by enacting laws and punishing those who violate them through sanctions that may include rehabilitative elements as well as acting as a deterrent to other potential wrongdoers. Because the government's power is great, due process safeguards have developed over the centuries in an attempt to create a fair criminal justice process. One consequence is that the offender's posture is defensive (and often passive) during the proceedings, while the government plays the active role. Criminal courts are arenas of battle in which the government is pitted against offenders in a high-stakes contest to determine whether the law has been violated and, if so, what form of sanctions should be imposed.

Figure 3.2 illustrates the more comprehensive understanding that restorative justice offers. There are actually four parties: victims, offenders, communities, and their governments. Every crime involves specific victims and offenders, and a goal of justice should be to help them come to resolution. In contemporary criminal justice, this dimension is largely left to the civil courts to address. However, restorative justice posits that the rights of victims should be vindicated and that offenders must make recompense to victims as part of a comprehensive response to crime.

Whereas Figure 3.2 addresses the "micro" dimension of crime (i.e., the response to particular victims and offenders), Figure 3.3 illustrates the "macro" response—government's and the community's efforts at crime prevention. Safety is sought through some combination of governmentally imposed order and community-built peaceful relationships. Where there is more community peace, less order will be required; where there is more order, community freedom will be externally limited to achieve safety. This dynamic relationship between government order and community peacebuilding is the basis for crime prevention strategies.

ORDER

RETRIBUTION
DETERRENCE
REHABILITATION

FAIRNESS

FIGURE 3.1

FIGURE 3.2

FIGURE 3.3

Combining Figures 3.2 and 3.3 reminds us that we need to consider the micro and macro responses together because they are interrelated. The victim's and offender's need for resolution and the government's and community's need for public safety must be addressed in the same process (Figure 3.4). This dual thrust contrasts with the separation of civil and criminal law in most modern jurisdictions, a separation that can force either/or choices for victims and the government in deciding whether and how to proceed against the offender.

Figure 3.5 shows the restorative justice goals that govern the relationship between the government and individual victims and offenders, as well as between the community and those individuals. The government helps re-establish order by ensuring that reparation takes place. It facilitates *redress* to victims through restitution and compensation while ensuring that offenders are treated with *fairness*. The community seeks to restore peace between victims and offenders and to reintegrate them fully into the community. For victims, the goals can be expressed as *healing*; for offenders, they can be expressed as *habilitation*.

The circular construction of the figures suggests the dynamic and dependent relationships that are necessary among the parties under restorative justice theory. Peace without order is as incomplete as recompense without vindication; healing without redress is as inadequate as habilitation without fairness. A society cannot select certain features of the model and omit others; all are essential. That very comprehensiveness is a fundamental aspect of the restorative pattern of thinking about crime. Restorative justice theory seeks to address and balance the rights, needs, and responsibilities of victims, offenders, communities, and the government.

■ ■ ■

Restorative justice theory seeks to address and balance the rights, needs, and responsibilities of victims, offenders, communities, and the government.

■ ■ ■

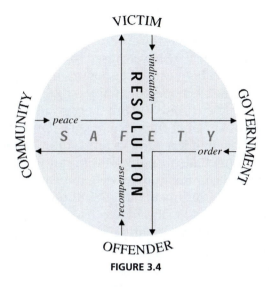

FIGURE 3.4

FIGURE 3.5

Conclusion

There are multiple conceptions of restorative justice. For some, its essence lies in encounters, the restorative processes in which parties may find healing. For others, it is a view of justice that insists that the harm caused by crime be repaired to the extent possible. For still others, it is a way of living that transforms relationships with others and with the social and physical environment. We hold to the reparative conception with the understanding that repair is best accomplished when the parties participate cooperatively in determining how that should be done.

Restorative justice focuses on repairing the harm caused by crime and reducing the likelihood of future harm. It does this by encouraging offenders to take responsibility for their actions and for the harm they have caused, by providing redress for victims, and by promoting reintegration of both within the community. Communities and the government accomplish this through a cooperative effort.

Restorative justice is different from contemporary criminal justice practice in a number of ways. It views criminal acts more comprehensively: Rather than limiting crime to lawbreaking, it recognizes that offenders harm victims, communities, and even themselves. It involves more parties: Rather than including only the government and the offender in key roles, it invites victims and communities as well. It measures success differently: Rather than measuring how much punishment has been imposed, it measures how much harm has been repaired or prevented. Finally, rather than leaving the problem of crime to the government alone, it recognizes the importance of community involvement and initiative in responding to and reducing crime.

Restorative justice responds to specific crimes by emphasizing recovery of the victim through redress, vindication, and healing, as well as recompense by the offender through reparation, fair treatment, and habilation. It seeks processes through which parties are able to discover the truth about what happened and the harms that resulted, to identify the injustices involved, and to agree on future actions to repair those harms. It considers whether specific crimes suggest the need for new or revised strategies to prevent crime.

Restorative justice seeks to prevent crime by building on the strengths of community and the government. The community can build peace through strong, inclusive, constructive, and just relationships. The government can bring order through fair, effective, and parsimonious use of force. Restorative justice emphasizes the need to repair past harms in order to prepare for the future. It seeks to reconcile offenders with those they have harmed, and it calls on communities to reintegrate victims and offenders.

Restorative processes and practices retain their restorative character as they reflect the values and principles of restorative justice. If these values and principles are lost or violated, then the result may not only be less restorative but also be destructive. Four of these values are particularly important: *inclusion*, *encounter*, *amends*, and *reintegration*. It is to these cornerpost values that we now turn.

Review Questions

1. What are the three conceptions used to define restorative justice, and which is most aligned with the authors' definition?
2. What are the three principles of restorative justice?
3. What are the four "cornerpost values" of restorative justice?
4. Does punishment have a place in restorative justice?
5. What are the elements in a restorative justice response to crime?
6. How does restorative justice seek to prevent crime? What are the roles of the community and the government?

Endnotes

1. Gerry Johnstone and Daniel W. Van Ness, "The Meaning of Restorative Justice," in Gerry Johnstone and Daniel W. Van Ness, eds., *Handbook of Restorative Justice* (Cullompton, UK: Willan, 2006).

2. The term and idea behind it is similar to essentially contested concepts, proposed by the philosopher W. B. Gallie and subsequently applied to political science by William Connolly. W. B. Gallie, "Essentially Contested Concepts," in M. Black, ed., *The Importance of Language* (Englewood Cliffs, NJ: Prentice Hall, 1962), 121–146 [first published in *Proceedings of the Aristotelian Society*, 56 (London, 1955–6)] and William E. Connolly, *The Terms of Political Discourse* (3rd ed.) (Oxford: Blackwell, 1993).

3. John Braithwaite, *Crime, Shame and Reintegration* (New York: Cambridge University Press, 1989), 172–173.

4. One of the important implications of the distinction between "community" and "victim" is that the community may not necessarily speak for the interests of the victim. But the opposite is also true: The victim does not necessarily speak for the community.

5. See Braithwaite, supra note 3, for an extended discussion of how shame can be both beneficial and destructive for offenders and the community.

6. Juan Cardenas, "The Crime Victim in the Prosecutorial Process," *Harvard Journal of Law and Public Policy* 9 (1986): 371.

7. There are, of course, other reasons why the government might use force, including most obviously its interest in protecting and advancing its own interests and the interests of its leadership and supporters. We are using "order" more narrowly than the term is often used, particularly when used by governments to justify repressive action. We do not include those uses in this definition.

8. John Braithwaite, "Principles of Restorative Justice," in Andrew von Hirsch, Julian Roberts, Anthony Bottoms, Kent Roach, and Mara Schiff, eds., *Restorative Justice and Criminal Justice: Competing or Reconcilable Paradigms* (Oxford: Hart, 2003), 9–13.

9. For example, the International Institute for Restorative Practices (http://www.iirp.edu).

10. Ivo Aertsen, "Who Is Afraid of Justice?" in *Report from Restorative Justice—Restorative Practices: Are They the Same?* Seminar conducted June 3, 2009, in Leuven, Belgium, 4.

11. Howard Zehr, *Changing Lenses: A New Focus for Crime and Justice* (Scottdale, PA: Herald Press, 1990), 63–82.

12. Gordon Bazemore, "Three Paradigms for Juvenile Justice," in Burt Galaway and Joe Hudson. eds., *Restorative Justice: International Perspectives* (Monsey, NY: Criminal Justice Press, 2002).

13. Conrad G. Brunk, "Restorative Justice and the Philosophical Theories of Punishment," in Michael L. Hadley, ed., *The Spiritual Roots of Restorative Justice* (Albany: State University of New York Press, 2001), 39.

14. Kathleen Daly, "Revisiting the Relationship between Retributive and Restorative Justice," in Heather Strang and John Braithwaite, eds., *Restorative Justice: Philosophy to Practice* (Burlington, VT: Ashgate, 2001).

15. Antony Duff, "Restoration and Retribution," in Andrew von Hirsch, Julian Roberts, Anthony E. Bottoms, Kent Roach, and Mara Schiff, eds., *Restorative Justice and Criminal Justice: Competing or Reconcilable Paradigms?* (Oxford: Hart, 2003), 43.

16. Howard Zehr, *The Little Book of Restorative Justice* (Intercourse, PA: Good Books, 2002), 59.

17. Frances Crook, testifying before the Home Affairs Committee of Parliament, February 24, 2009. The testimony can be found at http://www.publications.parliament.uk/pa/cm200809/cmselect/cmhaff/112/9022405.htm as of August 1, 2013.

18. Lawrence Sherman and Heather Strang, *Restorative Justice: The Evidence* (London: Smith Institute, 2007), 89.

19. A newer study, published in 2011 by the New Zealand Ministry of Justice, also found that "offenders who participated in restorative justice conferences … had a reoffending rate 20% lower than that of a similar group of offenders who did not receive restorative justice." *Reoffending Analysis for Restorative Justice Cases: 2008 and 2009—A Summary* (New Zealand Ministry of Justice, June 2011). See also the following 2011 book on the implementation of restorative justice programs with adult offenders in England and Wales: Joanna Shapland, Gwen Robinson, and Angela Sorsby, *Restorative Justice in Practice: Evaluating What Works for Victims and Offenders* (Oxford: Taylor & Francis, 2011).

20. Ibid.

21. Ibid.

The Cornerposts of Restorative Justice

4

Inclusion

KEY CONCEPTS

* Meaning and elements of inclusion
* Reasons for exclusion
* Accepted ways of including victims
* Giving victims legal standing to pursue reparation
* Inclusion of offenders
* Inclusion of community members

It is a familiar story with an overlooked subplot. A king faces a foreign army with a powerful leader and desperately seeks a champion willing to meet the hostile warrior in single combat. No one in the king's army will accept the challenge despite the king's offer of lavish rewards.

The story is from the Bible, the enemy warrior was Goliath, and the king's eventual champion was David. The fight between David and Goliath is well-known and is usually remembered as a metaphor for the courageous underdog who overcomes overwhelming odds. We return to that metaphor later, but the subplot that is of immediate interest is the account of how King Saul came to include David in his battle plans against Goliath and the Philistine army.

As the story goes, Goliath was a huge man, more than 9 feet tall, and so powerful that he struck fear in the king and his whole army. For 40 days, every morning and evening, Goliath had challenged the Israelites to settle their dispute in single combat. Despite his humiliating derision, no one in the Israelite army was willing to accept the challenge. King Saul offered a generous reward to the man who would defeat Goliath—great wealth, entry into the royal family through marriage, and freedom from taxes—but no one accepted. All were too frightened of this giant warrior.

Although David would later become a brilliant soldier and eventually king, when this story takes place he was too young to enlist in the army. He was the youngest of eight boys, and it was his three oldest brothers who served with King Saul. David lived at home and looked after his father's sheep. He would not even have been present at the battle except that his father had asked him to take food to his brothers and bring back news from the front. David arrived one morning just as the armies were taking battle positions, and as he was speaking with his brothers Goliath strode onto the battlefield and shouted his usual mockery. David was shocked to see the army of

Israel flee in terror. "Who is this foreigner," he asked, "that he should defy the armies of the living God?"

David was so outspoken about his willingness to accept Goliath's challenge that despite his brothers' opposition he was given an appointment with King Saul. The king was initially dismissive, but David argued that whereas Goliath might be unbeatable in conventional battle, he could be defeated by unconventional means. Saul's paradigm was warfare; David's was shepherding. Saul weighed odds of victory and wisely avoided combat when his army was at a disadvantage. It was better for him to wait than to engage the enemy on its terms. David, on the other hand, was a shepherd who had to act quickly to protect his sheep from predators more powerful than he; he had killed a lion and a bear that endangered his flock. His weapons were not designed to deter others or deflect blows; they were ones that could be used at a moment's notice, were lightweight, and portable. He used a staff, a sling, and stones. When faced with an enemy, his instinct was not to pause to look for strategic advantage but, rather, to rapidly protect his defenseless sheep. God had delivered him on those occasions, David argued, and God would help David triumph over Goliath.

We are not told why the king relented and consented to David's facing Goliath. It could be that there was something about David's demeanor that inspired confidence, perhaps Saul realized he had no other alternative, or maybe he came to see that David's approach was sound. But for whatever reason, he agreed to let the shepherd boy serve as Israel's champion against Goliath.

Saul offered to provide David with his best armor, but David was not accustomed to helmets, shields, and swords; he said they would hinder his ability to fight. So he took off the armor; seized his staff, his sling, and five smooth stones; and ran onto the battlefield. As Goliath moved forward to attack, David slung a stone at him, which hit him in the forehead and knocked him out. Using Goliath's own sword, David beheaded the giant.

What were the steps by which Saul came to include David in Israel's national strategy to defeat this foreign power? First, Saul issued an open invitation for someone to fight Goliath. It is obvious from the story that Saul was not interested in accepting Goliath's challenge himself, so his invitation was clearly sincere.

■ ■ ■ ━━━━━━━━━━━━━━━━━━━━━━━━━━━━━━━━━━

The promise of restorative justice lies in the inclusion of victims, offenders, and community members who have been touched by crime.

━━━━━━━━━━━━━━━━━━━━━━━━━━━━━━━━━━ ■ ■ ■

In fact, he bolstered the invitation with promises of reward, and he made sure that everyone in the army was aware of it. He acknowledged that he would need to appeal to the personal interests of would-be champions in addition to their altruistic love of country and king. David seems to have had mixed motives for volunteering; he expressed interest in the reward offered by Saul and also a desire to stand up for Israel and its God against the insults of Goliath. The "noble" motives of saving his country and defending the reputation of God were apparently not inconsistent with a more profane interest in personal wealth and advancement. Saul understood and appealed to both.

Third, he was willing to let David adopt an alternative approach. He made sure that David understood what he was getting into: "You are a boy and he has been a warrior all his life; are you sure this is what you want to do?" Furthermore, because David did not have armor of his own, Saul offered his own tunic and sword, and he also supplied a coat of armor and a helmet. Saul did what he could to prepare David for battle. However, David's lack of military experience meant that this equipment encumbered rather than empowered him. He could not move freely, and he did not know how to use the weapons. So he asked to approach the battle in his own way. He would fight with the weapons he had used before: his shepherd staff and his sling.

Saul invited David, acknowledged and appealed to his interests, and allowed him to use alternative approaches. We suggest that these are critical elements of any attempt at inclusion: *invitation, recognition and acceptance of the interests of the person invited*, and *willingness to adopt alternative approaches that better fit that individual.*

Restorative Justice and Inclusion

If we apply this story to the problem of crime and its consequences, Goliath stands for the enormity of crime and its resulting injuries within a society; David, for individual victims, offenders, and affected community members; and Saul, for the governmental "gatekeepers" responsible for determining how to respond to crime. The promise of restorative justice lies in the inclusion of victims, offenders, and community members who have been touched by crime.

When we speak of inclusion, we mean the opportunity for direct and active involvement of each party in the procedures that follow a crime. As discussed previously, in the usual practice of contemporary criminal justice, once a crime is reported, the victim and members of the community have minimal roles—they may participate as witnesses, if at all. The accused or convicted individual is reduced to a passive participant. The prosecution and defense attorneys, along with the judge, make virtually all the decisions and take all the actions (e.g., filing motions, deciding who will testify, examining and cross-examining witnesses, speaking to the jury, and communicating with the press). This legal maneuvering effectively prevents both victims and offenders from active engagement in clarifying the harms resulting from the crime, not to mention working out a way for the offender to take responsibility for making amends and addressing those harms.

Charles Barton puts it as follows:

The criminal justice system, which is epitomised by the traditional court process, is anything but empowering to the primary stakeholders. In their purported mission to protect the innocent and punish the guilty, contemporary criminal justice systems marginalise and disempower the very people who have most at stake in particular criminal justice interventions. Most significantly, victims and accused alike are discouraged and denied real opportunities to take an active role in the legal processing and resolution of their cases. In effect, they are reduced to the status of idle bystanders in their own cases in what, after all, is their conflict.[1]

■ ■ ■ ▬▬▬▬▬▬▬▬▬▬▬▬▬▬▬▬▬▬▬▬▬▬▬▬▬▬▬▬▬▬▬▬▬

By *inclusion*, we mean the opportunity for direct and active involvement of each party in the procedures that follow a crime. Critical elements of inclusion are invitation, recognition and acceptance of the interests of the persons invited, and willingness to adopt alternative approaches that fit the individuals and their situation.

▬▬▬▬▬▬▬▬▬▬▬▬▬▬▬▬▬▬▬▬▬▬▬▬▬▬▬▬▬▬▬▬▬ ■ ■ ■

In contrast to this, restorative encounter programs (e.g., those described in Chapter 5) invite all interested parties to participate, empowering them through opportunities to pursue their diverse interests.[2] Such programs occur outside the adversarial context of the courtroom and yet offer a structure that supports victim safety and respectful discussion. Their flexibility allows them to consider alternative approaches that fit the particular parties. These are so beneficial that some jurisdictions have adopted laws that grant victims the "right to access to restorative justice programs, including victim-initiated victim–offender dialogue programs offered through the department of corrections."[3]

This is particularly important for victims of crime. The great majority of crimes involve at least two individuals: the victim, who bears the brunt of the harm caused by the crime, and the perpetrator. The criminal justice process places the government, rather than the actual victim, at the center of the case against the accused offender. Victims who want to recover damages must file separate civil actions. As a result, a conflict exists between the government and the victim about "ownership" of the victimization experience—and nearly all criminal justice practices underscore the government's priority. The victim's role in criminal cases is typically limited to being a witness for the prosecution. The criminal proceeding is designed to serve public goals of incapacitation, rehabilitation, deterrence, or retribution. In that proceeding (legally speaking), the victim's personal interest in reparation and vindication is irrelevant and therefore ignored.

■ ■ ■ ━━━

Contemporary criminal justice puts the government, rather than the victim, at the center of the
case. The victim's role is to be a prosecution witness.

━━ ■ ■ ■

Whereas the prosecutor and defendant have formal roles in the criminal justice
process, victims have no standing to pursue their interests in recovering—and/or
reducing the likelihood of—further damages. Restorative justice theory, with its
emphasis on involving all parties and addressing all their harms, rejects this exclusion of victims and provides for their inclusion. It also insists that whenever more
conventional processes are used, they should be adapted to provide opportunities
for genuine inclusion of the victim.

Inclusion for Victims

The injustice of victims' exclusion from the criminal justice process has been a ral-
lying cry of the victims' rights movement and has resulted in a number of programs
and reforms since the 1970s. Among these are victim witness assistance, victim compensation funds, mandatory restitution legislation, and "victim bills of rights" granting victims rights to such things as information, presence in court, and victim impact
statements.

There are at least three ways that victims typically can be included in the criminal justice system. The least inclusive is simply to be given information about what is happening
in their cases. A second is to permit them to observe the proceedings as spectators if they
wish, even if they may later be called as witnesses. A third is to permit them to make a formal presentation at sentencing through a victim impact statement. All these have come to
be generally accepted.

A much more robust approach to victim inclusion is to give victims the right of full
participation—to give them legal standing in the criminal justice process in order to
pursue reparation. More will be said about this, but first let us briefly review the first
three ways to include victims (information, presence, and impact statements). Each is
an established right in many jurisdictions, often because of concerted activism on the
part of crime victims and their advocates.

Information

Crime victims have a basic need for information about the criminal justice process and
how it affects them. At least two categories of information are of obvious interest to victims: information about the services and rights they may expect and information about
the status of the criminal proceeding in their particular case. Included in the former is
information about crime victim compensation, victim services (e.g., emergency assistance, rape crisis centers, shelters, and general victim service agencies), the steps in a

criminal prosecution, contact information, and the victim's rights during the criminal proceedings.*

Information about the status of the prosecution against the accused offender can be provided at any number of stages in the criminal proceedings. The following are some of the junctures at which victims should receive notification:[4]

- Hearings (scheduled/postponed/rescheduled hearings on bail, pretrial release, sentencing, post-trial relief, parole, and commmutation)
- Bail release
- Pretrial release
- Dismissal/dropping of case
- Plea bargains
- Trial dates/times
- Final disposition/sentences
- Earliest possible release/parole dates
- Appeals process/proceedings
- Conditional release from prison
- Release from mental institution
- Parole
- Pardon/commutation
- Final release
- Escape/recapture of offender

Presence in Court

As a general rule, persons expected to testify as witnesses in a criminal trial are not permitted to attend the trial. The reason for this is to prevent witnesses from tailoring their

---

*Section 3.1.2 of *The United Nations Handbook on Justice for Victims: On the Use and Application of the United Nations Declaration of Basic Principles of Justice for Victims of Crime and Abuse of Power* (April 1998) provides that police

- *explain police procedures and the investigatory process;*
- *inform victims about how to protect evidence;*
- *inform victims of the possibility of infection with diseases or becoming pregnant as a result of a crime;*
- *provide information to crime victims about their rights, as well as the availability of crime victims compensation;*
- *immediately refer (verbally and in writing) to community agencies that offer emergency services to victims, as well as information about financial assistance. For example, a brochure should be developed in different languages and given to victims that includes information about emergency and long-term services, victim compensation, likely reactions to crime victimization, and information about the investigative process;*
- *ensure that the victim is personally contacted by telephone or in person 24–48 hours following the initial response in order to determine if assistance has been sought and/or received;*
- *ensure that the property of the victim is secured so that personal safety is not compromised as a result of crime;*
- *establish procedures to ensure that victims of violent crime are periodically informed of the status of investigations; and*
- *promptly provide crisis intervention and psychological first aid or referring to appropriate services.*

testimony to harmonize with what other witnesses have said. In other words, it is designed to ensure that witnesses' statements can be compared with those of other witnesses in an attempt to determine the truth about what happened. An exception to this rule exists for criminal defendants. Despite the fact that they may testify in their defense, their status as a party in the proceedings entitles them to attend the entire trial and to confront the witnesses against them. This exception, however, does not extend to the crime victim because the victim is not a party with legal standing or interest in the criminal case. If the victim is expected to testify for the prosecution, or for the defense, then the victim—like other witnesses—technically would not be permitted to attend the trial.

This exclusion can come as a surprise to victims or their survivors because these parties have a strong interest in observing the case and listening to the evidence and arguments. As a result of advocacy by victim rights organizations, a number of jurisdictions have modified this rule to allow victims to be present during part of the criminal proceedings. For example, victims may be permitted to attend the trial after they have testified. The rationale for this rule is that once they have offered their testimony, the issue of collusion is ended, and there is no longer any reason to keep them out of the courtroom. However, many defense attorneys, eager to keep these persons out of the courtroom lest they sway the jury as sympathetic persons, have taken to listing victims as potential witnesses for the defense—not because they actually intend to call the victims but to keep them out of the courtroom. To strengthen the victims' position, therefore, most U.S. states have adopted rules to permit the victim to attend all proceedings, although they typically give the trial judge the discretion to exclude the victim when the defendant's right to a fair trial would be jeopardized.

Victim Impact Statements

Presence in court and even testimony to support the criminal case against the defendant are not the same as the right for the victim's story to be heard. Many victims want the opportunity to tell criminal justice decision makers how the crime has affected them. Such testimony may be ruled irrelevant and unduly prejudicial to the defendant if offered during the criminal trial. Therefore, many jurisdictions have adopted provisions that permit the victim to make a statement either as part of the presentence investigation or as part of the sentencing hearing (or both). Some jurisdictions permit the victim to make a statement in a plea agreement hearing and provide for victim statements during hearings on pretrial release of the defendant. In addition, most jurisdictions in the United States permit the victim to make an oral or written statement at parole hearings.

■ ■ ■ ──

Many victims want an opportunity to tell criminal justice decision makers how the crime committed against them has affected them.

── ■ ■ ■

Typically, victim statements include evidence about the harm that they or their family suffered as a result of the crime. They may also discuss their views about the offense, the offender, and the punishment they believe would be appropriate. These statements may be given by the victim, the survivor of a homicide victim, or the parent or guardian of a victim who is a minor.

The provision allowing victim impact statements permits victims to express their views; however, the judge is required only to listen and is in no way bound to act on the victim information. In other words, the legal right of the victim is entirely procedural (to speak) and not substantive (there is no requirement that the judge use the information).

Is there a legitimate way for victims to take a more active and substantive part in the criminal proceedings? Under what circumstances and for what reasons could they do so? We propose that victims can pursue their interest in receiving reparation for the material harms resulting from the crime without compromising the justice process for the offender.

Giving the Victim Legal Standing to Pursue Reparations

If the primary issue in criminal justice is whether the offender violated the law, the victim's opinions, strictly speaking, are irrelevant. However, if the aims of criminal justice are modified to emphasize repairing the injuries caused by crime, the procedures of the criminal justice system should justly incorporate the interests of victims in reparation. A direct way of doing so would be to grant the victim legal standing to argue for restitution at sentencing, if the victim so chooses, and at any other stage in which that interest may be affected. Although this proposal would dramatically alter contemporary American criminal justice procedures, it would not be without precedent in our legal heritage.

In some ways, practice in the United States is already moving in this direction. Despite the traditional distinction between the punishment of criminal offenders through the criminal law and the compensation of crime victims through civil tort law, as a practical matter, the wide acceptance and use of restitution within the criminal justice system has already resulted in the partial merger of criminal and tort law. As a consequence, the victim can be viewed as having a direct interest of a restitutive nature in the criminal proceeding. To the extent that this is true, greater inclusion of the victim in criminal proceedings would be consistent with recent trends. It would also, we suggest, be consistent with legal tradition.

Victim and Prosecutor

Some would argue that the prosecutor adequately represents the victim's interest. However, according to the American Bar Association's *Standards Relating to the Prosecution Function*, the prosecutor's responsibilities are "to convict the guilty, enforce the rights of the public, and guard the rights of the accused."[5] Victims' interests are not mentioned and could be included (arguably) only within the broad category of "enforcing the rights of the public." If and when the public's interest conflicts with the victim's interest, the victim is clearly not represented. This is reflected in the American Bar Association's *Guidelines Governing Restitution to Victims of Criminal Conduct*:

> *The prosecuting attorney should advocate fully the rights of the victim on the issue of restitution to the extent such advocacy would not unduly prolong or complicate the sentencing proceeding, nor create a conflict of interest for the attorney acting as advocate for the government.*[6]

Sometimes the conflict between victims and prosecutors is not as nuanced as these examples. What happens when the victim disagrees with the prosecutor's position on sentencing, for example? According to *Dignity Denied*, a report published by Murder Victims' Families for Reconciliation (MVFR), victims who oppose the death penalty have been denied rights afforded to other victims. Three rights in particular were identified:

1. *The right to speak and be heard.* In one case, three relatives of a homicide victim asked to present their views to a parole board hearing on whether to grant a commutation of the death sentence imposed on the offender. The two who opposed the death penalty were denied the right to speak or to offer written testimony; the one who supported the death penalty was the only one afforded this right.
2. *The right to information.* Related to the first right, some prosecutors have refused to provide information about upcoming court proceedings, particularly the sentencing hearing, after learning that the victim opposed the death penalty.
3. *The right to assistance and advocacy.* The report documents a number of cases in which opposition to the death penalty meant that state victim advocates provided no support or assistance to the murder victim's relatives.[7]

The lead author of the study, who was also executive director of MVFR, was Renny Cushing, whose father had been murdered. Cushing was elected to the New Hampshire state legislature and in 2009 secured passage of the Crime Victims Equality Act, which prohibits discrimination against crime victims because of their opposition to the death penalty.[8]

Judith Rowland, a former prosecutor, has argued the need for "independent attorney advocates" to represent victims in the criminal justice system:

> *In our legal system, it may be a conflict of interest for one attorney to represent two clients in the same cause of action. A very real possibility is that such a conflict arises when a prosecutor represents both the victim and the state in the same criminal action when the aim of the prosecution is to obtain a conviction for the state.*
>
> *In whose best interest, for instance, is a "nolo contendere" plea, or the dismissal of counts affecting one or more victims while taking a plea to others? As to the former,*

the prosecutor will be the first to admit that the people's interest is in getting the plea ("nolo" being for the purposes of a criminal proceeding the same as guilty) and not in assisting the victim; in the latter example the risk is great that restitution, insurance, or victim compensation rights may be plea bargained away, lost, or compromised.[9]

What the prosecutor thinks is good for the public may be at odds with the victim's interest. This argues for victims being given standing to act independently of the prosecutor at any stage in the criminal justice process when their interests in recovering restitution and securing personal protection are at risk. Each victim would necessarily have the right to private representation for those stages of the criminal justice process that relate to the victim's pursuit of restitution or personal protection. This may actually help the prosecutor: It is obvious that prosecutors rely on victim cooperation to secure convictions. They may benefit, then, if the possibility of securing restitution encourages increased victim participation in the criminal justice process.

■ ■ ■ ━━━━━━━━━━━━━━━━━━━━━━━━━━━━━━━━━━━━━

What the prosecutor thinks is good for the public may be at odds with victims' interests.

━━━━━━━━━━━━━━━━━━━━━━━━━━━━━━━━━━━━━ ■ ■ ■

In summary, giving victims a formal role in the criminal justice system would result in both an explicit recognition that crime is also an offense against the victim while distinguishing between the legal interests of the victim and the government.

Victim Participation at Various Stages of Criminal Proceedings

Creating such a role would satisfy two of the three requirements of inclusion: invitation and acknowledgment of interests. The third element is acceptance of alternative approaches. What additional changes would need to be made in criminal proceedings if we add victims as a third party with recognized legal interests?

There is a growing body of literature in American journals on the role of victims in Western European criminal justice systems. This literature yields a wealth of suggested roles for victim inclusion in the criminal justice system of the United States. Although the stages of the criminal justice process vary from country to country, there is a basic process common to almost all jurisdictions—certainly to all common law jurisdictions. We discuss possible formal roles that victims and their counsel might play in the following key stages: investigation, bail, trial, plea bargaining, sentencing, and post-sentencing. In each of these stages, there are two basic forms that victim inclusion might take: (1) consultation with the prosecutor and (2) initiation of action independent of the prosecutor. The first requires direct access to prosecutors; the second, to the judge.

Investigation

The decision to prosecute normally rests with the public prosecutor for the reasons that historically gave rise to public prosecution: the need for even-handed and consistent prosecution and the importance of considering public interests over private interests in initiating criminal actions. The decision to charge a defendant nevertheless affects the future interests of the victim. If the prosecutor wants to pursue only one of several potential charges (e.g., charge the offender with a violent crime but not theft), the victim has an interest in negotiating with the prosecutor. Because a victim can secure restitution only after the defendant is found guilty, the victim clearly has an interest in what charges are brought against the accused.

European systems offer four basic options for such intervention: (1) The victim may ask the prosecutor to review an adverse decision, (2) the victim may appeal to the decision maker's superior or to an independent board of complaints, (3) the victim may appeal to the court, or (4) the victim may initiate a private prosecution. These methods of victim intervention employ formal administrative procedures, although few European jurisdictions have a formal appeal process.

An alternative approach is Minnesota's Office of Crime Victim Ombudsman, established in 1985 to assist victims needing assistance for redress of situations in which their statutory rights have been violated or they have been treated unfairly by the criminal justice system. This service continues under the Minnesota Crime Victim Justice Unit (CVJU), which investigates complaints, acts as a referral and information resource, and serves as a liaison between the victim and the criminal justice agency.

Arraignment through Presentencing

Decisions regarding bail could also affect the victim's interests. For example, victims may believe that their personal or family safety will be at risk should bail be granted. If so, they would be permitted to present supporting evidence to the judge (independent of the prosecutor) in the interest of limiting future harm at the hands of the defendant. In such a situation, victims could also request a restraining order against a defendant about to be released. But a victim might have a different objective request that the accused be released on bail in order to continue work and increase the likelihood of collecting future restitution.

Plea Bargaining

Victim involvement in the plea agreement stage is essential. The great majority of all cases are resolved by plea agreement. A plea agreement relieves the court and the prosecutor of the burden of a trial. It is typically an agreement among the prosecutor, defense counsel, and the accused to plead to reduced charges resulting in a lighter sentence. Of 100 felony arrests in the United States, 55 are carried forward. Fifty-two (95%) of these are disposed of by guilty plea. The victim has an interest in securing a plea that will maximize the potential restitution ordered. The interest of the state in obtaining a quick agreement may be at odds with the victim's interest in restitution.

However, the victim's interests and the prosecutor's interests may very well overlap. The victim's interest in restitution and the state's interest in efficient resolution of the case are not mutually exclusive. It is conceivable that restitution to the victim by the offender could satisfy at least a portion of the government's need for punishment. The payment of restitution also might be part of a bargain to reduce other charges.

Sentencing

A number of studies have indicated that victims are more interested in sentencing than in any other stage of the criminal justice process. Eighty percent of California victims interviewed indicated that the existence of their right to speak at felony sentencing was important to them.[10] It is at sentencing that the justice system moves from a legal determination of how to characterize the offender's behavior (did it violate the law?) to both the practical and symbolic act of deciding what to do about that lawbreaking. According to one study of burglary victims, three basic components make up victims' understanding of "fairness" when it comes to sentencing: the punishment the offender will be given, the compensation the victim will receive, and the rehabilitation services that will be made available to the offender.[11] Giving victims the right to intervene at sentencing to seek reparation, then, addresses at least one of these dimensions and arguably may address the other two as well. Restitution is often treated as an "add-on" to the real sentence, even though it is mandated in many jurisdictions. For it to be a meaningful sanction, judges must fashion sentences in which all components, including restitution, can be satisfied. For example, a sentence to incarceration may preclude the payment of restitution, whereas a sentence of intensive supervision probation would not. Sentencing should be constructed so as to increase the likelihood of restitution being paid. Restitution should be normative unless there is a compelling, overriding reason for it not to be.

■ ■ ■ ▬▬

Victims are more interested in sentencing than in any other stage of the criminal justice process.

▬▬▬ ■ ■ ■

Although it is commonly assumed that offenders cannot provide adequate compensation to their victims, studies have concluded that there are relatively few victimizations that are so costly as to negate the possibility of restitution, even after taking into consideration the extremely low income levels of some defendants. One comparative study of restitution programs found that the average compliance rate is 68%, suggesting that more offenders are able to comply than is generally believed. Moreover, this does not touch on the rate of compliance that might be achieved if restitution were given higher priority by sentencing and correctional authorities.

Post-Sentencing

Probation and parole violation hearings can affect the recovery of restitution. Victim interest in timely and full recovery is at risk if the offender violates the conditions of probation or parole and is returned to incarceration. The feasibility of restitution recovery from incarcerated offenders is clearly limited. It is not unreasonable, however, to expect offenders released into the community on probation or parole to pay restitution based on realistic payment plans and effectively monitored restitution collection. Both probation and parole supervision could be extended on an informal supervisory level until restitution is paid in full. In addition, currently recognized system deficiencies in monitoring and collecting restitution need to be addressed in order to provide a reparative framework of criminal justice.

Victim as Civil Claimant in Criminal Cases

In reflecting on how victims' restitution claims could be incorporated in the criminal justice process, it is worth considering the roles given to the victim in other countries, including France. Crime victims there can bring a civil action for damages as part of the criminal proceedings, using the *partie civile* procedure. A victim who brings such a civil action thus becomes a party to the related criminal action and can play an active role, through counsel, in asserting a right to civil damages. A significant number of victims seek this relief rather than instituting civil proceedings.

French experience has demonstrated the advantages of this one-court approach. Combining all the actions in one proceeding has been more efficient and has ensured that penal and civil decisions are consistent. For victims, the use of the criminal process has been faster, simpler, and cheaper than the civil proceeding. The prosecutor proves the guilt of the offender, so victims are relieved of that obligation.

A separate hearing on the victim's civil claim is held after the criminal charges have been settled. If the accused has been found guilty, the victim must (1) show that the injury he or she suffered was directly caused by the prosecuted acts and (2) prove the amount of the alleged damages to his or her person and property. If the accused has been found not guilty, the victim must show by a preponderance of the evidence that the damages suffered were directly caused by a violation of the Civil Code and were the result of the facts adjudicated at the preceding trial.

Victim rights advocates have achieved much during the past decades. These efforts have demonstrated that change is possible. Although we are proposing more comprehensive changes to expand victim involvement in the criminal justice process, it appears that this is not only a matter of basic fairness and justice but also feasible.

Inclusion of Offenders

Once an accused offender is apprehended, his or her initial inclusion is limited to the choice to cooperate with the investigation or not. Legal rights and protections are accorded to offenders for good reasons.[12] Yet these very protections can also shield the accused from participating in their own cases, including facing the harms, seeing the victims, making amends, and accepting responsibility for the crime and its consequences.

Certainly, in the legal process, it is wise for accused offenders to be guided by legal counsel in order to avoid having the prosecution take improper advantage of any words or actions that might prejudice their defense. However, opportunities for offenders to voluntarily enter into an alternative, restorative process outside the courtroom often lead to better outcomes in terms of accepting accountability, making amends, and even reducing the public expense of a protracted legal proceeding.

Chapter 5 describes several ways for offenders to engage in this way. One example, called a "circle," involves facilitated community meetings attended by offenders, victims, their friends and families, interested members of the community, and (usually) representatives of the justice system. Participants each have an opportunity to speak about the crime, including community conditions and related concerns. The focus is on finding an approach that leads to a constructive outcome, in which the needs of the victim and community are understood and addressed along with the needs and obligations of the offender, ending with consensus on a plan outlining the commitments required of the offender (and possibly commitments made by others such as family and community members). All involved understand that the offender will face consequences for noncompliance with the circle plan, including being returned to the circle or remanded to the court.

Restorative justice processes such as this are well established in many jurisdictions, but they are not prevalent enough to be an option in the majority of criminal cases. We contend that the invitation to offenders, their victims and members of the community to participate in such alternatives, is more likely to result in true "ownership" of their culpability and the obligations crime created. This should be a widely-available and commonly used option in criminal cases.

Inclusion of Community Members

Most crimes have an impact on the community where the crime took place—such as residents in the affected neighborhood or the teachers, students, and parents involved with the school system. Community members, like victims, are not generally included in a court process unless they testify for the prosecution or defense or sit on a jury. Although community members are not direct victims, the community may be threatened or disturbed and its members are therefore harmed by the offense. Furthermore, a crime can uncover social problems that need to be addressed in order to build a healthier community and lessen the potential for future offenses. Thus, communities have a stake in the outcome of the justice process and, as such, it makes sense for that stake to be represented.

In a restorative justice process such as a circle (described previously and in more detail in Chapter 5), representatives are present to speak on behalf of the community's interest and to ensure that any agreement includes due consideration of that interest. Furthermore, it allows for increased community understanding of the victim and the offender, and it makes it possible to engage members constructively in moving forward toward a better future. Community *involvement* in characterizing the harm resulting from the offense and working out a just way to address it by properly (and often creatively) holding the offender accountable provides greater incentive for *investment* in building toward a stronger, safer, better community for the future.

■ ■ ■ ──

Community *involvement* in characterizing the harm resulting from the offense and working out a just way to address it by properly (and often creatively) holding the offender accountable provides greater incentive for *investment* in building toward a stronger, safer, better community for the future.

──────────────────────────────────── ■ ■ ■

Conclusion

By *inclusion*, we mean the opportunity for direct and active involvement of the victim, offender, and community in the procedures that follow a crime. Critical elements of inclusion are invitation, recognition and acceptance of the interests of the persons invited, and willingness to adopt alternative approaches that fit the individuals and their situation.

Restorative programs outside the courtroom, such as mediation, conferencing, and circles, are able to be much more inclusive than the criminal justice system can be, and they provide opportunities for victims and community members to directly participate with offenders in explaining the impact of the crime and seeking accountability that addresses the direct harms involved. However, the criminal justice system could be changed so as to create a significant opportunity for inclusion in the court process for those victims who wish to take it. They are already involved as citizens and (possibly) witnesses. Moreover, the rise of restitution orders, victim impact statements, and other victim rights initiatives (e.g., the right to information and presence in court) have begun to give the victim a quasi-party role. A goal that is highly consistent with a restorative response to crime might be to expand and formalize a role for the victim as a party of interest in pursuing reparation. Such a goal would have at least four practical implications for the criminal justice system.

First, victims could obtain legal representation for those stages of the criminal justice process that relate to their pursuit of restitution or protection. This would avoid a potential conflict of interest that may impair the prosecutor's ability to represent the government as well as the victim, and it would symbolically and practically demonstrate the change in the victim's status.

Second, the decision to prosecute would remain with the prosecutor because it is that office which is charged with protecting the public's interest and also for practical reasons of efficiency and fairness. However, because the victim's interests are affected by that decision, there should be an avenue for appeal open to the victim who disagrees with the prosecutor's decision.

Third, sentences would be constructed so as to increase the likelihood of restitution being ordered and paid. In other words, restitution would be normative unless there is a compelling, overriding reason not to order it.

Fourth, care must be taken that rights given to victims do not diminish the defendant's rights or limit the prosecutor's duty to protect the public interest.

These are implications of expanding the criminal justice system to include a formal role for victims to pursue restitution. Victim inclusion addresses the injustice of excluding from the court proceedings those directly harmed by the crime; it moves the criminal justice system toward a more restorative focus.

Offenders, too, can benefit from opportunities to be meaningfully included in the disposition of their case. In the courtroom, counsel takes charge in order to protect the defendant's interests. However, an opportunity to voluntarily enter into an alternative, restorative process outside the courtroom, along with the victim and representatives of the community, often leads to much better offender outcomes in owning account-ability, making amends, and even reducing the public expense of a protracted legal proceeding.

Finally, community members have a stake in the case because of the impact of the crime on their community. Inclusion in restorative processes increases the likelihood of better outcomes for the victim and themselves, as well as potentially uncovering ways to strengthen the community's investment in its own well-being and safety.

Review Questions

1. Why is inclusion important and what are the elements of inclusion?
2. In what three ways are victims currently included in the criminal justice process?
3. What does it mean to give victims legal "standing" to pursue reparation?
4. How could offenders be fully included in their case?
5. Why do community members have a stake in the process?

Endnotes

1. Charles Barton, "Empowerment and Retribution in Criminal and Restorative Justice," in Heather Strang and John Braithwaite, eds., *Restorative Justice: From Philosophy to Practice* (Aldershot, UK: Dartmouth, 2000).

2. The benefits of inclusion and dialogue are not restricted to the parties in nonviolent crimes. See Susan L. Miller, *After the Crime: The Power of Restorative Justice. Dialogues between Victims and Violent Offenders* (New York: New York University Press, 2011).

3. New Hampshire HB 459 "An Act Relative to Access to Restorative Justice Programs by Victims of Crime." Approved July 29, 2009. Effective September 27, 2009.

4. Section 3.1.2 of *The United Nations Handbook on Justice for Victims: On the Use and Application of the United Nations Declaration of Basic Principles of Justice for Victims of Crime and Abuse of Power* (April 1998).

5. Josephine Gittler, "Expanding the Role of the Victim in a Criminal Action: An Overview of Issues and Problems," *Pepperdine Law Review* 11 (1984): 144.

6. American Bar Association, *Guidelines Governing Restitution to Victims of Criminal Conduct* (1988), 4.

7. Robert Renny Cushing and Susannah Sheffer, *Dignity Denied: The Experience of Murder Victims' Family Members Who Oppose the Death Penalty* (Cambridge, MA: Murder Victims' Families for Reconciliation, 2002).

8. New Hampshire HB 370 "An Act Relative to Equality of Treatment of Victims of Crime." Approved August 7, 2009. Effective October 6, 2009.

9. Judith A. Rowland, "Representation of Victims' Interests within the Criminal Justice System," in *The Attorney's Victim Assistance Manual: A Guide to the Legal Issues Confronting Victims of Crime and Victim Service Providers* (prepared for the Sunny von Bulow National Victim Advocacy Center in cooperation with the Attorney's Victim Assistance Project of the American Bar Association, Criminal Justice Section; 1987), 219.

10. Edwin Villmoare and Virginia V. Neto, *Victim Appearances at Sentencing Hearings under the California Bill of Rights: Executive Summary* (Washington, DC: U.S. Department of Justice, National Institute of Justice, February 1992).

11. Mark Umbreit, et al., *Victim Meets Offender: The Impact of Restorative Justice and Mediation* (Monsey, NY: Criminal Justice Press, 1994), 20.

12. In the United States, all who are charged with a crime have a right to counsel; for those unable to afford their own attorney, a "public defender" is assigned. However, recent studies have revealed that the quality and, indeed, availability of public defense is deeply compromised by excessive caseloads, lack of resources, and limited education and training in important advances such as DNA and forensic evidence. This lack of quality public defense has obvious and far-reaching implications for indigents accused of crimes. Justice Policy Institute, *System Overload: The Costs of Under-Resourcing Public Defense* (Washington, DC: Justice Policy Institute, July 2011). Available online at http://www.justicepolicy.org/uploads/justicepolicy/documents/system_overload_final.pdf as of August 1, 2013.

5

Encounter

KEY CONCEPTS

- Encounter programs: mediation, conferencing, circles, and impact panels
- Elements of encounter: meeting, narrative, emotion, understanding, and agreement
- Minimizing coercion

At the end of his epic poem *The Iliad*, Homer recounts an extraordinary midnight meeting between Achilles, the greatest of Greek warriors, and Priam, king of Troy. For 10 years, the Greeks have besieged Troy, and many warriors on both sides have died. Two recent deaths have particular importance to these two men. Achilles is mourning the death of his companion Patroclus, killed by Hector, Priam's son and the leader of the Trojan forces. Priam in turn grieves for Hector, killed by Achilles in battle as retaliation for the death of Patroclus. Achilles has denied burial to Hector's body, choosing instead to disgrace it by dragging it around the city of Troy at the back of his chariot and leaving it exposed to the sun and vulnerable to dogs and scavenger birds. The gods have protected Hector's body from decay and from being torn apart by animals, waiting for Achilles's anger to subside and for him to return the body to Troy for proper burial. However, Achilles's grief and anger do not dissipate, even after Patroclus's funeral and the daily humiliations of Hector's body. Finally, the gods order him to return the body, and they bring Priam to Achilles's tent under cover of darkness and their protection to negotiate the release of the body.

The two bitter enemies meet for the first time. Each considers himself to be the victim of a great loss, and they weep as they remember their dead loved ones. Priam appeals to Achilles by reminding him of his own father, who would long to have Achilles' body returned were he the one who had been killed. Stirred by pity, Achilles agrees to return the body, and he further agrees to a cease-fire for 12 days while Troy mourns the death of its hero.

In his description of this remarkable meeting, Homer paints a complete picture that depicts sharp emotions (grief, pity, anger, fear, admiration, and guilt), carefully chosen words, an awareness of nonverbal communication, and symbols of hospitality and respect. Achilles washes and covers Hector's battered body, afraid that Priam's natural resentment at its degrading treatment would provoke his own explosive anger. They eat together, and as they talk with and observe one another, each comes to a reluctant admiration for the other's strength and wisdom. Achilles prepares a bed for Priam and promises protection on his return trip to Troy.

This meeting offers only an interlude; war resumes at the conclusion of Hector's funeral. Within days, both Achilles and Priam are dead; Achilles is killed in battle before the walls of Troy, and Priam is killed in the following days when Troy is finally defeated. Interestingly, though, Homer did not include those events in *The Iliad*. Instead, he concludes with this dramatic meeting and a brief account of Hector's funeral. His theme, the dreadful consequences of Achilles's anger to both Greeks and Trojans, is completed as he describes the two men's encounter.[1]

Encounter is one of the cornerposts of a restorative approach to crime. It is greatly restricted in conventional criminal justice proceedings by rules of evidence, practical considerations, and the dominance of professional attorneys who speak on behalf of their clients. It is further restricted by the exclusion of key parties: primary and secondary victims. But even defendants are silent pawns in the courtroom, often failing to even comprehend what is taking place because of the arcane language and procedures used.[2]

The guarantee that accused offenders may confront their accusers in court is a well-established international human right. In recent years, some jurisdictions have increased the possibilities for victims of crime to express themselves in, or at least to listen to, court proceedings. Some jurisdictions allow victims to remain in the courtroom to hear testimony about their cases, even though they may themselves be witnesses. Others have given victims the right to address the sentencer (usually the judge) about the impact of the crime on their lives. These innovations are beneficial for victims, and they may have some indirect impact on the attitudes of offenders, but they—like the defendant's right of confrontation—are limited by the adversarial and judicial dimensions of courtroom proceedings and by the definition of crime as an offense against government.

In this chapter, we consider several approaches that permit parties to crime to encounter one another outside of the courtroom. We describe several such programs, including victim–offender mediation, conferencing, circles, and impact panels. We discuss both common and distinguishing elements among these approaches and consider strategic and programmatic issues to be explored as their use is expanded.

Mediation

Victim–offender mediation programs (VOMs) first appeared in the 1970s and were a direct contributor to the restorative justice movement. VOMs offer victims and offenders the opportunity to meet together with the assistance of a trained mediator to talk about the crime and to agree on steps toward justice. Unlike a court process, these programs seek to empower the participants to resolve their conflict on their own in a conducive environment. Unlike arbitration, in which a third party hears both sides and makes a judgment, the VOM process relies on the victim and offender to resolve the dispute together. The mediator imposes no specific outcome; the goal is to empower participants, promote dialogue, and encourage mutual problem-solving.[3]

■ ■ ■ ▬▬▬▬▬▬▬▬▬▬▬▬▬▬▬▬▬▬▬▬▬▬▬▬▬▬▬▬▬▬▬▬▬

Mediation offers victims and offenders the opportunity to meet one another with the assistance of a trained mediator to talk about the crime and come to an agreement on steps toward justice.

▬▬▬▬▬▬▬▬▬▬▬▬▬▬▬▬▬▬▬▬▬▬▬▬▬▬▬▬▬▬ ■ ■ ■

The first programs used the name "victim–offender reconciliation program" to emphasize that movement toward reconciliation was an optimal outcome, whether or not the parties actually achieved it. However, some objected to the word "reconciliation" as unnecessarily (and unhelpfully) value-laden. Victim support advocates were concerned that the term implied a duty on the part of victims to reconcile with their offenders. They preferred "mediation" or, even better, "dialogue" because those terms described the process rather than a possible outcome. Mark Umbreit suggested that the "primary goal of victim–offender mediation and reconciliation programs is to provide a conflict resolution process which is perceived as fair by both the victim and the offender."[4] For this reason, most programs now are referred to as victim–offender mediation programs. We follow this convention for several reasons. Many crimes involve victims and offenders who were strangers to one another before the offense and, hence, "reconciliation" is not applicable. Furthermore, many victims and offenders who complete the VOM process do not become friends. Apology and forgiveness after a relatively brief meeting can be offered in only a limited way. However, it is important not to lose sight of the fact that reconciliation—however incipient—is a possible result of the process of dialogue.

There is a basic structure to the VOM process, although, like other encounter approaches, its operation should "be dynamic, taking into account the participants and empowering them to work in their own ways."[5] The meeting allows the victim and the offender to pursue three basic objectives: to identify the injustice, to make things right, and to consider future intentions.[6] Identifying the injustice begins as both parties talk about the crime and its impact from their own perspective and as they hear the other party's version of the events. Some practitioners have called this "telling their stories." It is during this stage that the parties put together a common understanding of what happened and talk about how it affected them. Both are given the opportunity to ask questions of the other, the victim can speak about the personal dimensions of the victimization and loss, and the offender has a chance to express remorse. Discussion of how to make things right comes through identifying the nature and extent of the victim's loss and exploring how the offender might begin to repair the harm caused by the criminal act. This agreement is typically reduced to writing and specifies the amount of financial restitution, in-kind services, or other reparation to which both parties agree. Then the parties consider the future by, for example, setting restitution schedules, follow-up meetings, and monitoring procedures. Furthermore, meetings frequently include discussions about the offender's plans to make a better future by such actions as addressing alcohol or other drug problems; resisting negative family or peer pressures; and devoting time to productive activities such as work, hobbies, or community assistance.

Restorative justice program research to date underscores the, often remarkable, power of well-run victim–offender mediation. Such encounters help victims achieve a sense of satisfaction that justice is being done and cause offenders to recognize their responsibility in ways that the usual court process does not. Victims confront offenders, express their feelings, ask questions, and have a direct role in determining the sentence. Offenders take responsibility for their actions and agree to make amends to the victims. Offenders often have not understood the effect their actions had on their victims, and this process gives them greater insight into the harm they caused as well as an opportunity to repair the damage. Both victim and offender are confronted with the other as a person rather than a faceless, antagonistic force, permitting them to gain a greater understanding of the crime, of the other person's circumstances, and of what it will take to make things right.[7]

Conferencing

Family group conferencing (FGC), initiated by legislation in 1989 in New Zealand, was subsequently adapted in Australia and is now being used in one of its various forms throughout the world. This program actually has traditional roots—the New Zealand model was adapted from the "whanau conference" practiced by the Maori people. The conference process has been most extensively used in cases involving juveniles, although conferences involving adult offenders (sometimes referred to as community group conferences) are increasingly being used as well.

Conferences differ from VOMs in several ways. First, the process is facilitated, not mediated. The facilitator (or "coordinator" in the New Zealand model) assists the group, making sure the process remains safe for all involved and that it does not wander into irrelevant side issues. (Although this is also true of the mediation programs just described, it is not true of some programs that are far more directive and also use the VOM name.) Second, conference participants include not only the victim and offender but also their families or supporters, sometimes referred to as their community of care. The arresting police officer and other criminal justice representatives may also be present. A typical conference might have a dozen or more people in attendance, although conferences have been conducted with substantially more participants. Third, whereas many VOM programs emphasize the importance of pre-encounter preparation of the parties in individual meetings, conferences are usually conducted with minimal, if any, preparation of the parties.

Conferences open with the facilitator explaining the procedure. Then the offenders begin telling what happened in response to open-ended questions from the facilitator. The victims follow in a similar manner, and they describe their experiences, express how this has affected them, and direct questions (if they have them) to the offenders. The victims' families and friends, and then the offenders' families and friends, add their thoughts and feelings. Following this phase, the group discusses what should be done to repair the injuries caused by the crime. The victims and their families and friends have an opportunity to state their expectations, and the offenders and their supporters respond. Discussion continues until conference participants agree to a plan, which is then reduced to writing.

■ ■ ■ ───

Conference participants include not only the victim and offender but also their families or supporters, with a facilitator to assist them.

───────────────────────────────────── ■ ■ ■

Evaluation studies of conferencing indicate that victim satisfaction with conferences is very high. Restitution agreements are reached in virtually all cases, and these agreements are typically completed without police follow-up. Repeat criminal behavior is less than what would normally be expected. Offenders develop empathy for their victims; families of offenders report that their child's behavior has changed; support networks are strengthened; and the relationships between parents and police officers improve.

Circles

Circles are a community-based decision-making approach that is increasingly used in restorative programs. The basic model used for circles was derived from aboriginal peace-making practices in North America. Circles are facilitated community meetings attended by offenders, victims, their friends and families, interested members of the community, and (usually) representatives of the justice system. The facilitator is a community member (called a "keeper") whose role is primarily to keep the process orderly and periodically to summarize for the benefit of the group. Participants speak one at a time, and they may discuss and address a wide range of issues regarding the crime, including community conditions or other concerns that are important for understanding what happened and what should be done. The focus is on finding an approach that leads to a constructive outcome, in which the needs of the victim and community are understood and addressed along with the needs and obligations of the offender. The process moves toward consensus on a plan to be followed and how it will be monitored. Circles do not focus exclusively on sentencing, and the process often leads participants to discover and address issues beyond the immediate issue of a particular crime. When sentencing is involved, the circle plan outlines the commitments required of the offender and may also include commitments by others such as family and community members. Noncompliance with the circle plan results in the case being returned to the circle or to the formal court process.

The imprint of traditional rituals is visible on circle sentencing processes and structures, to

> *listen to conflicts to discover the potentials for positive change that they may hold for us. Conflicts are openings, doorways to new ways of being together. Because they occur within the whole, they bear a meaning that in some way relates to the whole. Perhaps the way things were wasn't entirely working; conflicts invite us to explore how to change them. Perhaps we've accepted norms that conflicts call us to reevaluate.*[8]

Because they do not have to focus solely on the crime, the victim, and the offender, participation in circles is not restricted to the immediate parties to the crime and those closest to them. Circles can include any community members who choose to participate. Every participant is heard—both in expressing their perspectives and feelings about the crime or other issues and in proposing and committing to solutions. The circle process allows for expression of its members' norms and expectations, leading to a shared affirmation by the circle—not just for the offender and victim, but for the community at large. This context offers renewed community identity and strengthens community life for its members through their participation.

■ ■ ■ ▬▬▬▬▬▬▬▬▬▬▬▬▬▬▬▬▬▬▬▬▬▬▬▬▬▬▬▬▬▬▬▬▬▬▬▬▬▬▬

> The circle process allows for discussion of its members' norms and expectations, leading to a shared affirmation by the circle—not just for the offender and victim, but for the community at large.

▬▬▬▬▬▬▬▬▬▬▬▬▬▬▬▬▬▬▬▬▬▬▬▬▬▬▬▬▬▬▬▬▬▬▬▬▬▬▬ ■ ■ ■

A circle process is initiated when an offender or victim makes application. Support groups may be formed for the victim and the offender. Multiple circles may be held with the support groups before the larger circle occurs. After the circle process has produced a plan by consensus of the whole circle, follow-up circles typically monitor it.

To date, relatively little research on sentencing circles is available, although stories abound to support the general benefits of these processes. Gordon Bazemore and Mark Umbreit report that a study by Judge Barry Stuart in Canada "indicated that fewer offenders who had gone through the circle recidivated than offenders who were processed by standard criminal justice practices."[9] However, it will be of considerable interest when research is available on a more comprehensive set of outcomes reflecting the circle process's objective to bring a measure of healing to the community, the victim, the offender, and their families.

Impact Panels

Not all offenders are caught. Moreover, even when a crime is "solved" by the conviction of the offender, the victim or offender may not wish to meet with the other, or there may be logistical problems that prevent such a meeting from taking place. In each of these instances, victim–offender panels may provide willing parties an opportunity for a kind of surrogate encounter.

A victim–offender panel (VOP) is made up of a group of victims and a group of offenders who are linked by a common kind of crime, although they are not "each other's" victims or offenders. In other words, where VOM and conferencing involve crime victims and their offenders, VOPs bring together groups of unrelated victims and offenders. The purpose of these meetings is to help victims find resolution and to expose offenders to the damage caused to others by their crime, thereby producing a change in the offender's attitudes and behaviors.

VOPs are much more varied in form and content than VOMs and conferencing. A program in England, for example, brings together victims of burglary with youthful offenders who have been convicted of unrelated burglaries. The two groups of four to six persons each meet for three weekly sessions of 90 minutes each. During the meetings, there is discussion and role-play involving all the participants.

■ ■ ■ ━━

A panel is made up of a group of victims and a group of offenders who are linked by a common kind of crime, although they are not "each other's" victims or offenders.

━━━ ■ ■ ■

In the United States, Mothers Against Drunk Driving (MADD) organizes Victim Impact Panels (or Drunk Driving Impact Panels, if offenders or other nonvictims are included) to expose convicted drunk driving offenders to the harm caused to victims and their survivors. The offenders are typically ordered to attend by a judge or probation officer. The victims are selected by MADD or other victim support groups based on two criteria: (1) whether the experience of telling their story is likely to be more helpful than harmful for the victim and (2) whether they are able to speak without blaming or accusing offenders. There is a single meeting, lasting 60–90 minutes, during which the victims speak. Carefully screened offenders may participate as panel members if they have shown remorse, have completed all aspects of their sentence, or have agreed that participation will not result in a reduction of their sentence, and if a screening committee has determined that the remorse expressed seems genuine and that the offender will be an effective speaker. There is no interaction between the victims on the panel and the offenders in the audience, although if the victims agree, there may be a brief question-and-answer period or informal conversation at the conclusion of their presentations.

The Sycamore Tree Project, a program run by Prison Fellowship organizations in New Zealand, England and Wales, Colombia, and a dozen other countries, brings groups of five or six victims into prison to meet with similar numbers of prisoners.[10] Using a prepared curriculum, they discuss issues including responsibility, confession, repentance, forgiveness, restitution, and reconciliation. At the end of the 6- to 12-week project, they draw from their experiences in the program to draft letters addressed (but not delivered) to their own victims or offenders. The program is a prelude to more direct encounters when possible and is an alternative when none is available.

Studies suggest that VOPs can be beneficial to victims and offenders who participate. Victims in the burglary panels reported that they were less angry and anxious as a result of the meetings. Offenders demonstrated a better understanding of the impact of their crime on victims: The number of offenders who believed that burglary victims were more upset about having a stranger come into their house than they were about losing property increased significantly. Research on drunk driving panels has shown a dramatic change in the attitudes of offenders and in the likelihood of recidivism, and it has also shown a significant benefit to the victim participants: 82% reported that it had helped in their healing. These results were even more dramatic when the participants were compared with a control group of nonparticipants after controlling for other variables (e.g., counseling and elapsed time since the crash); participants manifested a higher sense of well-being, lower anxiety, and less anger than nonparticipants. Studies of offender attitudes before and after participating in Sycamore Tree Project have found that offenders' thinking had become significantly less criminogenic.

Elements of Encounter

The previous descriptions are of prototypes or models. In practice, the apparent differences may very well disappear, depending on the circumstances. A "mediation" program may include family members and supporters, for example. Furthermore, some programs calling themselves "victim–offender mediation" or "conferences" may not include key elements of these models. For example, in some programs, the "mediation" consists of shuttle diplomacy by a mediator who meets with each party but does not bring them together. In some "conferences," the victim does not participate. Although there can be benefit to the participants in these practices, they cannot be considered fully restorative.

The illustration of encounter in Homer's *The Iliad* helps identify several elements that contribute to a process of restoration. The first, of course, was that Achilles and Priam actually met. This was not the story of shuttle diplomacy or of negotiation by proxies. Priam came to Achilles's tent for the meeting, and the two men talked and ate together. The second is that they spoke personally; each told the story from his own perspective. This personalized approach has been called *narrative*. They did not attempt to generalize or universalize but instead spoke with feeling about the particulars of the decade-long conflict that concerned them most. The third is related: They exhibited emotion in their communication. They wept as they considered their own losses. They wept as they identified with those of the other. They experienced not only sorrow but also anger and fear. Emotion played a significant role in their interaction. A fourth element is understanding. They listened as well as spoke, and they listened with understanding, which helped them acquire a degree of empathy for the other. Fifth, they came to an agreement that was particular to Priam's grievance and was achievable. Achilles agreed to turn over Hector's body for burial and in addition gave the Trojans time to conduct Hector's funeral.

These elements are also found in the encounter programs described previously. All involve meetings between victims and offenders in which dialogue takes place. In mediation, conferencing, and circles, the victims meet with their own offenders; with VOP, the meetings are between representative victims and offenders. This means that what takes place during the encounter directly engages the other party. This is in contrast to court proceedings, in which the best that will happen is that each party will be able to observe the other's statements to the judge or jury.

■ ■ ■ ━━━━━━━━━━━━━━━━━━━━━━━━━━━━━━━━━━━━━━━

The elements of encounter are meeting, narrative, emotion, understanding, and agreement.

━━━━━━━━━━━━━━━━━━━━━━━━━━━━━━━━━━━━━━━ ■ ■ ■

At the meeting, the parties talk to one another; they tell their stories. In their narratives, they describe what happened to them, how it has affected them, and how they view the crime and its consequences. This is a subjective rather than objective account;

consequently, it has integrity both to the speaker and to the listener. MADD suggests the following to victim panelists in drunk driving panels:

> *Simply tell your story.... After you've given the facts about the crash, talk about how you feel NOW—not yesterday or a week ago or when the crash happened. This will keep your story relevant and poignant and protect you from giving the same presentation over and over again. Speak what is true for you, and you can trust that it will be "right."*[11]

Narrative permits the participants to express and address emotion. Crime can produce powerful emotional responses that obstruct the more dispassionate pursuit of justice to which courts aspire. Encounter programs allow those emotions to be expressed. This can foster healing for both victims and offenders. All of the encounter programs described previously recognize the importance of emotion in training facilitators, preparing participants, and establishing ground rules. As a result, crime and its consequences are addressed not only rationally but also from the heart.

The use of meeting, narrative, and emotion leads to understanding. As David Moore observed about conferencing, "In this context of shared emotions, victim and offender achieve a sort of empathy. This may not make the victim feel particularly positive about the offender but it does make the offender seem more normal, less malevolent."[12] Likewise, for offenders, hearing the victims' story not only humanizes their victims but also can change the offenders' attitude about their criminal behavior.

Reaching this understanding establishes a productive foundation for agreeing on what happens next. Encounter programs seek a resolution that fits the immediate parties rather than focusing on the precedential importance of the decision for future legal proceedings. Therefore, encounter opens up the possibility of designing a uniquely crafted resolution reflecting the circumstances of the parties. Furthermore, they do this through a cooperative process rather than an adversarial one—through negotiation that searches for a convergence of the interests of victim and offender by giving them the ability to guide the outcome.

Do these elements—meeting, narrative, emotion, understanding, and agreement— yield reconciliation when combined? Not necessarily. Achilles and Priam's meeting did not result in the two men becoming friends, nor did it end the surrounding hostilities. However, it did increase their ability to view each other as persons, to respect each other, and to identify with the experiences of the other, and it made it possible for them to arrive at an agreement. In other words, some reconciliation had occurred. As Claassen and Zehr noted,

> *Hostility and reconciliation need to be viewed as opposite poles on a continuum. Crime usually involves hostile feelings on the part of both victim and offender. If the needs of victim and offender are not met and if the victim–offender relationship is not addressed, the hostility is likely to remain or worsen.... If however, victim and offender needs are addressed, the relationship may be moved toward the reconciliation pole, which in itself is worthwhile.*[13]

Issues

Encounters between victims and offenders have a number of advantages, as we have seen, but they also raise some important issues that should be considered carefully before implementing or using such programs. This chapter concludes with a review of three strategic issues of particular importance to policymakers and practitioners:

1. How to minimize coercion of participants
2. Whom to include in the encounter
3. Accountability for conduct and outcomes of encounters

Minimizing Coercion

One of the central attributes of contemporary criminal justice is that it is coercive: Government has the authority to punish offenders and to compel others (including victims) to participate in the process. Encounter programs, on the other hand, are committed to voluntary participation. There is an obvious difficulty in maintaining a truly voluntary process in the context of the highly coercive criminal justice system. Offenders may agree to participate in hopes of a more lenient sentence. This does not necessarily render the offender's participation involuntary or coerced. The existence of sentencing alternatives that produce results more onerous than those achieved by an encounter does not constitute coercion unless the alternatives are either nonexistent or unjust.

■ ■ ■

One of the central attributes of contemporary criminal justice is that it is coercive. Encounter programs, on the other hand, are committed to voluntary participation.

■ ■ ■

A poorly trained facilitator could exert pressure on the victim in an attempt to overcome early and natural resistance to meeting with the offender. Although pressure is wrong, it is appropriate and important that victims as well as offenders receive complete and accurate information about the alternatives they have for resolving the dispute. Eric Gilman suggests that mediation be only one of several options that are offered to victims. He describes the approach used by the Victim Offender Meeting Program of the Clark County Juvenile Court in Vancouver, Washington: Through a thoughtfully worded letter and/or phone contact, this initial connection with the victim seeks to

acknowledge the harm done to the victim and express the community's concern about the harm, and express the community's commitment to hold the offender accountable in ways that are meaningful to the victim (acknowledgment)

provide the victim with general information about the justice system and specific information about what is happening in their case (information)

> *offer victims the opportunity to talk about the impacts of the crime on them (a voice)*
> *provide choices for participation in the justice process (a choice to participate).*[14]

Those who choose to participate—victims as well as offenders—should do so because they believe that there is an advantage to taking this approach. The key, however, is to offer the option of an encounter process as honestly, objectively, and nonjudgmentally as possible so that those who choose otherwise can simply allow the criminal justice system to take its usual course.

Parties Involved

As we have seen, the various encounter approaches differ regarding the number of parties involved and the roles they play in the process. The VOM process typically includes a mediator, the crime victim, and the offender—those parties who are most directly involved. Sometimes the victim or offender asks to have parents or friends present or even (on rare occasions) to be represented by a surrogate. In some programs, the community may be formally represented through designated participants. When there are multiple victims, each victim has the opportunity to participate, and if it is decided that they should meet separately, there could be as many VOM processes as there are victims. Conferences, on the other hand, include family and friends of the parties as well as criminal justice representatives, along with the facilitator. When there are multiple victims and offenders, they and their families may be included in a single conference. Circles involve the offender, victim, support persons for each, criminal justice representatives, and community members—all facilitated by a community member.

Facilitators

In mediation, conferencing, and circles, facilitators are responsible for approaching the victims and offenders, helping prepare them for the meeting, and then guiding the actual meeting. Although many programs rely on trained volunteer facilitators, in the case of serious or violent crimes in which a greater level of therapeutic expertise is needed, professional facilitators may be used instead. In the meetings, facilitators help guide the interaction as needed, ideally following whatever process enhances communication between the victims and offenders and allows the parties to develop their own plan together. Facilitators will take corrective action if the process becomes physically or emotionally dangerous for anyone.

Facilitators do not decide what will happen, as judges or arbitrators do. Nor are they advocates for either the victim or the offender in achieving their goals for the reconciliation process. They do not press an offender to show remorse or a victim to speak words of forgiveness. Their function is to regulate and facilitate communication within the encounter setting to create a safe environment in which the parties can make their own decisions. This means that facilitators must remain alert to the potential for new harm to victims, either through the way the process proceeds or because the victims are not ready for the encounter. The victims' needs and the timing of the victims' recovery—particularly when the crime was serious or violent—are critical considerations in deciding when or whether cases should be brought to an encounter.

This description refers to the way that facilitators are expected to work when programs are run well. Training and selection of facilitators is an extremely important function of an effective program, as is in-service training and evaluation according to standards that reflect best practices and restorative values.

Victims

Victims who choose to participate in encounter processes have the opportunity to ask questions of the offender, express their feelings about what occurred, and suggest ways the offender can begin to make things right. According to one study, victims' three most important goals in entering an encounter process were to (1) recover some losses, (2) help offenders stay out of trouble, and (3) have a real part in the criminal justice process. However, once they had participated in the encounter, these goals changed:

> *[Victims] were most satisfied with (a) the opportunity to meet the offender and thereby obtain a better understanding of the crime and the offender's situation; (b) the opportunity to receive restitution for loss; (c) the expression of remorse on the part of the offender; and (d) the care and concern of the mediator. Even though the primary motivation for participation was restitution, the most satisfying aspect of the experience was meeting the offender.*[15]

A subsequent study found that 80% of victims who had participated in a mediation meeting reported that they had "experienced fairness," compared with fewer than 40% of victims who had chosen not to enter the program. These victims defined "fairness" as the right to participate directly in the process, as rehabilitation for the offender, as compensation for the victim, as punishment of the offender, and as the offender's expression of remorse. As noted previously, studies of family group conferences and circles indicate a similar degree of victim satisfaction.

■ ■ ■ ━━━━━━━━━━━━━━━━━━━━━━━━━━━━━━━━━━━━━━━

Eighty percent of victims who participated in a restorative encounter reported that they had "experienced fairness," compared with fewer than 40% of victims who had chosen not to enter the program.

━━━━━━━━━━━━━━━━━━━━━━━━━━━━━━━━━━━━━━━ ■ ■ ■

Although facilitators are trained not to side with either victims or offenders, the process recognizes that victims generally stand in a different moral position than the offenders, having been wronged as opposed to causing the harm.* There are several ways this

---

*This is not always true, of course, and what can emerge from a restorative encounter is a more complete picture of the dynamics and interaction between the victim and the offender than may emerge during a trial.

happens. First, offenders participate only if they have accepted responsibility for what they have done. Second, the process itself focuses on the wrongdoing by engaging the parties directly in conversation about it. Third, the parties examine the moral implications of the offender's actions.

Offenders

The encounter process puts offenders "in the uncomfortable position of having to face the person they violated. They are given the ... opportunity to display a more human dimension to their character and to even express remorse in a very personal fashion."[16] Genuine acceptance of responsibility can indicate the beginning of a change of heart in the offender, but such acceptance may take some time.

Encounter processes, however, do change offenders' attitudes. According to one study, offenders' reasons for agreeing to participate in encounters included avoiding harsher punishment, getting beyond the crime and its consequences, and making things right. After completing the process, however, they reported that their criteria for satisfaction had changed:

> [O]ffenders were most satisfied with: (a) meeting the victim and discovering the victim was willing to listen to him or her; (b) staying out of jail and in some instances not getting a record; (c) the opportunity to work out a realistic schedule for paying back the victim to "make things right." Strikingly, what offenders disliked most was, also, meeting the victim. This reflects the tension between, on the one hand, the stress experienced in preparation for meeting the victim, and, on the other hand, the relief of having taken steps "to make things right."[17]

It is not surprising that offenders experience this tension because of what they have done. Allowing the offender and the victim to address what happened in a nonjudicial context gives the offender freedom to repair some of the damage he or she caused by the crime and thus gain a better moral footing in the situation.

Support Persons and Community Members

The presence or absence of support persons and community members is a significant difference between the prototypical models of VOMs, conferences, and circles. In VOMs, the principal parties are the victim and offender. In conferences, the family, support group members (the "community of care"), and criminal justice professionals are full participants and play an active role in the process up to and including agreement on a plan of action. In circles, this involvement is expanded to include anyone interested in attending for whatever reason, including community members who have no relationship with the victim or offenders (the "community of interest").

Government Representatives

In both conferencing and circle models, government representatives may participate. These may include the arresting police officer, a social worker, the prosecutor, or the judge—although typically not all of these individuals. In some instances, these people serve as facilitators, and in others they are merely participants. Declan Roche recommends that justice system personnel not serve as facilitators because their decision-making roles within the coercive criminal justice system make it difficult for them to be perceived as neutral conveners.[18]

One might ask whether the state should have a participatory role in a restorative process and, if so, why. As discussed in Chapter 3, the government and community make different contributions to establishing safety. The government's responsibility is to provide a just order, whereas the community's is to build a just peace. Order is established in several ways: first, through the use of coercive power when necessary to bring about order in a chaotic environment, such as after a natural disaster or civil disturbances; second, by creating orderly processes for dealing with crimes and their aftermath; and third, by providing in legislation a clear statement about the conduct that society deems to be criminal. It is in this latter role that government representatives may participate; they bring the perspective of society at large, which means, as Roche suggests, that victims are free to be forgiving if they wish, without sacrificing the principle that criminal behavior is harmful and wrong.[19]

Accountability for Conduct and Outcomes of Encounters

In criminal cases, accountability is generated in several ways. First, the parties are allowed representation by attorneys, who may make motions concerning the process and outcome in court, may object if they believe the judge or other party is taking inappropriate action, and may appeal to a higher court if the judge rules against them. In addition, adult court proceedings are typically open to the public and media, which means that all participants are vulnerable to public exposure. Encounters, on the other hand, typically take place in private and usually without lawyers present. Although a well-trained facilitator can help ensure effective practice, the question arises about the accountability of the facilitator and parties to participate in good faith and in keeping with restorative principles and values.

Roche[20] explored this issue in a research project involving 25 programs in six countries. He found that several forms of accountability are present during encounters. One is what he calls deliberative accountability, which stems from the nature of the encounter process. Each party becomes accountable to the others to explain their positions because decisions are made on the basis of consensus. Consequently, it is necessary for participants to explain their point of view in order to persuade the others. This creates a kind of balance of power in which no party is able to dominate the others. This informal accountability was supplemented in most programs by the availability of an alternative forum if a party was unhappy with the deliberative process. For example, offenders could choose to leave the restorative encounter and demand a hearing in open court.

This is not the only check against domination by parties over others in the encounter. Another is to include friends and supporters of the parties to offer them encouragement and assistance. This might be particularly useful when parties feel intimidated by other parties or when one of the parties has difficulty expressing opinions and perspectives. Some programs allow professional advocates to participate, such as in Australia, where offenders may bring lawyers and victims a victim advocate. In Belgium, attorneys routinely attend encounters in order to advise their clients during the proceedings. A third approach identified by Roche is to carefully prepare the parties before the encounter and screen out those who would not be able to participate without dominating or being dominated. This preparation can include provision of legal information.

In addition, the meeting can be structured to reduce domination. One example Roche offers is of a conferencing scheme that provides for a short break in the middle of the meeting so that young offenders may talk with their families. This allows them to express any concerns privately to their families that they may be reluctant to bring to the attention of the whole group.

More traditional forms of accountability are useful as well, according to Roche.[21] He reports that some of the programs he researched allow observers, although they differ with regard to who may observe. Others permit some form of external review. *The United Nations Basic Principles on the Use of Restorative Justice Programmes in Criminal Matters* states that after an encounter, the agreement should be reviewed by the law enforcement or judicial officials who referred them in the first place. Roche proposes, however, that this review be only procedural and not substantive so that the officials do not substitute their opinions about the outcomes but merely ensure that the process itself is protected.

Conclusion

Encounter programs offer the parties to crime an opportunity to face one another. The formal criminal justice system separates the parties and limits their contact, reduces the conflict to a simple binary choice of guilty/not guilty, and deems irrelevant any information related to the conflict and the individuals that does not directly prove or disprove the legal elements of the crime charged. An encounter, on the other hand, offers victims, offenders, and others the chance to decide what they consider relevant to a discussion of the crime. The encounter tends to humanize them to one another and permits them substantial creativity in constructing a response that deals not only with the injustice that occurred but also with the futures of both parties.

Review Questions

1. What makes an encounter "restorative"?
2. Why is coercion an important issue?
3. What parties are typically involved in an encounter process?

Endnotes

1. Analise Acorn, in *Compulsory Compassion: A Critique of Restorative Justice* (Vancouver: UBC Press, 2004), has criticized our use of this story, accusing us of both misunderstanding and misappropriating the account in an attempt to present Homer as "a fellow booster of their agenda. There is a quackery here—a kind of false advertising—that we ought not to overlook" (p. 92). Her assertion is that we suggest that Achilles and Priam achieved reconciliation to right their relationship, although she inconsistently concedes that we place the story in context as an interlude in a decades-long war that concludes soon thereafter with the death in battle of both men. She complains that we fail to present all of Achilles's motives in returning the body: Pity might have been part of his motivation, but so were gifts brought by Priam and especially the insistence of the gods that he return the body (although we had mentioned the gods' order in previous editions, we have underscored it in this edition so there can be no mistake).

   The premise of Acorn's book is that "[t]he seductive vision of restorative justice seems, therefore, to lie in a skilful deployment—through theory and story—of cheerful fantasies of happy endings in the victim–offender relation, emotional healing, closure, right-relation and respectful community. Yet, as with all seductions, the fantasies that lure us in tend to be very different from the realities that unfold. And the grandness of the idealism in these restorative fantasies, in and of itself, ought to give us pause" (p. 16). Having adopted this view of restorative justice and its advocates, she assumes that this is what we had in mind; that this story is an attempt to weave "cheerful fantasies of happy endings." Based on that assumption, she complains that we have not gotten the story right and that our failure to do so was intentional.

   However, we do not believe that restorative justice promises or even is primarily about happy endings. We make this explicit in the last two paragraphs on page 89 (paragraphs that appeared in previous editions as well). Happy endings may emerge for some participants in restorative processes but certainly not for all, as we have stated in this chapter and elsewhere in all three editions of this book. And as Acorn grudgingly acknowledges, we have emphasized that this late-night meeting was a brief, nonviolent encounter in the midst of a savage war. So why do we use this story to begin the chapter on encounter? Because it offers remarkable insights on what can happen when adversaries meet and communicate authentically. The tension, barely contained anger, pragmatic negotiations, grudging admiration, and nonverbal communication so powerfully presented by Homer ring true. This was a true encounter of adversaries and neither a formalized negotiation by proxies nor a judicial proceeding before the gods in which neither party speaks to the other. It includes features that are often found in restorative encounters.

   But, asks Acorn, in what way is this justice? The answer is that it is not. Neither Priam nor Achilles has admitted guilt, a prerequisite of virtually all restorative encounters. Although Acorn believes that Achilles is at fault (as, presumably, do most who read this story), Achilles himself does not. He views this as simply a meeting between adversaries with comparable moral standing. That is not the case in restorative encounters. It is the admission of one of the parties to wrongdoing that makes an encounter justice.

2. One of this book's authors (Van Ness) is an attorney who practiced criminal law for a time. On one occasion, the family of an indigent client awaiting trial in the county jail contacted Van Ness; he agreed to represent the accused. The next court date, which was simply a status hearing in which the judge would determine whether the case was ready to go to trial, was the following day. During that hearing, Van Ness informed the judge that he would be representing the client, and that he had not yet received a transcript of the preliminary hearing from the prosecutor but that the other discovery had been made available that morning. The prosecutor indicated that the transcript would be available in 2 weeks. Following local custom, Van Ness stated that, notwithstanding that delay, the defense was answering ready for trial and demanding trial under the Speedy Trial Act. The judge continued the case for another 30 days but (again following local custom) did not mark the case ready for trial. The next hearing would be another status hearing.

   When Van Ness spoke with his client after the hearing, it became clear that he had no idea what had taken place. He had heard his previous lawyer, a public defender, demand trial at the last court appearance, and he had therefore assumed that the trial would commence that day. Van Ness explained that the demand for a trial simply triggered the Speedy Trial Act, which provided that if he were not tried within 120 days he would be released. The demand for trial was made solely to protect his right to a speedy trial and not because either side was in fact prepared to go to trial. That was not the only point of confusion: The defendant (understandably, as no one had ever explained it) had no idea what discovery was or why it was important. He remembered the preliminary hearing as a court appearance in which something more than usual happened, but at the time he had thought it was the trial and had been surprised that the public defender representing him had not permitted him to testify. He was shocked to learn that the case would not be going to trial even on the next court date, and he was dismayed to learn that it would probably not be tried until the 120-day period was nearly over.

3. Note that there are differences between mediation conducted by community-based nonprofit organizations and those conducted by judicial authorities. We will not discuss the differences here because the role of the judicial authorities is very different in civil law and common law countries. For discussion of this issue, see Martin Wright, "Restorative Justice: For Whose Benefit?" and Jacques Faget, "Mediation, Criminal Justice and Community Involvement: A European Perspective" in The European Forum for Victim–Offender Mediation and Restorative Justice, ed., *Victim–Offender Mediation in Europe: Making Restorative Justice Work* (Leuven, Belgium: Leuven University Press, 2000). The process we describe here will be more familiar to those in common law countries. Furthermore, some programs call themselves "victim–offender mediation" but use a process of "shuttle diplomacy" between the victim and the offender. In these programs, the mediator acts as an intermediary in negotiating a restitution settlement, and the victim and offender are unlikely to meet. These programs are undoubtedly an effective way to determine how amends will be made, and they provide limited opportunities for indirect communication. They may be very useful when one or both of the parties do not want more contact. However, because the contact is only indirect, we do not include these programs as encounters. We suggest that they should instead be considered as processes leading to amends.

4. Mark Umbreit, "Mediation of Victim Offender Conflict," *Missouri Journal of Dispute Resolution* (Fall 1988): 85, 87.

5. Howard Zehr, "VORP Dangers," *Accord: A Mennonite Central Committee Canada Publication for Victim Offender Ministries* 8(3) (1989): 13.

6. While directing the VORP of the Central Valley program in California, Ron Claassen developed mediator training that presents the basic components as they are discussed here. We are indebted to Claassen for a number of the following insights concerning mediation.

7. Victim–offender dialogue (VOD) can occur even in cases of severe violent crime. An organization called Just Alternatives did a study of best practices for the use of VOD in such cases, based on information gathered from program administrators of 18 established state programs. Findings are published online in the *VOD Guide to Best Practices* (March 2006) available online at http://justalternatives.org/research-project-work/vod-guide-to-best-practices as of August 1, 2013.

8. Kay Pranis, Barry Stuart, and Mark Wedge, *Peacemaking Circles: From Crime to Community* (St. Paul, MN: Living Justice Press, 2003), 77.

9. Gordon Bazemore and Mark Umbreit, *Conferences, Circles, Boards, and Mediations: Restorative Justice and Citizen Involvement in the Response to Youth Crime* (Washington, DC: Office of Juvenile Justice and Delinquency Prevention, U.S. Department of Justice, September 1, 1999), 28.

10. The England and Wales version has been modified due to prison regulations. In that version, one victim participates and the offender group can be as high as 20.

11. Janice Harris Lord, *A How to Guide for Victim Impact Panels: A Creative Sentencing Opportunity* (Irving, TX: Mothers Against Drunk Driving, 1990), 23.

12. David Moore, "Evaluating Family Group Conferences," in David Biles and Sandra McKillop, eds., *Criminal Justice Planning and Coordination: Proceedings of a Conference Held 19–21 April 1993* (Canberra: Australian Institute of Criminology, 1994), 213. Paper may be found at http://www.aic.gov.au/media_library/publications/proceedings/24/moore.pdf as of August 1, 2013.

13. Ron Claassen and Howard Zehr, *VORP Organizing: A Foundation in the Church* (Elkhart, IN: Mennonite Central Committee, U.S. Office of Criminal Justice, 1989), 5.

14. Eric Gilman, "Victim Offender Meetings: A Restorative Focus for Victims," *Restorative Justice Online*, December 2004. Available at http://rjonline.org/editions/2004/December as of August 1, 2013.

15. Mark S. Umbreit, "The Meaning of Fairness to Burglary Victims," in Burt Galaway and Joe Hudson, eds., *Criminal Justice, Restitution, and Reconciliation* (Monsey, NY: Criminal Justice Press, 1990), 50.

16. Mark S. Umbreit, "Mediation of Victim Offender Conflict," *Missouri Journal of Dispute Resolution* (Fall 1988): 9–10.

17. Robert Coates and John Gehm, "An Empirical Assessment," in Martin Wright and Burt Galaway, eds., *Mediation and Criminal Justice* (Newbury Park, CA: Sage, 1989), 254.

18. DeclanRoche, *Accountability in Restorative Justice* (Oxford: Oxford University Press, 2003), 105–106.

19. Ibid., 105.

20. Ibid., 81–103.

21. Ibid., 188–225.

6

Amends

- Apology
- Changed behavior
- Restitution
- Generosity

Ebenezer Scrooge is the archetype of a tightfisted, misanthropic miser. Charles Dickens's story *A Christmas Carol* tells of the conversion of Scrooge by the spirits of Christmas. To help us understand the dramatic change this produced, Dickens begins with a powerful description of the coldhearted, irascible skinflint:

> *Oh! But he was a tight-fisted hand at the grindstone, Scrooge! a squeezing, wrenching, grasping, scraping, clutching, covetous old sinner! Hard and sharp as flint, from which no steel had ever struck out generous fire; secret, and self-contained, and solitary as an oyster. The cold within him froze his old features, nipped his pointed nose, shriveled his cheek, stiffened his gait; made his eyes red, his thin lips blue; and spoke out shrewdly in his grating voice. A frosty rime [coating] was on his head, and on his eyebrows and his wiry skin. He carried his own low temperature always about with him; he iced his office in the dog-days; and didn't thaw it one degree at Christmas.[1]*

Scrooge's sins against humanity seem endless. He abuses his clerk, Bob Cratchit, paying him the paltry sum of 15 shillings a week and providing miserable working conditions (a single burning coal in mid-winter to warm his working station). He refuses to provide any bonus or other concession to Christmas day aside from the day off, which he grants only grudgingly as "picking his pocket." He spurns any contact with his family because there is no financial profit in spending time with them. He refuses to contribute to a fund for the poor on the grounds that he already pays taxes for prisons and workhouses. When reminded that many poor cannot go there and others would rather die than do so, he grumbles, "If they would rather die, they had better do it, and decrease the surplus population."[2] His demeanor is so hostile that no one ever greets him in the street, no beggar approaches him, no child asks the time, and no stranger ever seeks directions. Seeing-eye dogs lead their blind owners into doorways and courtyards to avoid passing by Scrooge.

Scrooge was not always this way. He was a lonely child who buried himself first in books and then, as he grew older, in work. He fell in love, but he delayed marriage so often in order to pursue wealth that his fiancée finally called off the wedding. His first employers were generous to their employees, but as he became an employer himself he viewed such generosity as wasted profit. It was not until he was visited by the ghost of his former partner Jacob Marley, and taken on journeys through time and space with the Spirits of Christmas Past, Present, and Future, that he realized the moral bankruptcy of his life. The purpose of life is not to gain money but, rather, to become "a good friend, a good master, and a good man". How those experiences could lead to such a radical transformation is an interesting and profitable matter for reflection. However, that is not why we begin this chapter with Scrooge's story.

After his night of visions, Scrooge awakens on Christmas morning a changed man. As this final chapter of the story begins, Dickens emphasizes two points: the tangible reality of Scrooge's surroundings compared to the visions of the previous night and the equally clear truth that Scrooge is now different. "Yes! and the bedpost was his own. The bed was his own, the room was his own. Best and happiest of all, the Time before him was his own, to make amends in!"[3]

Making amends. That is what interests us about this story. For Scrooge's efforts to repair the harm of his previous life parallel closely the ways in which he had harmed others in his former life. Before Christmas, he had chased away a boy who sang carols in hopes of a tip; after Christmas, he enjoys an excited conversation with another boy and pays him handsomely to purchase a holiday turkey. Before Christmas, he had abused his employee Bob Cratchit; after Christmas, he anonymously sends him the turkey, gives him a raise, and provides him with enough coal to warm his workstation. He even arranges for medical treatment for Cratchit's son, Tiny Tim, so that he does not die as was prophesied by the Christmas Spirits.

■ ■ ■ ▬▬▬▬▬▬▬▬▬▬▬▬▬▬▬▬▬▬▬▬▬▬▬▬▬▬▬▬▬

Making amends does not undo the past, but it takes steps to repair the harm caused.

▬▬▬▬▬▬▬▬▬▬▬▬▬▬▬▬▬▬▬▬▬▬▬▬▬▬▬▬▬ ■ ■ ■

Before, he was unwilling to contribute to charities serving the poor; after, he makes a very large contribution. Before, he spurned people in the street; after, he greets people with a smile, pats children on the head, questions beggars, and finds that it all gives him pleasure.

Before, he ignored his relatives; after, he attends their Christmas celebration and enjoys himself completely. Before, his response to Christmas was "Bah, humbug!"; after "[i]t was always said of him, that he knew how to keep Christmas well, if any man alive possessed the knowledge."[4]

■ ■ ■ ▬▬▬▬▬▬▬▬▬▬▬▬▬▬▬▬▬▬▬▬▬▬▬▬▬▬▬▬▬

There are four elements to making amends: apology, changed behavior, restitution, and generosity.

▬▬▬▬▬▬▬▬▬▬▬▬▬▬▬▬▬▬▬▬▬▬▬▬▬▬▬▬▬ ■ ■ ■

In making amends, Scrooge did not try to undo the past but instead took steps to repair the harm his behavior had caused. Scrooge apologized to Bob Cratchit and to the charitable solicitors. His change was demonstrated behaviorally by attending his nephew's Christmas party; by paying attention to people in the street, beggars, and little children; by adopting more humane work practices; and by learning to celebrate Christmas well. He made monetary and in-kind restitution by increasing Bob Cratchit's salary and spending more on fuel at the office. He generously sent the large turkey to the Cratchits as an anonymous gift, gave substantially to charity, and paid for Tiny Tim's medical treatment.

These four elements—apology, changed behavior, restitution, and generosity—are the elements of making amends.[5] In restorative processes such as mediation, circles, and conferencing, all four play an important role. An evaluation of conferencing in Australia found that 89.7% of conferences involved a verbal apology, 34.2% involved a commitment not to reoffend, 23.9% involved direct restitution, 17.9% involved voluntary work for the victim, and 36.8% involved community work.[6]

Apology

What is an apology? Carl D. Schneider suggests that apology has three elements.[7] The first is *acknowledgment*: "It was wrong and I did it." There is an admission that a norm was violated and that the person making the apology is responsible for that violation. This is different from simply expressing sorrow about the aggrieved person's beliefs (e.g., "I am sorry that she feels she was injured") because that admits neither the wrong nor the wrongdoing.

The second element is *affect*: "I am troubled by what I did." Julie Leibrich has found that private remorse is the most powerful factor in an offender's decision to stop offending.[8] A person may express regret or shame in words or by his or her demeanor. Victims who witness this can find it a validating, healing experience. However, we need to understand that regret and the expression of regret are two separate things. A low capability to express regret, although diminishing the impact of the apology for the victim, does not necessarily mean that there is no regret.

The third element of apology is *vulnerability*: "I am without defense." The effect of an apology is to make the wrongdoer powerless before the person wronged. The victim may accept the apology and extend at least a measure of forgiveness, or that may not happen. The apologizer cannot know until the apology is offered. When an attempted apology fails to incorporate the element of vulnerability by shifting into an explanation and attempting exoneration, it falls short.

Understood in this way, we can see why an apology is an "exchange of shame and power between the offender and the offended."[9] Where offenders have previously exerted power to the disadvantage and shame of their victims, in offering an apology offenders shame themselves and give the victim power to accept or reject the apology.

An apology is an important part of making amends, even in individualist cultures such as the United States. A Japanese researcher asked 117 American and 198 Japanese students whether an apology would be important to them if someone had stolen $500 from their home. Sixty-nine percent of the Americans and 95% of the Japanese students agreed or strongly agreed that the apology would be important. Only 16% of the Americans and 3% of the Japanese said that an apology was "not necessary."[10]

How can we know for sure that the apology is genuine? This is a reasonable question but a difficult one to answer because it depends so much on correctly understanding the meaning of the words and affect of the person apologizing. But apologies that include the three elements discussed previously are more likely to be genuine than those that do not. David Walker, a coordinator of a restorative justice program operating in prisons in England, had the following response to the question of genuineness:

> *I attended a session in a well-known, inner-city prison full of local, inner-city, young men with all the airs and graces of inner-city life, drugs, violence and gang culture. These things don't cease upon sentencing—if anything they can sometimes be more intense on a prison wing than on the street. Status can be everything on the wing and a new pair of trainers will do wonders for you on the respect scale.*
>
> *To see a young man in an environment like this full of masculine front stand up to read a letter he has written to the parents of another young man he had beaten up in a gang-related incident. To see this man physically shaking and weeping in front of the room I have described. To see some of the other men welling up at what they are hearing. To hear the regret that the realisation of their actions has induced: a realisation not at all prompted by the court process. To witness all this is the only way to have that big question answered. This is what I witnessed and I have absolutely no doubt as to their sincerity.[11]*

Yael Danieli has argued in the context of human rights abuses by governments that an apology alone is insufficient. It must be accompanied by restitution of some sort, even in token amounts:

> *It's not the money but what the money signifies—vindication. It signifies the governments' own admission of guilt, and an apology. The actual value, especially in cases of loss of life, is of course, merely symbolic, and should be acknowledged as such. The money concretizes for the victim the confirmation of responsibility, wrongfulness; he is not guilty, and somebody cares about it.[12]*

This may be true for other crimes as well. Most restorative processes result in agreements that require more than an apology from the offender. These elements are mutually reinforcing. Changed behavior, restitution, and generosity underscore the sincerity of the apology.

Changed Behavior

A second way to make amends is to change behavior. Minimally, this means to stop committing crimes, but the change can be more constructive than that. One of the reasons crime victims give for becoming involved in restorative processes is to help "turn the offender around" in order to keep others from becoming victims. This interest in rehabilitation has little to do with sentimental feelings for the offender and more to do with a concern that others not suffer the same fate as they did.

Genuine change has two components: *changed values* exhibited in *changed behavior.* Scrooge's values changed in the course of his three visitations, but his change was not complete until he transformed his new understanding into action the next day. The same is true for offenders.

Three strategies for changing behavior are to change the environment, learn new behaviors, and reward positive change. These elements are discernable in agreements negotiated in many restorative encounters. For example, the offender may agree to stay away from certain places or (more positively) to attend school or work. This changes the environment of the offender and makes it less likely that the offender will repeat patterns of behavior that lead to crime. Offenders learn new behaviors by taking anger management courses, completing drug treatment, or signing up for training in a work area that interests the offender. One type of reward is the follow-up meeting that takes place after many encounters, during which offenders receive positive reinforcement of their efforts to satisfy the agreement.

■ ■ ■ ──────────────────────────────────────

Genuine change has two components: changed values demonstrated by changed behavior.

────────────────────────────────── ■ ■ ■

Restitution

As a formal way of holding an offender accountable, restitution is a prime way for the justice system to respond restoratively to the harm done to victims. Restitution requires the offender to *recompense the victim* for the harm sustained.[13] Restitution is typically made by returning or replacing property, by financial payment, or by performing direct services for the victim.

As discussed in Part I, restitution was an important part of criminal justice in the past. Even after the shift in thinking that led to the offender becoming the passive recipient of sanctions imposed by criminal courts, calls for restitution sanctions continued to be raised. In his 1516 book, *Utopia,* Sir Thomas More proposed that convicts be sentenced to labor on public works for pay in order to have funds from which to reimburse their victims. The eighteenth-century philosopher Jeremy Bentham argued for mandatory restitution in money or in-kind services in all property crimes. In the latter part of the nineteenth century, a succession of reformers proposed the revival of restitution to international penal conferences. Such calls continued into the twentieth century. In some instances, they were based on the principle of fairness to victims; in others, they were based on the beneficial effects to the offender. It was not until the 1980s, however, that restitution became firmly established legislatively in the United States and elsewhere. For the most part, however, it is still only of secondary importance to other, more traditional sanctions in the criminal justice system.

A number of issues need to be addressed for restitution to assume primary importance in a justice system. We consider some of these later in this chapter.

Generosity

The final component of making amends is generosity. Generosity means *going beyond the demands of justice and equity*. Scrooge sent the Cratchits an enormous turkey for Christmas, one that was far larger than they needed. He gave a surprisingly large gift to charity, one that left the fundraiser stunned by its size. In doing more than he needed to do, he showed both the genuineness of his conversion and his desire to make up for the kind of person he had been: He told the fundraiser that there were many years of back payments in his gift.

Albert Eglash addresses this dimension of making amends by proposing something he called "creative restitution," which means going beyond the required. It involves "going the second mile." This is a form of restitution negotiated by the offender and victim, in which the offender voluntarily takes on a duty that does more than "balance the books."[14]

Examples of generosity often involve the offender offering services that do not necessarily benefit the victim and only tangentially relate to any debt to the community as a whole. For example, the offender may agree to provide artwork for a community center or participate in a home renovation project for a person in need. Because this community service is not directly related to the harm caused, it is difficult to consider it restitution. It looks less like a debt being repaid and more like a contribution being made. Nevertheless, it is clearly intended to be part of how the offender makes amends.

Issues Related to Restitution

The full restorative potential of restitution comes when it is the result of an agreement made in an encounter. This is because in those circumstances, offenders are able to take *active* responsibility by choosing to make restitution, whereas if restitution is simply ordered by a judge, the offenders are only *passively* responsible. Furthermore, in an encounter the parties are able to settle a number of issues for themselves: How much restitution is enough? Who should receive it? What if the offender does not have the resources to pay the victim?

■ ■ ■ ━━━━━━━━━━━━━━━━━━━━━━━━━━━━━━━━━━━━━

The full restorative potential of restitution comes through an encounter agreement, when an offender takes an *active* part in choosing to pay back the victim rather than simply being given a court order.

━━━━━━━━━━━━━━━━━━━━━━━━━━━━━━━━━━━━━ ■ ■ ■

However, in light of contemporary sentencing policies, which are offender-focused, requiring courts to give primacy to restitution would be a significant reform that would move criminal justice in a restorative direction. If that were to happen, policy decisions would need to be made concerning a series of important questions. Let us consider some of those.

Who Should Receive Restitution?

At first glance, the answer to this question seems obvious: the victim. However, there is seldom a single person harmed; there are usually other, secondary victims as well. What about them? If we imagine a series of concentric circles around each crime, the direct victim—the one against whom the crime was perpetrated—would be in the center circle. Other victims could be placed in the remaining circles based on their proximity to the primary victim. Secondary victims or co-victims (e.g., homicide survivors) would be in the second circle. The local community in which the crime took place would be in the third. Insurers or employers would fall into the fourth circle. Society would be in the outside circle.

What can we say about the idea of an injury to society? Should this be recognized in restorative justice, and if so, how is that injury redressed? In a helpful article, Antony Duff[15] argues that criminal cases involve not only the injuries to victims but also injuries that have been caused by *wrongful* action. Wrongful acts are *public* harms, not in the sense that the wrong against the public should be set against the wrong to the victim, but that the public is rightly concerned about what happened to the individual victim. Society is concerned because the wrongful act violates agreed-to moral values captured in the criminal law. He goes on to explore a number of implications that follow from this. One is that the wrongfulness of the behavior can be redressed in ways that offer restitution and restoration to the victim. Another is that repairing the harm caused to the victim may not be a great enough sanction in light of the seriousness of the offense, or conversely, repairing the actual harm to the victim might be far more onerous than the seriousness of the offense would require.

The difficulty arises in attempting to quantify the harm to society. Andrew von Hirsch proposed, in connection with a different but related issue, that harm could be established by determining how it impedes the standard of living of the typical person.[16] How does a particular kind of crime infringe on the typical victim's physical integrity, material support and amenity, freedom from humiliation, and privacy? One possibility would be to convert this calculation into a common denomination, such as a certain number of working days' wages for the average worker. However expressed, this average infringement, less the actual harm to the particular victim, might be considered the public dimension of the harm. This assumes that the overall harm is relatively constant, and that the proportion of harm that is public, as opposed to belonging to the victim, depends on the actual harm experienced by the victim.

However it is calculated, one might conceive of a court requiring a defendant to pay restitution to a victim and some other amount, representing the public dimension of the harm, into a restitution fund that could be available for victims whose offenders are not caught or have not paid.

In some ways, restorative justice theory offers a more useful approach, and that is to handle the issue of a societal harm by allowing a government representative to participate in the restorative encounter. In the same way that reparation to the victim can be negotiated with the victim, and that local communities can be represented (e.g., in circles), so too can the broader societal interest be addressed by including a government representative. This approach is procedural rather than substantive; the emphasis is on who is invited to the restorative process rather than on precisely what harm was caused to society.

Must a criminal sanction of restitution include all the victims in each of these circles? Can it do so? The claim to restitution loses intensity and practicality as the harm involved becomes more indirect, but it does not follow that those claims must be ignored or minimized; after all, criminal laws express the public's censure of behavior that violates the common good. Even more, criminal laws and the institutions of the criminal justice system encourage a public expectation of safety and security that is violated when crime occurs.

We suggest, as a general principle, that those who have suffered the most direct and specific injuries should be the first to receive restitution in criminal proceedings. Therefore, the more indirect or general the injuries, the lower the expectation should be that a judge will order restitution. For practical reasons, it may be useful for legislatures to establish categories of victims and injuries that are eligible for restitution so the decision need not be made on a case-by-case basis, and such categories should reflect the principles of *directness* and *specificity*. This will be particularly important in deciding whether community service should be considered a form of restitution. It is sometimes described as restitution for intangible harm done to the community. However, without first defining with some precision the harm done to the community, calling it restitution is more a rhetorical and imprecise name than a meaningful reality. For example, if a burglar who destroyed a school's computer equipment is sentenced to "community" service picking up highway trash, how can this be described as restitution? It is not at all clear who is being compensated (is it the highway department? taxpayers in general? the people who use the highway?) or how they were directly and specifically injured (or even indirectly injured) by the crime. On the other hand, it would be easier to understand if the community service was to key in data lost when the equipment was destroyed.

■ ■ ■ ▬▬▬▬▬▬▬▬▬▬▬▬▬▬▬▬▬▬▬▬▬▬▬▬▬▬▬▬

Victims who have suffered direct and specific injuries should receive restitution in criminal proceedings.

▬▬▬▬▬▬▬▬▬▬▬▬▬▬▬▬▬▬▬▬▬▬▬▬▬▬ ■ ■ ■

One group of restorative justice practitioners and researchers has suggested that the presence of the following factors makes community service more likely to be restorative:

- Direct involvement by the victim and offender in a restorative process
- Involvement of the community in determining community service that is meaningful to both community and offender
- Community members and offender working side by side
- Public acknowledgment of offender's contribution

- Opportunities for reflection that help offender and community understand and accept community service as "giving back"
- Opportunity for offender to gain or enhance skills or competencies[17]

What about cases in which an offender has been identified but is never convicted of the particular offense? For example, offenders sometimes plead guilty to certain outstanding charges in return for the prosecution's dismissal of other counts. Should restitution be ordered for those charges that were dismissed? In the late 1980s, the Criminal Justice Section of the American Bar Association examined the legal boundaries and precedents related to restitution and established *Guidelines Governing Restitution to Victims of Criminal Conduct*.[18] These require that the offenses be adjudicated before restitution can be ordered. However, the commentary prepared with the guidelines concludes that this merely requires that a court review and sanction the restitution order. Victims in cases dismissed as a result of the plea bargain could receive restitution as part of the overall plea agreement under the guidelines. However, the more remote the claimants are from the case in which the defendant is pleading guilty, the less appropriate it is to pursue restitution as part of the plea.

Should Restitution Reflect the Seriousness of the Offense or of the Injury?

Some actions are more detrimental to public order than others. The relative seriousness of a crime is not necessarily reflected solely in the physical damage that results. For example, an act of vandalism, an aborted attempt to break into a building, and a failed assassination attempt may each result in a broken window. However, in the latter two cases, replacing broken glass is not the only issue that must be addressed. This is reflected in the charges that will be brought in each case as well as in the sentences imposed. Standards of lawful conduct must be reinforced by considering both the seriousness and nature of the offense as well as the nature of harm suffered by the victim and the community in which it occurred.

Courts throughout the United States have used these considerations to design many sentences that are primarily nonincarcerative for a wide range of serious, even violent, offenses. When such sentences include restitution, they address the harm done to the victim and reinforce the unacceptability of the behavior.

Previously, we mentioned von Hirsch's proposal to quantify the seriousness of an offense by calculating the average impact of that kind of offense on victims' standard of living. This might be a useful approach when the matter is before a judge. The other alternative we proposed was procedural: The seriousness of the offense would determine which parties must be present in order to have a satisfactory encounter and agreement on amends. In the most serious crimes, a government representative must be present in addition to the victim, offender, and community representative.

For Which Injuries Should Restitution Be Provided?

The government has a legitimate interest in prohibiting behavior that causes or threatens harm to persons or communities. If preventing harm is one of the justifications for making and enforcing laws that prohibit criminal behavior, then it is reasonable to expect that the penalties or sanctions for breaking the laws would include duties to repair the harm. But what kinds of harm can properly be redressed through criminal sanctions? The American Bar Association's *Guidelines* give judges a great deal of latitude, within broad limits, in deciding which harms should be considered. The limits are that the damages should be directly related to the criminal conduct of the defendant and that they should be easily quantified. Claims for damages that lie outside those limits are better resolved in civil court.

We have suggested that a guiding principle for restitution be that the most direct and specific harms suffered should be the first to be redressed through sentences of restitution. For example, if a victim misses 2 weeks of work due to hospitalization for injuries sustained from a robbery, the lost property and hospitalization expenses are more direct than are the lost wages. They are also more specific than the trauma that may have resulted from the crime.

When Restitution Is Not Feasible

Few offenders have the income or resources at hand to repay their victims. This discourages many victims or prosecutors from requesting restitution orders. Studies have shown, however, that restitution is most effective as a sentence when courts and correctional authorities are committed to it as a sentencing priority.[19] For example, prisoners in Belgium were given opportunities to perform community service inside the prison, with the government paying the equivalent of a wage into a restitution fund for the victims of those prisoners based on how long the prisoners work. When probationers complete their probation period but still owe restitution, they could be given extra time to finish their payments without continuing other conditions of community supervision. If a victim's need for redress is immediate and the victim cannot wait for the offender to pay, the victim could receive funding from a victims' compensation fund with the offender reimbursing the fund over time.

In some jurisdictions, these compensation funds are established using monies paid by offenders for whom no direct victim needed payment and by excess funds accumulated when sentences exceeded the restitution due the victim. Victims who cannot recover damages from their offenders can be repaid from this fund. Forfeiture laws can be applied so that seized assets are used to support compensation funds or assist communities ravaged by crime. The important thing is that offenders make restitution and that victims receive it—directly when possible, indirectly when necessary.

A commitment to restitution involves a commitment to making it feasible. Committed government and community agencies working together can overcome many impediments to restitution. Often, an offender's inability to pay is simply accepted, and the victim's hope of redress is set aside. The government, local businesses, vocational educators, and others can cooperate to address the reasons why an offender has no means. When rehabilitative interventions are needed, human services agencies could also be involved. The community setting provides a potential network of services and opportunities that can help make restitution work.

Once incarcerated, most offenders have virtually no means of making restitution or paying family support. This is why we believe nondangerous offenders should serve their sentences in the community, where they may have a better opportunity to redress the harm caused by their crimes. However, what about those offenders for whom the risks and stakes are so high that they must be incarcerated? We suggest that prisons become a place in which prisoners are encouraged to engage in meaningful work.

■ ■ ■ ▬▬▬▬▬▬▬▬▬▬▬▬▬▬▬▬▬▬▬▬▬▬▬▬▬▬▬

A commitment to restitution for victims means we must make it possible for offenders to make amends.

▬▬▬▬▬▬▬▬▬▬▬▬▬▬▬▬▬▬▬▬▬▬▬▬▬▬▬ ■ ■ ■

What kind of work can be considered "meaningful"? We suggest that the following four factors distinguish meaningful work from other forms of prison industry. Each corresponds to one of the four parties addressed by restorative justice: offender, victim, community, and government:

- Meaningful work fosters training in the work ethic and compensates inmates fairly for their labor, preferably at market wages.
- Meaningful work fosters payment of restitution. The primary benefit to victims of prison industries is the restitution they may receive; if offenders are able to work for decent wages, they have an opportunity to make amends, both financial and symbolic, to their victims.
- Meaningful work fosters development of a productive workforce in the community.
- Meaningful work fosters well-managed correctional institutions by reducing costs and prisoner idleness.

Conclusion

Amends are an important feature of restorative justice. An offender can make amends through apology, changed behavior, restitution, and generosity. Because of the victim's direct harm, a restorative process that involves an encounter with the victim offers the offender the best opportunity to accept responsibility for making amends and provides a method by which they may agree on how this will be accomplished. However, when an encounter is not feasible or appropriate, courts may require the offender to make amends. Restitution is the most obvious and direct way of doing that, although community service, in the right circumstances, may serve as well.

A restorative system is more concerned with repairing harm than with punishment that ignores the need and obligation to make restitution. It also attempts to reduce the likelihood of future harms. This means that when incarceration must be used to restrain exceptionally dangerous individuals, the criminal justice process should maximize the likelihood of timely restitution to victims while effectively managing the potential risk to public safety.

Sanctions should first redress the harm to victims. The risk and needs of offenders as well as the seriousness of offenses can be addressed in ways that do not defeat this primary purpose. Furthermore, the most direct victims should be considered first, and the most specific harms suffered should be the first to be redressed. Therefore, if complete deprivation of liberty is not necessary to manage the risk and stakes, it should not be imposed. This is because a commitment to restitution involves a commitment to making it feasible.

To manage high-risk offenders, restitution programs must be designed with, and given sufficient resources to establish and maintain, supervision components that will meet the risk involved. Finally, a restorative system will strive to develop and maximize the use of restitution sanctions while guarding victims' and offenders' interests in an efficient and timely disposition of their cases.

Incarceration need not be the standard against which all punishments are measured. In a restorative system, restitution provides that gauge. If restitution for the harm done to victims is returned to its central place in the sentencing process, programs will do more than divert nondangerous offenders from prison; they will ensure that offenders make restitution to victims so that a measure of restoration occurs.

Review Questions

1. What are the four elements to making genuine amends?
2. Why is each element important?
3. Who should receive restitution?
4. What are obstacles to restitution and how might they be addressed?

Endnotes

1. Charles Dickens, *The Annotated Christmas Carol*, with introduction and notes by Michael Patrick Hearn (New York: Clarkson N. Potter, 1976), 58, 60.

2. Ibid., 65.

3. Ibid., 163.

4. Ibid., 172.

5. Linda Radzik, in her insightful book *Making Amends: Atonement in Morality, Law, and Politics* (New York: Oxford University Press, 2009), presents *amends* comprehensively as the moral obligation of a wrongdoer to take atoning steps that open the possibility of "moral reconciliation" with the victim and/or the victim's community. Because wrongdoing causes not just material but also *relational* harm, the elements of amends also include consideration of the victim's moral claims. It is not sufficient to prescribe a set of restitutionary steps for the wrongdoer (as if to repay a monetary debt); the wrongdoer must demonstrate a commitment to moral transformation that looks to future values and behavior as well. Furthermore, the prerogatives and responsibilities of the victim to accept the wrongdoer's sincere and proportional amends are essential to the equation, if there is to be genuine repair of the relationship (or *redemption*, in her terminology). Our example does not delve into, for example, Bob Cratchit's view of the harms he endured under Scrooge's unredeemed behavior and the moral obligations Cratchit and his family would perceive as essential to achieving a genuine relationship with Scrooge.

We take Radzik's point. Yet in practical terms, combining our four elements of apology with encounter (as explained in Chapter 5), reintegration (Chapter 7), and inclusion (Chapter 5) creates the conditions under which moral reconciliation can occur to a significant degree (as Radzik acknowledges, p. 159).

6. Hennessey Hayes and Tim Prenzler with Richard Wortley, *Making Amends: Final Evaluation of the Queensland Community Conferencing Pilot* (Brisbane, Queensland, Australia: Queensland Department of Justice, Juvenile Justice Branch, 1998), 34.

7. Carl D. Schneider, "What It Means to Be Sorry: The Power of Apology in Mediation," *Mediation Quarterly* 17(3) (Spring 2000): 265–280.

8. Julie Leibrich, "The Role of Shame in Going Straight: A Study of Former Offenders," in Burt Galaway and Joe Hudson, eds., *Restorative Justice: International Perspectives* (Monsey, NY: Criminal Justice Press, 1996); see also Julie Liebrich, *Straight to the Point: Angles on Giving Up Crime* (Dunedin, New Zealand: University of Otago Press, 1993).

9. Aaron Lazare, "Go Ahead, Say You're Sorry," *Psychology Today* (January/February 1995): 40–43, 76–78 at 42 (cited in Ibid).

10. Kate Elmwood, "Cultural Conundrums: Sorry to Have Made You Apologize," *Daily Yomiuri Online* (April 16, 2012), available at http://cafe.daum.net/japanologist/Gd1/3198?docid=rj xGd1319820120417102417 as of August 1, 2013.

11. David Walker, "So How Do You Know That an Offender Means It When They Say Sorry?" Blog entry for Prison Fellowship England and Wales, February 21, 2011. Available online at http://prisonfellowshipew. blogspot.com/2011/02/so-how-do-you-know-that-offender-means.html as of August 1, 2013.

12. Yael Danieli, "Healing Components: The Right to Restitution for Victims of Gross Violations of Human Rights and Humanitarian Law," in D. Pollefeyt, G. J. Colijn, and M. Sachs Littell, eds., *Hearing the Voices: Teaching the Holocaust to Future Generations* (Merion Station, PA: Merion Westfield Press International), 219–233.

13. In some countries, the term *compensation* is used instead of *restitution*. See, for example, Lucia Zedner, "Victims," in Mike Maguire, Rod Morgan, and Robert Reiner, eds., *The Oxford Handbook of Criminology* (New York: Oxford University Press, 1994), 1237, 1239. However, we use that term more narrowly to refer to payments made by the government or by another party unrelated to the offender, in an amount typically based on the nature and extent of the harm.

14. Albert Eglash, "Beyond Restitution: Creative Restitution," in Joe Hudson and Burt Galaway, eds., *Restitution in Criminal Justice* (Lexington, MA: Heath, 1977). See also Albert Eglash, "Creative Restitution and Mutual Help Programs: A Historical Contribution to a Workshop on Family Violence," submitted to the Workshop on Restorative Justice and Family Violence, July 2000, Canberra, Australia, 8–9 (manuscript in author's possession).

15. Antony Duff, "Restoration and Retribution," in Andrew von Hirsch, Julian Roberts, Anthony E. Bottoms, Kent Roach, and Mara Schiff, eds., *Restorative Justice and Criminal Justice: Competing or Reconcilable Paradigms?* (Oxford: Hart, 2003), 43–60.

16. Andrew vonHirsch, *Censure and Sanctions* (Oxford: Clarendon, 1993). He was exploring the link between the seriousness of an offense and a particular punishment. Crimes can be listed in order of seriousness, as can potential sanctions. However, it is extremely difficult to connect a particular crime with a particular sanction. Von Hirsch suggested that looking at effect on standard of living might be one way to do that.

17. K. Pranis, G. Bazemore, M. Umbreit, and R. Lipkin, *Guide for Implementing the Balanced and Restorative Justice Model* (Washington, DC: U.S. Department of Justice, 1998), 54.

18. American Bar Association Criminal Justice Section, *Guidelines Governing Restitution to Victims of Criminal Conduct* (including commentary on the guidelines) (Chicago: American Bar Association, 1988).

19. See Catharine M. Goodwin, "Imposition and Enforcement of Restitution," *Federal Probation* (June 2000), available online at http://www.ussc.gov/Education_and_Training/Guidelines_Educational_ Materials/cgLALrest6-00.pdf as of August 1, 2013.

7 ⸬

Reintegration

KEY CONCEPTS

- Elements of reintegration: safety, respect, help, and care
- Victim needs
- Offender needs and responsibilities
- Meaning and means of reintegration

One of the central characters in Victor Hugo's classic story *Les Misérables* is Jean Valjean, a man who stole bread for his starving nephew and ultimately served 19 years in prison. After his release, Valjean's prospects were hindered by the requirement that he present documentation of his "convict" status wherever he goes, with the result that he was repeatedly denied work and shelter. This practical burden only compounded the bitterness and hardness of heart that Valjean had developed over the years. Physically, he was an exceptionally strong man, but he had become stunted in spirit and filled with hatred.

His redemption began one night after police arrested him for a theft committed earlier in the evening. He had robbed a poor but generous bishop who had given him food and shelter, making off with the household silver. When the police discovered the bishop's silver, they forced Valjean to return to the bishop's house to be confronted by the churchman. If the bishop denounced him, Valjean was doomed to either more years in the wretched conditions of prison or execution. However, instead of accusing Valjean of robbery, the bishop told the police that the silver was a gift to Valjean and publicly made a further gift of two valuable silver candlesticks. He bade Valjean to go in peace as an honest man and to return any time as a welcome guest. The bishop addressed Valjean as "my brother," telling him "you belong no longer to evil, but to good."[1]

Nearly faint with shock and relief at this utterly incomprehensible turn of events, Valjean, as if by habit, stole money from a child only a short time later. The contrast between the identity called out for Valjean by the bishop and the perversity of this petty theft finally broke through his hardness of heart:

> [T]his last misdeed had a decisive effect upon him; it rushed across the chaos of his intellect and dissipated it, set the light on one side and the dark clouds on the other, and acted upon his soul, in the condition it was in, as certain chemical reagents act upon a turbid mixture, by precipitating one element and producing a clear solution of the other.... He beheld himself then, so to speak, face to face, and at the same time, across that hallucination, he saw at a mysterious distance, a sort of light which he took at first to be a torch. Examining more attentively this light which dawned upon his conscience, he recognised that it had a human form, and this torch was the

bishop.... He filled the whole soul of this wretched man with a magnificent radiance. Jean Valjean wept long.... While he wept, the light grew brighter and brighter in his mind—an extraordinary light, a light at once transporting and terrible.... He beheld his life, and it seemed to him horrible; his soul, and it seemed to him frightful. There was, however, a softened light upon that life and upon that soul.[2]

The bishop had given Valjean four critical gifts. First, he provided for his safety by telling the police that the silver in Valjean's possession was a gift. Second, he demonstrated respect for Valjean's dignity and worth. This impoverished man bore the label "convict" and because of that was unable to re-enter society. The bishop called him "brother." Third, despite his own straitened means, he provided practical and material help to Valjean, freely giving him food, a bed, and his valuable silver. Lastly, the bishop provided a moral and spiritual beacon by forgiving Valjean, challenging him to be better than he had been, and demonstrating faith that such change was possible. These four things—safety, respect for dignity and worth, practical and material help, and moral and spiritual guidance and care—worked together to transform Valjean's image of himself in relation to the hatefulness of society. His life course was altered; he became a responsible person (although haunted by his "convict" past) and one who lived out a commitment to be generous to others despite the bitterness he encountered in them. Valjean's anger and hatred had defined him and his perception of the world until the bishop gave him the wherewithal to change.

■ ■ ■ ▬▬▬▬▬▬▬▬▬▬▬▬▬▬▬▬▬▬▬▬▬▬▬

The elements of reintegration are safety, respect for dignity and worth, practical and material help, and moral and spiritual guidance and care.

▬▬▬▬▬▬▬▬▬▬▬▬▬▬▬▬▬▬▬▬▬▬▬ ■ ■ ■

Crime and its aftermath can be defining moments for both victims and offenders, for profoundly different reasons. Victims suffer both practical and emotional losses as well as potential physical harm and the social stigma associated with being a "victim." Offenders often retreat (as Valjean did) into a forest of bitter rationalization that is compounded by the barriers facing people with a "record." Restorative justice places a high value on taking the steps needed to help both victims and offenders re-enter their communities as whole, productive, contributing members.

It may seem counterintuitive to discuss reintegration of victims and offenders in the same chapter. Their needs are different, and their moral positions in relation to the crime are different as well. Nevertheless, victims and offenders often share at least one common problem: The community treats each as an outcast; each is stigmatized. Both victims and offenders find that they threaten many around them. Victims make nonvictims feel more vulnerable ("If it happened to her, it could happen to me."). Offenders arouse anger and fear ("If he did it once, he will do it again."). Therefore, without equating their status at all, we focus on how the community might, like Valjean's bishop, be a catalyst for reintegration of victims and of offenders. First, however, it is important to understand the issues and injuries victims and offenders may carry with them as they begin the process of reintegration.

Victims

The most immediate need for victims of crime is safety. If the offender still has power to harm the victim, as in domestic violence, stalking, kidnapping, and so forth, the victim needs to be rescued from the peril and made safe. Even if the offender does not have that power, victims may feel frightened and vulnerable in the aftermath of a crime. Of course, much of this protective work is done by the police in securing the crime scene, but there are additional needs related to safety that often are met by community and nonprofit organizations. For example, domestic violence shelters provide a safe haven for partners and children of abusers who are in danger of further violence. Many of these are operated by nongovernmental organizations with financial support by the government. Other victims may need assistance in securing their homes in the aftermath of a burglary. Still others may need to move or may want an escort when they must be in places that make them feel vulnerable, such as parking lots at their places of employment. Steps taken to help victims feel safe are important not only because they increase their actual safety but also because they allow the victims to deal more effectively with trauma they may have experienced.

There are also financial costs related to victimization—costs that are greater than the loss sustained in the course of the crime. The UK Commissioner for Victims and Witnesses, Louise Casey, conducted a survey of 36 families bereaved of a loved one through murder, manslaughter, or culpable road death to determine the total financial costs they faced. These costs included inquests, civil prosecutions, accommodations, counseling, trial transcripts, and travel to hearings. The costs averaged approximately £37,000 ($56,500) per family, or £113K ($137,340) if lost earnings were included. The costs continued to accumulate for long periods of time; the average duration was 5 years.[3]

Crime victims are widely diverse in terms of demographics, prior history of victimization, and personal stability preceding victimization. According to Dean Kilpatrick, "most studies show that victims' demographic characteristics such as gender, race, and age have little (if any) impact on crime-related psychological trauma."[4] However, prior victimization (especially in cases involving violence or crimes against the person) does increase the incidence of serious trauma for victims. Post-traumatic stress disorder (PTSD) and depression are among the symptoms identified for such victims. Even in cases in which serious psychological trauma is not likely, victims frequently experience a crisis reaction for which some form of intervention is indicated. Arlene Bowers Andrews offers the following description of victims in crisis:

> *Persons in crisis tend to be emotionally aroused and highly anxious; often they are weepy. Occasionally they will act extremely controlled and noncommunicative as*

a way of coping with high anxiety, but most often they will express despair, grief, embarrassment, and anger. Their thoughts are disorganized, leading to trouble in relating ideas, events, and actions. They may overlook important details, or may jump from one idea to another, making communication hard to follow. They may confuse fears and wishes with reality. Persons in crisis may not be able to perform routine behaviors such as basic grooming. They may avoid eye contact, and may mumble. Some persons may act impulsively. People in crisis have reported feelings of fatigue as well as appetite and sleep disruptions. They are socially vulnerable, which means that a helper can have significant influence, but so can people with exploitive motives. People in crisis act in ways similar to people with certain forms of chronic mental illness, but it must be emphasized that the crisis state is time limited, usually lasting no more than a few days to six weeks.[5]

For a victim in crisis, the isolation and disorientation may be limited by time, as Andrews indicates. A source of support and understanding, as well as practical links to available resources, can mitigate the intensity of the crisis as well as its duration, and in so doing lessen the damage to relationships, employability, and other factors related to the victim's long-term readjustment. For a victim experiencing psychological trauma, crisis intervention can involve referral to mental health resources in order that the trauma may be assessed and appropriately treated. Many crime victims do not spontaneously recover without treatment.

Beyond the crisis or trauma resulting from the crime itself, there is also a negative self-identity that sometimes occurs for victims. Morton Bard and Dawn Sangrey have devoted a chapter of *The Crime Victim's Book* to "The Mark: Feelings of Guilt and Shame." They quote a robbery victim:

I just hate to think of myself as a victim. It's like when I lost my job—I hadn't done anything wrong, but it was so embarrassing to have to tell people that I had lost my job. And when this happened, I felt the same way. It was like a guilty secret. I didn't want to talk about it.[6]

Furthermore, Bard and Sangrey point out that crime victims are commonly viewed as having failed to protect themselves. Criminal justice procedures often reinforce this negative view that somehow the victim is responsible for the crime. This stigma may have long-term, unexpected negative results in a victim's life. Once the immediate crisis has passed, victims are left with an ongoing battle to preserve their sense of self-control and dignity.

Independent of whether there is significant emotional trauma, victims often confront a range of practical concerns, such as emergency assistance, crime scene cleanup, transportation, help filling out insurance forms, explanations about the criminal justice process, and so forth. Just as Valjean needed practical assistance, many victims need this as well.

Furthermore, crime can create a spiritual or moral crisis for victims as they try to make sense of what happened to them and how they will respond. Many wonder why this happened to them, what they did to deserve this. Others find that they have had a rather benign view of humanity, a view that is now seriously undermined. Others must come to terms with their fantasies of and desires for revenge: Is this healthy and is it justified? If they were practicing members of a religion, their faith may be challenged by what took place. Each of these instances provides an opportunity for growth, but wise assistance may be needed to clarify the issues and come to resolution.

■ ■ ■ ━━━

Criminal justice procedures sometimes reinforce the view that somehow the victim is responsible for the crime. This stigma may have long-term, unexpected negative results in a victim's life.

━━━ ■ ■ ■

Reintegration for victims, then, focuses first on crisis intervention and help with the trauma resulting from the crime and then on ongoing support as life is resumed in the new "normal" patterns, while coping with the resurgence of crisis symptoms from time to time. A stabilizing family or community in which the victim feels secure and cared for offers the victim an environment in which to work out the feelings and fears following victimization and in which to redefine and redirect his or her life.

Offenders

We all must take responsibility for the choices we make in life. This is true for offenders; they must face honestly what they have done, accept accountability, and recognize the effects of their crime on others—the victim, the offender's family, and the community. This, however, should not blind us to the often overwhelming personal, societal, and spiritual obstacles faced by offenders when it comes to reintegration—obstacles for which the community may have some responsibility. As recidivism rates indicate, too few offenders establish themselves in productive, crime-free lives following their prison sentence. Huge numbers of prisoners are released daily. This group represents the most stigmatized offenders, and those perhaps in most need of reintegration. Although not all offenders face the same burdens as transitioning ex-prisoners, the differences are more in degree than in kind. The label of "convict" follows all who have been convicted, not just prisoners.

Prisoners possess an assortment of needs upon release from incarceration. Some of these existed prior to their crime and subsequent incarceration; others are caused or exacerbated by their status as ex-offenders. Together, these needs can present nearly overwhelming obstacles to successful reintegration. Some released prisoners face hostility and potential violence when they return to their communities because of unresolved matters with their victims or the fear of people in the community. (One example is the challenge of finding community placements for pedophiles when their prison sentence is completed.) Although an overt threat of violence may affect only a small number of released prisoners, all face immediate discrimination by society, and this is often compounded for ethnic minorities. One of the most difficult challenges an ex-prisoner encounters is finding employment. A large percentage of ex-offenders lack start-up money for food and clothes, reliable transportation, suitable shelter, adequate education, psychological counseling, and drug treatment. Other difficulties include the lack of societal acceptance or approval, lack of positive role models, peer pressure, unrealistic expectations, an excessive or deficient sense of sin and guilt, fear of failure, distrust of others, hopelessness, and the lure of addictive behaviors. They often do not connect with or have access to resources for overcoming obstacles. Many released prisoners are not aware of public or private agencies that could help, and even when they are, those agencies are overworked.

More than half of all American prisoners will have to rely on somebody else for support and a place to live when discharged. Ex-prisoners who live alone or with their parents generally have more problems than those who live with their spouses and children. A majority of marriages or significant relationships break up while one partner is incarcerated. Even prisoners with intact marriages often experience serious marital discord in the post-prison home environment or an absence of warmth, trust, and support. Offenders may have weak prosocial skills that hinder their relationships with family as well as with friends, neighbors, and employers; many have developed inappropriate relationships, antisocial values, ethical insensitivity, destructive habits, and an inability to make decisions or plan ahead.

■ ■ ■ ──

Prisoners have an assortment of needs upon release. Some existed prior to their crime; others were caused by their having been in prison. Together, these needs can present overwhelming obstacles to successful reintegration.

── ■ ■ ■

These problems are increased by the specific effects of incarceration, where most decisions—both important and trivial—are made for the prisoner. The regimen inside prison walls produces the so-called "institutionalized mentality" that can make even simple matters on the outside paralyzing to the ex-offender. Matters such as paying an electric bill, pumping one's own gas, or choosing among various brands at the supermarket are overwhelming, let alone more complex matters such as holding a job or forming a healthy relationship with a significant other. The expectation that offenders can emerge as law-abiding citizens ready to assume a responsible place in the community—even if the community were prepared to accept them as such—is fanciful. Offenders are isolated from the community by their own problems as well as by public distrust and cynicism.

In summary, victims and offenders both experience alienation that results from emotional distress, family tension, physical dislocation, loneliness, and stigmatization. For victims, the sense of isolation adds an additional injury to the crime. Offenders who have "paid their debt to society," but find that they are still excluded from it, experience this exclusion as an injustice. Like Jean Valjean, victims and offenders need help reintegrating into the community.

Reintegration

When we speak of reintegration, we mean re-entry into community life as whole, contributing, productive persons. This means more than being tolerant of the person's presence; it means acceptance of the person as a member. It requires action on the community's part but also on the part of the offender and/or victim involved. For many individuals faced with transition, particularly offenders, reintegration is a misnomer. Their previous immersion in lifestyles characterized by drugs, crime, and other disintegrating realities make it questionable whether real integration was present even before they entered the criminal justice process from which they are now emerging. Furthermore, their experiences in the criminal justice system frequently increase their alienation from the norms and institutions that are viewed as positive and constructive elements of community life. Nevertheless, we use the term *reintegration* to include those situations that might be better described as "integration."

We believe that the work of John Braithwaite on what he calls "reintegrative shaming" can help us understand the roles both the community and the one being reintegrated may play.[7] Although Braithwaite's work focuses on how to respond to offenders, many of his observations on the factors that support reintegration can apply to victims as well. For both victims and offenders, a critical next problem is the community's failure to reintegrate them. For offenders, this goes beyond help with re-entry (although that may be needed); it means finding ways for them to rejoin the community as contributing members, not outcasts. For victims, this goes beyond providing services; it means permitting the individual to leave behind his or her "victim" status and to successfully re-enter community life.

Braithwaite suggests that for reintegration to take place, the relationship between the one reintegrated and the reintegrating community must be characterized by at least three traits: (1) mutual respect for one another, (2) mutual commitment to one another, and (3) intolerance for—but understanding of—deviant behavior.[8] Implicit in these three is that the person being reintegrated and the community feel safe from harm. Interestingly, these four traits are closely related to the four gifts of the bishop to Valjean: safety, respect for his dignity and worth, practical and material help, and moral and spiritual guidance and care.

Reintegration places unusual demands on communities because it requires that we view others and ourselves as a complex mixture of good and evil, injuries and strengths. Furthermore, it means that while we resist and disparage evil and compensate for weaknesses, we must also recognize and welcome the good and make use of strengths.

Building a Reintegrative Response

What might a comprehensive reintegrative response look like? First, services would be readily available for those who need them as soon as the need arises. These might range from highly intensive support tailored to particular individuals to services that are generally available to all citizens, such as social welfare assistance. A victim or offender support worker would be assigned to work with the person; this individual would be skilled at obtaining assistance, listening sympathetically, and understanding and being able to explain the criminal justice process. Third, a support group would be organized, if necessary, including families, friends, the victim or offender support worker, and providers of needed services.

■ ■ ■ ▬▬▬▬▬▬▬▬▬▬▬▬▬▬▬▬▬▬▬▬▬▬▬▬▬▬▬▬▬▬▬▬▬

Reintegration means re-entry into community life as whole, contributing, productive persons. This means acceptance of the person as a member of the community.

▬▬▬▬▬▬▬▬▬▬▬▬▬▬▬▬▬▬▬▬▬▬▬▬▬▬▬▬▬▬▬▬ ■ ■ ■

Victims would find that human and financial resources are available from the moment the crime is reported. The victim support worker (who might be salaried or volunteer) would maintain regular contact and communication with the victim. The two would problem-solve together, and the support worker could serve as advocate for the victim, if necessary, with the employer, families, and so forth.

Susan Herman[9] describes such an approach as "parallel justice." She suggests that criminal justice is offender-oriented and that efforts to include victims, although important, are inadequate. Restorative justice, which Herman equates to restorative encounters, may be beneficial for victims, but she believes they fall short because they are available to only a small number of victims, are often offender-oriented, do not address all the important needs of victims, and do not provide a role for government in helping rebuild victims' lives. She proposes that there should be a parallel justice response for victims that would focus on ensuring that victims are safe, assisting them as they recover from the trauma of their crimes, and making resources available to help them rebuild their lives. She lists four principles that should guide the response to victims:

First, when a crime is reported, the safety of the victim should be a high priority for police and other criminal justice agencies.... Second, every victim of crime should be offered immediate support, compensation for losses, and practical assistance.... Third, all crime victims should have an opportunity to explain what happened to them, the impact the crime had on their lives, and what resources they need to get back on track.... Fourth, case managers should coordinate all available resources to meet victims' needs.[10]

In a similar way, the resources needed by offenders must be identified and structured so they are readily available to those who need them. These could be coordinated by probation and parole personnel but require other governmental and community assistance as well. Furthermore, some offenders may require intensive supervision and support because of the risk they pose to the community and, sometimes, the potential danger the community poses to them. A case in point is Circles of Support and Accountability, part of an intensive reintegration process for high-risk sex offenders returning to the community following the completion of their sentences. The Mennonite Central Committee (Canada) developed the approach under contract with the Correctional Service of Canada. It involves volunteers (primarily from the faith community) forming support groups for transitioning ex-offenders in the context of a structured reintegration program. The Circles of Support and Accountability work cooperatively with the police, neighborhood groups, and treatment professionals to reduce recidivism by individuals convicted of sexual offenses, to help them reintegrate into the community, and to reassure their victims and neighbors. The ex-offenders involved are known to present high potential risk, and this creates understandable fear on the part of the community and the returning ex-offenders. The Circles of Support and Accountability provide specific mechanisms for dealing with the many issues involved and aim to help the ex-offenders establish positive lives in the community—lives that offer greatly reduced risk to the safety of others.[11]

Reintegrating Communities

Braithwaite's work (discussed previously) has been criticized on the grounds that reintegrative shame does not work as well in urbanized and individualistic societies as it does in more communitarian cultures. Much of the discussion on this has focused on the lack of potency of shame, but perhaps a more difficult challenge has to do with the reduced likelihood of reintegration in such societies. If reintegration requires relationships characterized by mutual respect, mutual commitment, and "understanding intolerance" for deviant behavior, then the problem we face has a great deal to do with the lack of such relationships. It is relatively easy to think of ways to stigmatize offenders even in our individualistic society, and such shaming efforts are done today. The problem we face is less how to shame than how to reintegrate. Where can we look for persons willing to offer the respect, commitment, and understanding that is required?

Families and Supporters

The families and supporters of the victim or offender are often the first community to which they look for help and support. Often, however, they are overwhelmed themselves by their own trauma resulting either from the victimization of their loved one or by the injuries they have sustained from the offender. Consequently, their ability to provide assistance is limited by their own issues and needs.

The Huikahi Circle, developed in Hawaii by Lorenn Walker, was designed for incarcerated people as they prepare for release. It brings together their supporters, at least one prison representative, and a facilitator to prepare a re-entry plan for the incarcerated individual. The incarcerated people determine their goals, and the group helps them decide the best way to achieve those goals. According to Walker, it produces better outcomes for people than traditional case planning and case management programs in which professionals make the decisions for the incarcerated people.[12]

The process is strengths-based and consequently does not focus solely on the problems to be overcome. However, it does recognize that the supporters themselves have been harmed by the incarcerated person and that this harm must also be addressed if they are going to be able to provide assistance and encouragement during the time of re-entry. The purpose of the circle is to deal with the harms and to help the offender prepare a plan that will address those.

The circle begins with the facilitator inviting the incarcerated person to tell the group about something he or she is especially proud of having achieved while in prison. The rest of the group is then invited to create an inventory of the person's strengths. When this is completed, the facilitator helps the group to transition to a discussion of the ways they have been harmed by the incarcerated individual's actions. This conversation begins with the prisoner and continues with the supporters speaking of their injuries and steps the offender could take to make amends. The offender is then invited to consider other people not in the circle who were also harmed by the crime. The group discusses whether an apology letter to those individuals might or might not be helpful.

The group then transitions into a discussion about how the prisoner can meet the needs faced in transitioning back into the community. From this discussion, they prepare a transition plan, which includes a date and place to hold a follow-up circle. The group concludes with each participant sharing something positive they learned or observed about the prisoner in the course of the meeting.

This process was designed for incarcerated individuals, but it would be interesting to consider what something similar would look like for victims of crime and their supporters. It would give them all an opportunity to discuss the trauma of the crime and set realistic plans for how to help the victim recover.

Support and Assistance Groups

Another source of help is to look to others who have been in a similar situation to create a community for at least some part of the journey toward reintegration. These affinity groups demonstrate that the significant relationships necessary to reintegration need not have existed prior to reintegration. The common struggle to deal with a crisis and to re-establish oneself in light of that crisis can provide the basis for such relationships.

Self-help and support groups have been developed for both victims and offenders. Because of common experiences (including shared alienation from the broader community), members of these groups find strength in meeting together to talk with and encourage one another.

■ ■ ■ ──────────────────────────────────────

Self-help and support groups exist for both victims and offenders. Members of these groups find strength in meeting together to talk with and encourage one another.

────────────────────────────────────── ■ ■ ■

An example of a nationally organized effort for victim support is Parents of Murdered Children. There are many other locally organized groups for victims focused on specific needs or shared experiences such as battering, rape, and other violence. Shelley Neiderbach described the effect of victim group counseling sessions as follows:

> *The degree of victim isolation cannot be overestimated. Crime victims feel lost not only within themselves but within the human community as well. Therefore, the conversion of the ... [crime victim's] counseling group into what became a virtual subculture and "intentional family" was swift, predictable, and enthusiastically determined by the participants. This fairly immediate sense of group identity laid the groundwork for the more acute and profound psychological revelations that victims then permitted to surface as the sessions continued.*[13]

Neiderbach distinguished such support groups from "most publicly funded victims' services," the object of which is to promote the welfare of the victim "in the service of converting victims to witnesses, so that prosecution rates can be higher."[14] Although such programs may perform important services and may be staffed by highly motivated and compassionate people, Neiderbach's point was that they do not create the kind of relationships necessary to aid in what we have called reintegration. They have a different purpose. Support groups are able to meet some of those unmet needs.

Offenders, too, can benefit from the support, encouragement, and accountability offered by peers in overcoming the challenges of re-entry and reintegration. There are a number of re-entry and aftercare efforts that organize and equip groups of ex-offenders in communities throughout America, providing encouragement and accountability in staying crime-free and establishing stable lives. Ex-offenders who have successfully reintegrated and achieved stability often lead these groups.

However, there are limitations to affinity groups. Support groups for victims or offenders offer validation to those recovering from their experiences with crime and can be a source of strength for them as they work to re-enter their community. However, for reintegration to be complete, similar relationships must be forged with members of the wider community, not simply with others who feel alienated from it or who have shared an experience of need. Otherwise, all that exists is a subculture.

One place to find people in the wider community who are willing to walk alongside persons needing reintegration is faith communities. Churches, synagogues, temples, and mosques are located in most communities, and they are usually already meeting local needs.[15] Ram Cnaan of the University of Pennsylvania performed an extensive study of social services in the United States and documented "the massive involvement of the religious community in social services provision" for a wide range of needs.[16] Cnaan and colleagues present strong evidence that religious-based services can and do produce positive results, suggesting the contours of a "limited partnership" between government and faith communities for the meeting of needs. The bishop in *Les Misérables* recognized all the dimensions of Valjean's bitterness and alienation and was able to respond to his spiritual needs while also meeting his very basic and practical needs for shelter and food. This help was key to his reformation. Communities of faith can offer victims and offenders who seek it a similar chance for help, reaching multiple dimensions of need in the reintegration process.

Faith Communities as Reintegrating Communities

Faith communities have the potential to be agents for reintegration for both victims and offenders. We understand that there are significant obstacles to such an undertaking. Christian churches, the faith community with which we are most familiar, have often been better at proclaiming love than demonstrating it. They are fragmented; they are viewed with suspicion by many nonmembers as more interested in wealth or politics than in sacrificial service; and some of their members too often give simple, glib answers to the searching and questioning that follows a crisis. Nevertheless, the church's strong and extensive *history of involvement* with those in need, its *traditions* that speak of both the call and the resources to undertake such a task, and its *presence* in virtually every part of the world make it a promising agent for reintegration. We discuss Christian faith traditions to illustrate this point because that is where our research and experience are most extensive. Others with different expertise may be able to test our hypothesis with other faith communities.[17]

History

For two millennia, and in a variety of cultures and nations, many churches have served as reintegrating communities for those who are alienated. That has certainly been true in the United States, where the church has been actively involved in issues ranging from the abolition of slavery to the humane treatment of criminals. It was Quakers in Philadelphia who convinced the city to establish what is generally credited as the first penitentiary—a place of penitence—in 1790 as an alternative to cruel corporal punishments. They believed that crime resulted from a negative moral environment, and that the foundation for reformation was to provide a solitary, moral environment.

■ ■ ■ ▬▬▬▬▬▬▬▬▬▬▬▬▬▬▬▬▬▬▬▬▬▬▬▬▬▬▬▬▬▬▬▬

Faith communities have the potential to be agents for reintegration for both victims and offenders.

▬▬▬▬▬▬▬▬▬▬▬▬▬▬▬▬▬▬▬▬▬▬▬▬▬▬▬▬▬▬ ■ ■ ■

The first nationally recognized prison expert was Louis Dwight, whose work distributing Bibles for the American Bible Society had taken him into jails, where he was shocked into action by the unconscionable conditions he found. He became a leading proponent of what was called the "Auburn System" of corrections (the first major alternative to the Pennsylvania approach), which emphasized collective treatment of offenders in religious revival meetings, religious teaching, and congregate labor. Since that time, religiously motivated individuals have proposed and implemented new ways of improving the effectiveness of those prisons through rehabilitative programs.

Although it is clear that prisons as we now use them will never accomplish such rehabilitative purposes, we should not forget the context in which these proposals were raised. These early reformers argued against the inhumane punishments of the time; they proposed, raised support for, and initiated whole new approaches that were designed to be reintegrative. There are important lessons to be learned in why prisons became places of exclusion and disintegration rather than avenues toward reintegration, but the failure of the efforts should not blind us to the significance and enormity of the effort and its intent.

It is also true that religious people and institutions have often been all too happy to relegate to others the responsibility for "law and order," including increasingly punitive measures against lawbreakers. Gerald Austin McHugh leveled the following indictment in his 1978 book, *Christian Faith and Criminal Justice*:

> *Throughout its history, the Christian Church in America has endorsed, tacitly approved, or at the very least been shamefully ignorant of the inhumanities of our criminal justice system. Even after the explicitly religious penal models of the penitentiary movement have faded into history, it was (and is) widely assumed that the punishment of criminals is in some way a holy duty.… And where Christians have been concerned with justice, it has all too frequently been the selective vengeance we have sanctioned as retribution, as opposed to the all-encompassing righteousness which is known as justice in the bible. It is not at all unusual to hear a Christian minister decry the rising tide of crime and immorality in print or in the pulpit, but it is rare indeed to hear a Christian minister exhorting the faithful to actually dare to love their enemies.*[18]

Nevertheless, there has been a significant increase in the past 30 years in the numbers of Christians who are actively involved in service to victims and offenders. Prison Fellowship, founded by Charles Colson after his incarceration for Watergate-related crimes, has become one of the largest volunteer organizations in the world, with affiliates in 127 countries. The U.S. Office for Victims of Crime has worked with faith communities since 1982 to help them respond to the needs of crime victims. An increasing portion of the Christian faith community is becoming involved in criminal justice services.

Tradition

The Judeo-Christian tradition teaches care for the outcast, relief for those in need, and the intrinsic value of human beings as created and loved by God. Biblical tradition and stories show God's desire that all should be redeemed. The commandments to love one's neighbor and (even more) to love one's enemy are compelling reasons for churches to rise to their responsibility for assisting with reintegration.

The New Testament story of the Good Samaritan is a direct lesson in caring for a victim of crime. It instructs church members to be good neighbors by offering to assist victims (and other persons in need) in moving toward physical, emotional, and spiritual recovery. As victims deal with their crises, their anger, hurt, disorientation, and isolation may be mitigated by the caring presence of someone willing to help in whatever way the victim needs and wants. Furthermore, some victims may desire to explore the spiritual or theological aspects of what happened to them.[19] This is undeniably a difficult and sensitive area; victims who are angry and vulnerable may say or do things that many church members would find distressing or even heretical. When well prepared, however, those people of the church can form communities of reintegration.

We previously mentioned the thousands of church volunteers who are currently involved in reaching out to offenders. Much of this work is going on in prisons and jails, but a great deal of it is also happening within communities. For those who have developed friendships or mentoring relationships with prisoners, it is a hard fact of life that many hopeful and determined prisoners fail to succeed after they are released. Throughout the world, churches and church members are stepping forward to help those coming back from prison toward reintegration. Halfway houses, job training and placement efforts, alcohol and other drug treatment programs, life skills training, and mentoring are some of the ways church members are getting involved.

■ ■ ■ ▬▬▬▬▬▬▬▬▬▬▬▬▬▬▬▬▬▬▬▬▬▬▬▬▬▬▬▬▬

> When victims or offenders feel stigmatized and isolated, a faith community can be a source of support. Both can benefit from practical assistance, emotional support, and spiritual nurturing in a context of trust and concern.

▬▬▬▬▬▬▬▬▬▬▬▬▬▬▬▬▬▬▬▬▬▬▬▬▬▬▬▬▬ ■ ■ ■

Presence

There are approximately 350,000 places of worship in the United States. They are visible in every community. This fact has been noted recently by policymakers who recognize that community-based groups, including faith communities, have a potential for delivering social services that may far outstrip government programs in effectiveness. Religious influence—even simple attendance at church or a Bible study—has been shown to mitigate a whole variety of social ills, from drug use, disease, and depression to delinquency and crime.[20] This positive association offers hope for reintegration for both victims and offenders, who could benefit from a touch of the "faith factor." When victims and offenders feel stigmatized and isolated, a faith community can be a source of positive personal contact and support. Both can benefit from available practical and physical assistance, emotional care and support, and spiritual nurturing in a context of trust and concern.

For victims of crime, crisis services can help lessen the duration and severity of the stages of victimization by (1) helping the victim rebuild a sense of safety and security, (2) allowing the victim to ventilate questions and feelings and validating those feelings, and (3) preparing the victim for what he or she might experience through the crisis. There is no formula for healing. The road to recovery will be different for individual victims, and they must be empowered to work toward it in their own ways.

[A] "helpful" person who tries to second-guess the victim, imposing what the helper thinks the victim wants, can add to the sense of violation.… Really helping a person

in trouble requires extraordinary sensitivity and discipline. People who really want to help must focus on the victim, listen carefully for the victim's expression of his or her needs and then respond to that expression—without imposing their own suggestions or judgments or perceptions. The ideal helper is one who is able to create a climate in which victims will be able to ask for and get whatever help they want.[21]

In the impact stage of victimization, victims may need a variety of practical services, such as transportation to a hospital or clinic; crime scene cleanup; help with police and insurance forms; calling friends or clergy; help with burial arrangements; and assistance with emergency food, clothing, shelter, and finances. Some victims need help navigating the maze of the criminal justice system; therefore, someone able to explain the criminal justice process may be crucial. Because prosecutors' offices are often unable to notify victims adequately about the progress of their cases, volunteers can work with these offices to keep victims informed of upcoming hearings.

In the crisis phase, victims have emotional needs as well as physical or practical ones. Research has consistently shown that the most significant intervention to crime victims is for someone to demonstrate human care and compassion for them. In all stages of victimization, just having another person on hand can be important. A primary role of the caregiver is to be a friend to the victim. Because victims frequently feel a loss of dignity and control, compassionate care can help restore a sense of worth and self-respect. Although victims may not want to hear answers to their cries of anger and distress, the freedom to express these feelings in a supportive context is deeply needed.

For offenders, basic personal and practical assistance in the critical weeks and months of initial transition to the community can be the key to beating the recidivism odds. In the first months after release, short-term, practical assistance may be urgently needed. This includes the very basics: money, food, clothes, housing, and transportation. However, because of the effects of incarceration and previous life experiences, most prisoners are confused about what to do to meet these basic needs. The stress of the re-entry process can heighten the risk of alcohol or other drug abuse and personal conflict. Many returning prisoners lack the skills and life experience to cope positively with stress and conflict; behaviors that are "normal" in the prison context are starkly different from what is expected in a workplace, for instance. Thus, there is also a significant need for a coach, advisor, or mentor during this period to help with orientation, encouragement, and follow-through.

In order to deal most effectively with this crisis period, practical planning can help the person in transition see beyond the immediate needs to a strategy that will diminish the crisis, build confidence, and promote independence. Over time, some of these basic needs may stabilize, but there may be longer term issues involved in reintegration. In the following months and years, although crisis times do occur, needs generally have more to do with sustaining a stable residence and job, developing and maintaining healthy relationships with family and friends, setting and meeting personal goals, and reorienting life patterns. The kinds of needs—and their intensity—will vary among individuals, based largely on the support systems they already may have in place.

In addition to the practical and social issues that complicate the re-entry process, there is also a spiritual dimension to both the problems and the resources of ex-offenders. This dimension is evident in the reverberating effects of child abuse and violence and in the chokeholds of addiction and depression. The temptation to take shortcuts or escape routes rather than dealing honestly or effectively with problems and obstacles reflects more than just "bad habits"; they may also have spiritual dimensions. Twelve-step programs have recognized this fact for years; this is arguably one reason for their long-standing success. Ex-offenders in transition need spiritual as well as practical and emotional resources in order to reintegrate successfully into the community and to overcome the many hurdles leading up to that success. Spiritual nurturing and a supportive faith community are beneficial for transitioning offenders in their personal growth and maturation as members of families and society. Faith communities are able to give offenders a place to learn, grow, and gain strength in an atmosphere of both accountability and support.

Faith communities face internal and external challenges when they are confronted with the needs of prisoners and victims. Perhaps the most difficult issues arise when dealing with offenders who have a history of sexual abuse. Because children and other vulnerable people attend faith communities and need to be safe while doing so, churches and states are grappling with the best way to create safety. North Carolina, for example, has made it illegal to be within 300 feet of a church nursery, which makes attending church impossible. Meanwhile, the Seventh Day Adventist church has issued guidelines providing that sexual abuse offenders may be restored to membership only if they are not given unsupervised contact with children. The desire is to balance protection of the congregation with the desire to support abusers' freedom of worship.

By providing practical assistance and opportunities to discuss spiritual and emotional issues in a supportive context, faith-based programs can assist victims and offenders in moving beyond their alienation to greater emotional, physical, and spiritual health. Of course, ethnic, religious, and cultural backgrounds of victims and offenders are important factors. They may have varying cultural assumptions about managing anger, grief, and stress. They may be deeply involved in other religions or may be hostile to religion. Programs offering a spiritual component must be sensitive to this and able to help the victim or offender gain access to the resources of their own tradition and support network.

Conclusion

We have shown that both victims and offenders wrestle with stigmatization and other issues as they face their futures, and we have suggested that faith communities are a potential resource in every community. Whether it is faith communities, other community organizations, or government agencies that provide the services, the important point is that for restoration to occur, victims and offenders need to find wholeness and establish themselves in the community as participating members. To do so, each has barriers to overcome, and it is our view that it is part of the community's role to take some responsibility for assisting with the needed reintegration. It is not sufficient simply to see that a victim is paid back—although that is an important goal. The victim's other harms also need to be addressed within the context of a caring community. It is not enough simply to hold offenders accountable for the harms they have created—although that is also a very important goal. The offender must also be offered a real opportunity to gain a full place in the community. In each case, both victim and offender will frequently need attention and assistance from the community in order for the reintegration process to occur.

As the illustration from *Les Misérables* reminds us, there are four areas of assistance that a caring community can offer those in the process of reintegration. First, those individuals need protection and other steps to make them *safe*. Second, they need concrete affirmations of *respect for their dignity and worth* so that they are no longer treated as outsiders but, rather, as acknowledged members of the community. Third, they need *practical and material help* dealing with immediate challenges and needs. Fourth, they need *moral and spiritual guidance and care*, providing hope for a future that is not determined by the past. Each contributed to bringing Valjean into a new life as a responsible, participating member of society. In working toward the reintegration of both victims and offenders, communities can provide encouragement, practical help, and avenues of hope and purpose, despite the ravages of the past. This not only strengthens the victims and offenders but also serves to reinforce the values and resiliency of the community.

Review Questions

1. What are the four elements of reintegration illustrated in the scene from *Les Misérables*?
2. What issues do victims experience?
3. What is meant by reintegration?
4. How can communities assist with reintegration?

Endnotes

1. Victor Hugo, *Les Misérables*, translated by Charles E. Wilbour (New York: The Modern Library, 1992), 92.
2. Ibid. 98-99.
3. Louise Casey, "Meeting the Service Needs of Families Bereaved by Homicide" (United Kingdom Ministry of Justice, 2011), available online at http://www.justice.gov.uk/downloads/news/press-releases/victims-com/families-bereaved-homicide.pdf as of August 1, 2013.
4. Dean G. Kilpatrick, "The Mental Health Impact of Crime: Fundamentals in Counseling and Advocacy," in materials for the 1996 National Victim Assistance Academy, sponsored by the U.S. Department of Justice Office for Victims of Crime.
5. Arlene B. Andrews, "Crisis and Recovery Services for Family Violence Survivors," in Arthur J. Lurigio, Wesley G. Skogan, and Robert C. Davis, eds., *Victims of Crime: Problems, Policies, and Programs* (Newbury Park, CA: Sage, 1990).
6. Morton Bard and Dawn Sangrey, *The Crime Victim's Book*, 2nd ed. (Secaucus, NJ: Citadel Press, 1986).

7. The concept of "shaming" is highly controversial. Some critics believe that shaming is inherently negative, dehumanizing, and counterproductive. In this view, even if shaming techniques are found to produce desirable results, the shaming of a person is always an illegitimate means to that end. Others (following Braithwaite) make much of the distinction between stigmatizing shaming and reintegrative shaming. In this view, there are positive and legitimate ways to acknowledge the wrongness of a deed for which the offender should rightly be ashamed. This is a way of affirming the community's values and its sense of right and wrong and also inculcating internal controls. The critical key distinguishing reintegrative from stigmatizing shaming is that the experience of shame is then linked with concrete steps to bring the offender into a new status as a fully accepted individual. Theologians are familiar with this process in the concepts of repentance and justification. In any event, as Howard Zehr has observed, by the time a restorative process has ended, shame should have been lifted.

8. John Braithwaite, *Crime, Shame, and Reintegration* (Cambridge, UK: Cambridge University Press, 1989), 64–75.

9. Susan Herman, "Is Restorative Justice Possible without a Parallel System for Victims?" in Howard Zehr and Barb Toews, eds., *Critical Issues in Restorative Justice* (Monsey, NY: Criminal Justice Press, 2004), 75–83.

10. Ibid. 80–81.

11. For information on the operation of Circles of Support and Accountability, see Andrew McWhinnie, *Circles of Support and Accountability: Guide to Project Development, Project Guide 2003* (Ottawa, Ontario, Canada: Correctional Service Canada, 2003).

12. This description comes from Lorenn Walker, "Huikahi Restorative Circles: Group Process for Self-Directed Reentry Planning and Family Healing," *European Journal of Probation* 2(2) (2010): 76–95.

13. Shelley Neiderbach, *Invisible Wounds: Crime Victims Speak* (New York: Harrington Park Press, 1986), 9.

14. Ibid.

15. See Pat Nolan, *When Prisoners Return: Why We Should Care and How You and Your Church Can Help* (Lansdowne, VA: Prison Fellowship, 2004).

16. Ram A. Cnaan with Robert J. Wineburg and Stephanie C. Boddie, *The Newer Deal: Social Work and Religion in Partnership* (New York: Columbia University Press, 1999), 298. Of particular interest is Part Two ("Provision of Religious-Based Social Services: Theological Underpinnings, Historical Trends, and Current Findings"), 91–276.

17. There are many faith-based organizations that assist offenders, and the number offering services for victims is growing. Catholic Charities, for example, offers many types of help that are needed in the reintegration process—whether or not they specifically target victims and offenders (http://www.catholiccharitiesusa.org). The Salvation Army, too, is active in providing a great many services in locales throughout the United States and throughout the world (http://www.salvationarmy.org), and it has particular programs for incarcerated persons and their families. Kairos, Inc., is another well-established organization active in prisoner ministry in the United States and Canada (http://www.kairosprisonministry.org). The Coalition of Prison Evangelists (COPE) is a network organization for more than 550 Christian ministries in the field of corrections (http://www.copeministries.org). Jewish Prisoner Services, International, helps organize assistance for Jewish prisoners and their families (http://www.jewishprisonerservices.org). The Human Kindness Foundation, based in North Carolina, has been working since 1973 on the Prison Ashram Project in the United States and its corollary, Kindness House (http://www.humankindness.org). Muslim and Islamic programs for prisoners and ex-prisoners are abundant, often working through local mosques or Islamic organizations. The Crime Victims Advocacy Council (CVAC) in Atlanta is an outgrowth of the United Methodist Church, offering support services and advocacy for victims through churches, community organizations, and concerned individuals (http://www.cvaconline.org). Its founder, Bruce Cook, was a recipient of the Justice Department's Crime Victim Service Award for activism in victim support in April 2000. These are only some examples of the variety of faith-based efforts that have recognized the needs of victims, offenders, and their families.

18. Gerald A. McHugh, *Christian Faith and Criminal Justice: Toward a Christian Response to Crime and Punishment* (New York: Paulist Press, 1978), 133.

19. A unique and excellent anthology discussing the theological issues and pastoral implications of victimization and caring for victims is found in Lisa Barnes Lampman and Michelle Shattuck, eds., *God and the Victim: Theological Reflections on Evil, Victimization, Justice, and Forgiveness* (Grand Rapids, MI: William B. Eerdmans, 1999).

20. See, for example, T. D. Evans *et al.*, "Religion and Crime Reexamined: The Impact of Religion, Secular Controls, and Social Ecology on Adult Criminality," *Criminology* 33 (1995): 195–217; J. Gartner, D. B. Larson, and G. D. Allen, "Religious Commitment and Mental Health: A Review of the Empirical Literature," *Journal of Psychology and Theology* 2(1991): 1115–1123; E. L. Idler and S. V. Kasl, "Religion, Disability, Depression, and the Timing of Death," *American Journal of Sociology* 97 (1992): 1052–1079. See also Chapter 9, "Who Escapes? The Relation of Churchgoing and Other Background Factors to the Socio-Economic Performance of Black Male Youths from Inner City Tracts," in Richard B. Freeman and Harry J. Holzer, eds., *The Black Youth Employment Crisis* (Chicago: University of Chicago Press, 1986), 353 ff.

21. Bard and Sangrey, supra note 6, at 38.

The Challenge of Restorative Justice

8

Making Restorative Justice Happen

- Gaining support
- Coalition-building
- Strategic goals for change
- Evaluation of processes and outcomes
- Resistance

Can the current practices of criminal justice really change? It can seem that inertia has entrenched for good the old ways of thinking and doing in criminal justice. But in fact, as we discussed in Chapter 2 and will consider again in Chapter 9, significant reforms are taking place at local and national levels throughout the world. Restorative justice advocates are effectively promoting change in public policy debates, within government agencies, and through nonprofit organizations. They are helping turn restorative vision into restorative practice. The following strategies, drawn from their frontline experience, can help others develop plans, generate momentum, make midcourse corrections, and create opportunities to widen the circle of influence for restorative justice action.

Build Support for Restorative Justice

One of the keys to successful implementation of restorative practices is to build support for restorative justice. That support is needed at multiple layers. The first layer is at the core—the agency, nonprofit organization, or legislative committee in which the reforms will be implemented. Staff, volunteers, oversight board members, and other participants in the core agency or group need to be informed and engaged to support the restorative initiative.

The next layer is made up of the surrounding organizations and individuals who work directly with the core group and whose backing is needed for the program or practice to work. These supporters include, for instance, funders, referral agencies, or partners in other programs. Their support is needed because they provide the backdrop against which the restorative initiative plays out. Their resistance would be highly detrimental to the initiative; indifference could hamper it; support will make implementation much easier.

Finally, there is the broader community, which is only indirectly affected by the program or practice. Backing from the community is important because it will reinforce support sought from the core and supporters, and lack of support can create political problems at times of resistance.

Kay Pranis, a restorative justice veteran of agency as well as community activism, has outlined six recommendations for those who wish to generate support at each of these layers.[1]

First, find your natural allies. These are people whose values, experiences, and interests
resonate with restorative justice values. They are predisposed to be supportive and simply
need information about the vision and values of restorative justice. Find these people by
listening to what community members have to say. Think about how restorative principles apply to their concerns. Learn their language—the terminology that they use—so
that you can communicate effectively. Then, explain the vision and values of restorative
justice, showing how it is similar to approaches they are already aware of and interested
in. For example, educators may be interested in the potential for restorative justice to help
with discipline in schools. Law enforcement officials may view this as related to the move
toward community policing. Business people may respond to discussion about effective
government and prudent fiscal policy.

In light of the political support that "get tough" policies seem to have, one might
wonder whether the public is likely to be interested in a restorative response to crime.
Public opinion surveys in the United States suggest that the public is concerned about
crime and wants something done. If the only option offered is getting tough, the public
will support that as better than doing nothing. However, when people are given options,
they are strongly inclined to favor responses to crime that are restitutionary, rehabilitative,
and sensitive to victim issues. Thus, promoting such viable options is an important step
toward making them a reality.

*Second, avoid becoming identified with a particular political, ideological, or sectarian
label.* Associating strongly with a particular political party, for example, will reduce
chances of building broad-based support. It may keep some people who agree on restorative justice from joining the efforts to implement it because of disagreement on collateral
matters. It may also cause people to assume that restorative justice is of interest only to
persons of one political party or of particular religious groups. They may not consider
restorative ideas if they do not identify themselves as part of those groups or affiliations.
Therefore, it is wiser to find ways to use terms and highlight concepts that appeal to the
values of multiple groups without too closely adhering to the vernacular of any one of
them. For instance, political conservatives will resonate with the restorative emphasis on
personal accountability and limitations on the role of government. Political liberals will
respond to the community-building potential of restorative justice and the emphasis on
habilitation of offenders to ease reintegration. Religious people will be interested in the
ways that restorative justice reflects themes within their traditions and also in the spiritual
dimension of encounters. Nonreligious people will agree with the themes of respect for the
individual and recognition of common values of people in the community.

Third, listen to those who disagree. Although the first point was to find and work with natural allies, it is a mistake to ignore those who disagree. Listen to the concerns of opponents,
and try to understand the objections they raise. This is important in part because these
people are part of the community, and they deserve to be heard with respect, but also
because it may be possible to learn from them and to reshape or improve the proposed

program or policy in light of what they have helped you see. It is possible to turn some adversaries into allies by finding the truth in their point of view and incorporating it into the proposals.

■ ■ ■ ━━

Victim concerns and issues should be at the center of work for restorative justice, and not ancillary.

━━ ■ ■ ■

Fourth, put victims first. If the people raising objections are victims or victims' advocates, then pay exceptionally close attention to their concerns. Travel to meet with them if necessary. Ask them to listen as you repeat in your own words what you understand their concerns to be. A sympathetic victim advocate might participate in the meeting to help clarify the concerns and assist with communication. Ask victims and victim advocates for their ideas and suggestions about the program, and incorporate as many as possible. Learn about the issues that victims face and the impact of crime on victims. Use victim stories in presentations and materials. Be sure victim concerns and issues are core to the work for restorative justice, and not ancillary.

Fifth, focus on values and vision, but be flexible on practice. There are always multiple ways to achieve goals; if the old approaches are not working or better options emerge, it can be useful to adopt new strategies. This can make it possible to take advantage of opportunities that arise quickly, even if those are not part of a long-term plan.

Finally, be aware of assumptions and stereotypes. Everyone is constrained by their own paradigms, and those who pursue restorative concepts and practices may need to do some fresh thinking themselves (as we discuss further in Chapter 10). Without taking time to monitor attitudes and preconceptions, restorative justice advocates may miss new opportunities or allies because they simply do not see them.

The media certainly helps shape public opinion and can be a strategic ally in building social support for restorative justice both at the grassroots and more broadly. Recognizing this, the European Forum for Restorative Justice produced a downloadable media toolkit for restorative justice organizations to use in creating and executing a media plan.[2] The forum emphasizes that if approached appropriately, both social and traditional media have powerful potential for getting compelling stories and persuasive information to both the public and policymakers. Strategic stories at critical times are able to bring restorative perspectives into the open and stir up attention around relevant, timely issues.

Increase the Use of Restorative Practices

Restorative justice practices are used in many localities but often in isolated contexts. A school or school district may use restorative practices. A small nonprofit may accept referrals from judges at the juvenile or adult levels. However, because of their isolation, they are not influencing the community in the way they might. Mark Umbreit and

Marilyn Peterson Armour proposed a number of initiatives that they believe will increase the availability and acceptance of restorative justice in communities. These include the following:

1. Giving those who are victims of all but the most serious violent crime the opportunity to choose a restorative justice response before going to the criminal justice system (see Chapter 9)
2. Creating hybrid restorative practices to accommodate individual needs and circumstances
3. Increasing the use of surrogate victim–offender-community dialogue when the actual offender has not been caught or the victim or offender does not want to participate
4. Using restorative practices in school settings from elementary level through college
5. Using restorative practices in workplace settings
6. Offering more support for victims of severe violence
7. Building ever-increasing bridges between the dominant culture and the many ethnic groups and communities of color within our society
8. Using restorative justice principles and practice to create new approaches for addressing racism, severe political violence, the death penalty and other chronic problems confronting communities
9. Using neighbors in community-based restorative initiatives as a way to strengthen the community

Develop a Credible Coalition

Those working for restorative justice do well to create broad coalitions to reflect the concerns of victims, offenders, the community, and law enforcement officials. There are two reasons for doing this. First, members of a locality are the best people to design local restorative programs. Involvement by people with diverse interests will generate creative ideas and build consensus. Second, proposals made by a coalition have more credibility than those urged by a single interest group. This is particularly true in criminal justice matters, in which advocacy is often as adversarial as the justice process.

This is an obvious idea but not easy to accomplish. Restorative justice proponent Mark Carey suggests that part of the problem is a "we–they" attitude between the community and the justice system.[3] He reviews a number of factors that insulate the justice system from the community, including limited disclosure of information, removal of emotion from the justice process, and intimidating physical surroundings (e.g., courtrooms) in the justice system. Add to this list the professionalization of justice, with its special language and practices, and the community's general mentality that the justice system and its agents should solve justice problems. All these factors are reinforced by defining and handling crime as lawbreaking—an offense against the government to which the government must respond.

By raising awareness of the personal and community dimensions of the harm resulting from crime, and opening up options for addressing that harm, restorative justice helps the justice system and community find common cause. Restorative justice practices begin to draw the community and justice system together, each doing what it does best, in order to achieve a safe, fair, and constructive outcome.

Another group that may be alienated or isolated from the justice system and wary of restorative justice initiatives is the victim community. Many crime victim advocates are cautious about restorative justice, fearing that victims' interests will be subordinated by an overriding (even if not explicit) concern for offender rehabilitation. This is a reasonable fear because many restorative justice advocates come from law enforcement, correctional agencies, or nonprofit organizations whose work has traditionally been offender-oriented. In addition, the criminal justice system is so offender-oriented that it is very easy to find restorative justice programs failing to be as victim-centered as they have intended or promised. This is why it is essential to have victims and victim advocates involved in discussing, planning, managing, and evaluating restorative programs.

■ ■ ■ ━━

By raising awareness of the harm to people and communities that results from crime, and by providing options to address that harm, restorative justice helps the justice system and community find common cause.

━━ ■ ■ ■

Pursue Strategic Goals

The failure of contemporary criminal justice is not one of technique but of purpose; what is needed is not simply a new program but a new pattern of thinking. Criminal law does not adequately recognize the harms to the victim, to the community, or to the offender. The offender's punishment seldom redresses the harm done to the victim or ameliorates the conditions that may have contributed to the crime in the first place. Victims have little or no legal standing in criminal court; their role is limited to assisting the prosecution (when necessary) to convict the offender, although in some places they may also offer an impact statement prior to sentencing.

Given the challenges and impediments to implementing a restorative approach, moving forward will require careful thought and clear strategies. In developing these strategies, it is important to distinguish between the restorative justice vision and the strategies for implementing that vision. Strategic goals should be set but not confused with the ultimate objective; their value depends ultimately on whether they bring the system closer to a societal response to crime that reflects the restorative vision. In other words, planners need to be clear about the ends they seek and the means used to get there—and then to remain clear about the differences between ends and means.

The following are suggested strategic goals that would redress the imbalanced focus on government and offenders in most criminal justice policies and practices. These goals may appear as unbalanced as the system they are meant to remedy. This is because they provide counterweights needed to create balance. The goals emerge from the cornerpost restorative values discussed in Chapters 4–7.

Strategic Goal 1: Give every victim and offender the opportunity to participate in an encounter program. Encounter programs offer a structured opportunity for victims, offenders, and others to meet, discuss the crime, and work out an acceptable agreement to make things right. Participation in encounters benefits victims and offenders in several ways. It enables each to become an active participant in the justice process. Victims usually receive some form of amends, and they report a higher degree of satisfaction with the justice process after such an encounter. Offenders are given an opportunity to learn how their crimes injured people and not just an impersonal system, to apologize, and to make amends.

Encounters should not be forced on either party, but they hold great healing potential for those who take the opportunity. Therefore, these programs should be available to any victim or offender who wants to use them. Although no one should be pressured into an encounter, no one should be denied the opportunity to participate in one because the means are unavailable. For this reason, every community should establish and maintain sufficient encounter programs to meet local demand.

■ ■ ■ ━━

Give every victim and offender the opportunity to participate in an encounter program.

━━ ■ ■ ■

Strategic Goal 2: Expect offenders to pay restitution and make it possible for them to do so. Accountability includes assuming responsibility to make reparations; therefore, restitution should be a key part of any criminal sentence. However, few offenders have the resources to repay their victims, particularly if they are imprisoned. Furthermore, prisons seldom prepare prisoners to be productive after release. This means that few victims can really expect to receive restitution in contemporary criminal justice systems. This should change. Offenders who do not present a serious risk to the community should be sentenced to community-based supervision in settings that allow them to work, repay their victims, avoid the debilitating conditions in prison, and save the community the tax burden of unnecessary incarceration.

Three factors should be considered in sentencing decisions. The seriousness of the offense should determine the amount of the sanction. The harm to victims should determine the form of the sanction, ensuring an emphasis on reparation. The risk the offender poses should be a limiting factor influencing the amount of restraint the government will place on the offender. Objective criteria need to be established to identify those offenders deemed too dangerous to stay in the community, using a standard such as "high likelihood of seriously threatening criminal behavior." Even categories as crude as violent versus nonviolent suggest that a substantial portion of those now in prison might be sentenced differently under this standard. Criminal justice systems should be accountable for ensuring that amends are collected from offenders and delivered to victims in a timely manner, just as they should be for the care and reintegration of offenders.

■ ■ ■ ——————————————————————————————————————

Expect offenders to pay restitution and make it possible for them to do so.

—————————————————————————————————————— ■ ■ ■

Strategic Goal 3: Let victims be parties in criminal cases, if they wish, in order to pursue restitution. Victims should be given the opportunity to seek restitution in criminal proceedings. They could be given legal standing to protect this interest; they should have the opportunity to be represented by attorneys at any stage at which their stake in restitution could be affected. This would be a complete departure from criminal justice practice in many common law countries, although it is similar to the rights offered to crime victims in some European countries. It offers at least three advantages over the current criminal/civil distinction in law:

1. The criminal process is more speedy and less costly than the civil process.
2. Permitting victims to seek amends represents institutional recognition that the harm to victims should be repaired.
3. Granting victims legal standing ensures a clear distinction between the legal interests of the victim and those of the government.

■ ■ ■ ——————————————————————————————————————

Let victims be parties in criminal cases, if they wish, in order to pursue restitution.

—————————————————————————————————————— ■ ■ ■

Strategic Goal 4: Provide every victim and offender the help they need to reintegrate as whole and productive members of the community. Most crime victims need assistance of some kind from the moment a crime is committed. They may receive help from family or friends, but often their needs go beyond what those informal networks can provide. The immediate and long-term effects of serious crime can be devastating, but they are reduced if immediate aid is available. Crisis intervention services such as emergency shelter, financial assistance, child care, and referrals to social service agencies exist in many places. However, most of these are unable to provide victims with comprehensive help due to staff and funding shortages. Communities must augment these system-based victim assistance programs.

Offenders also need help in reintegrating into the community. This need is particularly acute when the offender has been imprisoned, but it exists for many who have served community-based sanctions as well. In addition to barriers the offender may have faced before, he or she now carries the stigma—and in many cases the legal disabilities—that come with being a convicted felon.

In order to meet the challenge of helping victims and offenders reintegrate, communities need to orchestrate cooperative ways to make services known and available to those who need them. This may require networking among various nonprofit, governmental, and even for-profit agencies with a specific emphasis on helping victims and offenders to get ready access to needed help. Faith communities have much to offer victims and offenders. Almost every community has local churches or other faith groups (in some urban communities, they are virtually the only viable nongovernmental institution available), and service to victims and offenders is consistent with their missions. They are currently a largely unused resource in criminal justice, but the factors that have contributed to that underuse may be overcome. Faith communities can offer relationships of acceptance and accountability that are an essential foundation to helping victims or offenders reintegrate into the community as whole contributing members.

■ ■ ■ ━━━

Provide every victim and offender the help they need to reintegrate as whole and productive members of the community.

━━━ ■ ■ ■

If these four strategic goals were creatively pursued and progress on them charted and evaluated, the pattern of thinking that shapes our society's response to crime would begin to change. Both system and community responses would open up to new possibilities for recognizing victims' harms and offenders' accountability, for recognizing the personal dimensions of crime and ways to respond to them, and for ensuring that both victims and offenders are able to access reintegrative programs and community relationships.

Revisit the Vision and Evaluate Impact

Work on strategic goals to help restore balance to the system can nonetheless produce programs that fail to reflect restorative principles. For example, victim involvement in criminal trials is a strategic goal, but if such involvement increases the isolation and antagonism of victims and offenders, it would conflict with restorative values of collaboration and resolution. Therefore, it is important to evaluate policies and programs regularly, in terms of both their success at redirecting society's response to crime and the extent to which they help achieve restoration of victims, offenders, and communities. Even if they start well, policies and programs can lose their original focus as they respond to pressures and changes in environment, personnel, and resources. Therefore, restorative justice advocates would be wise to revisit previously enacted policies and programs to assess the effectiveness of their strategies and outcomes and make adjustments to keep them on track. One expedient reason for evaluation is that arguments for restorative justice depend on practical examples and cost–benefit analysis. Future arguments rest on past accomplishments, and past accomplishments are only as strong as their practical outcomes. Therefore, an ongoing commitment to evaluation based on the principles and values of the restorative justice vision builds the necessary research and experience base to secure the future of restorative justice as well as keeping current efforts on track.

Impact evaluations may be highly formal or quite simple, but they are the best way to determine objectively whether a program or policy accomplishes what it set out to do. Evaluation begins with program design, guides the development of ideas into actions, and provides an objective framework for testing whether the program's features produce the intended benefits or outcomes. Although program administrators may feel threatened when undergoing an evaluation that asks tough questions about the translation of principles into practice, evaluation is the backbone of a healthy program. It provides the opportunity to improve on program strengths and to correct unsatisfactory performance before it weakens the whole program. Evaluation data are the best "proof" to funders, justice officials, and even critics who want objective verification of the benefits of the program.

Evaluation is more easily done when clear goals and measurable objectives have been established at the outset. The discipline of careful planning is a great advantage. The principle of "go slow to go fast" is applicable to those charting the course for restorative justice in practice. Advocates may be eager to accomplish change, but they will only know what they have accomplished if they know what they set out to do, how their methods relate to their goals, and how they will benchmark and measure progress. For restorative justice to take root and bear fruit, its policies, practices, and programs must be observably and measurably connected to the vision—and this will remain true through the inevitable process of growth and adaptation to changing times, new challenges, and fresh opportunities.

■ ■ ■ ━━━

It is important to evaluate policies and programs regularly to monitor how well they help achieve restoration of victims, offenders, and communities.

━━━ ■ ■ ■

One way to generally monitor whether a policy or program is consonant with the vision and values of restorative justice is to use a simple checklist. The following checklist, for example, could be used to assess the relative "restorativeness" of policies or programs.[4] It is unlikely that any effort would receive a perfect score on every point below, but the more elements that are substantially included, the more restorative the effort will be.

1. Does it guide victims, offenders, and communities toward restoration and away from further harm?
   * Leaders and program staff understand and act on the restorative mission and goals.
   * Restorative directions for all parties are identified and included.
   * Procedures and policies further the accomplishment of reparative and/or reintegrative goals.
   * The victim and the offender are invited and enabled to participate fully.

- A mechanism is provided for community participation.
- Victim safety and dignity are diligently protected.
- Offenders are given respect and are not dehumanized or threatened.
- The community's legitimate need for safety is acknowledged and incorporated.

2. Does it produce restorative outcomes for victims, offenders, and communities?
   - Measurable objectives directly related to the restorative purposes of the program or policy are set, tracked, and fed into a continuous improvement process.
   - Analysis of program data gives an honest picture of the program's restorative nature and activities.
   - Reports are made available to others who are seeking to build restorative justice so that a collective body of experience and knowledge is increasingly available.

3. Does it invite participation by all parties but function in a restorative direction even when some do not participate?
   - It invites full participation by victims, offenders, and the community.
   - It offers alternatives to compensate for the lack of (or limited) participation by any of the parties while still pursuing restorative ends.

4. Does it encourage voluntary involvement but function in a restorative direction even when coercion is necessary?
   - It is noncoercive in offering participation to victims and offenders.
   - Its social controls, when necessary, interfere as little as possible with the restoration of the victim and offender.

5. Does it harmonize with the role of the state in maintaining a just order and the role of the community in achieving a just peace?
   - It facilitates effective community–government cooperation.
   - It effectively coordinates public and private resources.
   - It successfully maintains the restorative vision as it encounters adverse political and institutional forces.
   - Mechanisms are in place to recognize and address injustice or imbalances when they appear.

This kind of checklist can help identify areas needing adjustment or additional resources. A next step would be to go beyond a general assessment of the processes and work to measure (qualitatively and quantitatively) the actual impact and benefits to the victims, offenders, and communities who are involved with the restorative justice program or effort. We suggest collaboration with local universities or foundations that can help implement and resource this kind of evaluation.

Realign Vision and Practice

Evaluation provides a means to test the link between vision and practice. Claims about a program's restorativeness must stand the reality test. Proponents of the penitentiary believed sincerely that the penitentiary was the logical, moral, and humane response to lawbreaking—especially in contrast to the prevailing practices of the day. In reality, the penitentiary failed to match the vision from which it sprang. Although prisons have not delivered their desired results, confinement has remained a dominant feature of the corrections landscape. Contemporary citizens only rarely question the value of confinement as the "normative" mode of punishment for any crime deemed serious. There is a lesson here. For the Quakers, confinement was a practical way for penitents to focus on their wrongs and change their lives apart from pressures, temptations, and distractions. Instead, it became a means of isolating wrongdoers from their communities. In restorative justice practice, we must be prepared to be creative, flexible, and nondogmatic about program features while holding firmly to the vision, principles, and values of restorative justice. The way to do that is to pay attention to the results and then modify the program to better achieve the vision.

Stay Connected

One of the remarkable features of restorative justice has been how similar ideas and programs have emerged spontaneously in different areas of the world. Family group conferencing developed without an awareness of restorative justice; that theory helped locate conferencing within the field of criminology, but it did not produce the program.

A second feature has been the exceptional appeal of restorative justice in diverse cultures and places. One could accurately say, as the British once did of their empire, that the sun never sets on restorative justice. This means that developments of theory, practice, and programs are proceeding at a great rate. This contributes to the dynamic creativity of the movement, but it also means that its practitioners and advocates need to exchange experiences and discoveries. This need has led to formation of associations such as the Victim–Offender Mediation Association, the European Forum on Restorative Justice, the International Network for Research on Restorative Justice for Juveniles and the National Association of Community and Restorative Justice. It explains why national and international conferences on restorative justice are so well attended. Internet sites on restorative justice and related issues provide yet another means of exchanging information.[*]

■ ■ ■ ━━

Restorative justice will continue to be relevant and vital only if it stays in touch with its vision, tests its practices, stretches its applications, and grows with the diversity and creativity of its proponents.

━━ ■ ■ ■

Those pursuing the restorative vision will gain much by learning from, collaborating with, and challenging each other as well as those who hold other visions and agendas.

[*]One such site is Restorative Justice Online (http://www.restorativejustice.org), maintained by Prison Fellowship International's Centre for Justice and Reconciliation, of which Van Ness is executive director.

Restorative justice will continue to be relevant and vital only if it stays in touch with its vision, tests its practices, stretches its applications, and grows with the diversity and creativity of its proponents. Otherwise, this new pattern of thinking and its practical applications will become isolated and marginalized.

Expect Resistance

Machiavelli, in his famous book *The Prince*, counseled,

> *[O]ne should bear in mind that there is nothing more difficult to execute, nor more dubious of success, nor more dangerous to administer than to introduce a new order of things; for he who introduces it has all those who profit from the old order as his enemies, and he has only lukewarm allies in all those who might profit from the new.*[5]

Many of the themes of restorative justice are appealing. In fact, what restorative programs seek—redress for victims, recompense by offenders, development of peaceful communities, increased participation in criminal justice, reintegration, and reconciliation—will have wide appeal (if not dismissed by initial skepticism). However, wide appeal is not the same as deep commitment, and that can have a significant impact on the success of restorative programs.

Restitution is a good example. It enjoys almost universal support from victim rights organizations, prisoner rights groups, liberals, and conservatives. Although this makes it a highly attractive feature for restorative justice advocates, countervailing political forces may in the end be more powerful. As researchers Alan Harland and Cathryn Rosen noted in their research on the promise and realities of early enthusiasm for restitution in the 1980s and early 1990s,

> *If winning popular support for the system is a rationale for using the criminal justice process to compensate victims, however, questions arise again as to the likely fate of restitution when it conflicts with other powerful items on the public popularity agenda. How, for example, are individual decision makers and policymakers to rank public support for victims against the omnipresent mandate to get tough on crime, if imprisoning more offenders means destroying or deferring for long periods whatever earning capability they may have had to repay their victims?* [6]

This applies as well to restorative justice. Support for restorative measures can dissipate rapidly if the measures become the focus of political controversy.

The criminal justice system, like any bureaucratic system, resists change. Modern prosecutors are agency administrators with their own political and administrative agendas. So too are leaders of all other parts of the criminal justice system, from law enforcement to corrections. Each has its own interests, which are at least as important to it as an overall societal objective for the system. The challenge to restorative justice advocates is to draw from existing public support to establish programs that reflect restorative justice ideals, using those programs to illustrate their value and thus promote deeper public commitment, and building ongoing accountability for maintaining the vision in the implementation of programs.

■ ■ ■ ▬▬▬▬▬▬▬▬▬▬▬▬▬▬▬▬▬▬▬▬▬▬▬▬▬▬▬▬▬▬▬▬▬

The challenge is to draw from public support to establish programs that reflect restorative justice ideals and then use the successes of those programs to build deeper public commitment.

▬▬▬▬▬▬▬▬▬▬▬▬▬▬▬▬▬▬▬▬▬▬▬▬▬▬▬▬▬▬▬▬▬ ■ ■ ■

Conclusion

Restorative justice will not just happen. However, two phenomena in particular are creating openness to this new pattern of thinking. First, the sheer cost of incarceration puts pressure on public budgets. In the attempt to contain the rising costs, correctional, educational, and medical programs are being squeezed. Innovation—particularly if it can demonstrate better results than the status quo—is viewed with interest. Second, people are better connected through online services and other communication technologies that offer instant information and the ability to discuss it in a wide variety of forums.

As restorative programs and approaches are developed for responding to crime, they must anticipate and compensate for the pressures and realities of social change. Program managers must be willing to evaluate their efforts to determine whether the programs deliver as promised and produce restorative outcomes. The ultimate test of any policy or program will be whether it helps achieve the overarching goal of restoration—one person at a time as well as in the wider social process. The changes now underway demonstrate the promise of restorative justice. Much more is possible.

Review Questions

1. What are the six recommendations for gaining support for change?
2. Why is coalition-building strategic?
3. What are the four strategic goals for change, and how would achieving them help bring balance to criminal justice policies and practices?
4. What is the value of ongoing evaluation, and what is important to monitor?

Endnotes

1. Kay Pranis, *Building Community Support for Restorative Justice: Principles and Strategies* (1995). Available online at http://rjonline.org/10fulltext/pranis-kay.-building-support-for-community-justice-principles-and-strategies; also http://www.iirp.edu/article_detail.php?article_id=NDcx as of August 1, 2013.

2. Brunilda Pali, *Media Toolkit for Restorative Justice Organisations* (Leuven, Belgium: European Forum for Restorative Justice, 2007). Available online at http://www.euforumrj.org//assets/upload/Media_Toolkit.pdf as of August 1, 2013. A companion report is also available offering information about how

to make a compelling case for restorative justice, exploring previous research about both public opinion and political dynamics. See Brunilda Pali and Christa Pelikan, *Building Social Support for Restorative Justice* (Leuven, Belgium: European Forum for Restorative Justice, 2007). Available online at http://www.euforumrj.org//assets/upload/Final_Report_Building_Social_Support_for_RJ.pdf as of August 1, 2013.

3. Mark Carey, "Taking Down the Walls: Measures to Integrate the Objectives of the Justice System with the Community's," originally published in *Community Corrections Report* (1997). Available online at http://www.ojp.usdoj.gov/nij/topics/courts/restorative-justice/local-system/taking-down-walls.htm as of August 1, 2013.

4. Howard Zehr proposed a similar list of questions in *Changing Lenses: A New Focus for Crime and Justice* (Scottdale, PA: Herald Press, 1990), 230–231. Those questions are (1) Do victims experience justice? (2) Do offenders experience justice? (3) Is the victim–offender relationship addressed? (4) Are community concerns being taken into account? and (5) Is the future being addressed?

5. Niccolò Machiavelli, *The Prince*, Peter Boudanella and Mark Musa (trans.) (New York: Oxford University Press, 1984), 21.

6. Alan T. Harland and Cathryn J. Rosen, "Impediments to the Recovery of Restitution by Crime Victims," *Violence and Victims* 5(2) (1990): 127–140.

Toward a Restorative System

KEY CONCEPTS

- Conditions for a restorative system: consent, safety, and fundamental rights
- Models for merging restorative and contemporary criminal justice
- How restorative justice is applied within the contemporary criminal justice system
- Assessing the "restorativeness" of a system

Could the restorative practices and values we have discussed in this book be combined to make a restorative system—that is, a system that responds as restoratively as possible to all or substantial portions of crimes, harm, victims, offenders, and communities? In this chapter, we consider what some of the prerequisites for such a system might be, outline possible ways restorative justice might integrate with contemporary criminal justice, review how restorative justice processes are currently being incorporated into each phase of contemporary criminal justice, and identify strategic issues that must be considered in pursuing those models. We conclude by proposing a framework with which to assess the degree to which systems reflect a restorative character.

The Conditions for a Restorative System

Before discussing the variety of models for a system that integrates restorative approaches, it is useful to consider the conditions or prerequisites for such systems. We suggest that three elements are so essential that it is difficult to imagine a system that integrates restorative approaches that would not include these three: consent, safety, and fundamental rights.

Consent

Previously, we noted that encounter programs should be voluntary; the parties should not be required or forced to participate. This makes encounter programs different from the criminal justice system, which must operate regardless of the willingness of particular victims, offenders, and community members. Consent, not coercion, is required.

In part, this is a reflection of the values of restorative justice, but there are also practical reasons for this. Coercing an unwilling offender to participate can disappoint victims and community members if the accused individual denies responsibility or simply refuses to speak. Creating a context in which an offender may be compelled to make incriminating statements means that attorneys would have to be actively involved in the encounters, which could then become more formalized and "legalized." Insisting that the victim participate can impede his or her recovery from the crime because the experience of powerlessness of the crime is continued into the response to that crime.

In reality, there is not always a vast gulf that separates a voluntary decision from one the party feels compelled to make. Choices might be positioned on a continuum ranging from entirely voluntary to entirely coerced. A voluntary choice is one motivated by personal beliefs and values. A coerced choice is one that a person would not make except for another person's threat or promise. Between these two lie a host of circumstances in which considerations, incentives, inducements, pressures, and even threats influence a person's choice. Examples include peer pressure (e.g., when a teenager engages in certain behavior in order to fit in), the threat of public exposure (e.g., when professional associations publish the names of members appearing before the disciplinary committees), and incentives for good behavior (e.g., when insurance rates decrease for good drivers). Many choices are motivation by a blend of internal values and external norms reflected in customs, policies, laws, or regulations.

This is why we proposed that in assessing the "restorativeness" of a program or policy, two indicators are (1) whether it offers but does not compel participation and (2) whether the social controls it exerts interfere as little as possible with the restoration of the parties. When both indicators are true, we can describe the choice to participate as freely and voluntarily made.

How can this value be incorporated into a restorative system? The United Nations' (UN) *Basic Principles on the Use of Restorative Justice Programmes in Criminal Matters* provides that

> *restorative processes should be used only where there is sufficient evidence to charge the offender and with the free and voluntary consent of the victim and the offender. The victim and the offender should be able to withdraw such consent at any time during the process. Agreements should be arrived at voluntarily and should contain only reasonable and proportionate obligations.*[1]

It further provides that "neither the victim nor the offender should be coerced, or induced by unfair means, to participate in restorative processes or to accept restorative outcomes."[2]

When the state of Alaska adopted legislation providing parties the opportunity to present negotiated agreements at sentencing, it required the consent of both parties. It also provided that an additional determination be made by the judge "that the victim has not been intimidated or coerced in reaching the agreement."[3] This raises the second condition for restorative justice: safety.

Safety

Crime is an indication that some people, at least, are not safe. Someone has been victimized. One of the objectives of restorative justice is to create a safer community. As discussed in Chapter 3, there are two approaches to creating safety. One is through the imposition of order by the government; the other is through creation of a peaceful community. If the mechanism for moving from vulnerability to safety is to be a restorative one, then the parties need to feel safe as they go through that process.

One of a facilitator's most important functions is to create a safe environment within which the parties may meet. This involves preparation of all the potential participants to explain the restorative process, answer questions they may have, and determine their interest in taking part. This may include exploring what they would like to say to the other party, which means that the facilitator needs to be able to deal with expressions of strong emotion and to create a context in which the emotion can be shared in a constructive way with the other parties. A good facilitator builds relationships and trust with the parties so that they are able to exert influence in the meeting without dominating it, but he or she will also know when it is time to take a break or end a meeting if physical or emotional injury becomes likely. The parties need to know that they will be safe when going into the meeting.

The need for safety extends beyond the meeting to the process of reintegration of the victim and the offender into their communities. In Chapter 6, we stated that this was so important that it needed to be considered an element of reintegration, along with respect, practical and material assistance, and moral and spiritual guidance. Similarly, in assessing the "restorativeness" of programs and policies, we suggested that an important factor is whether the intervention guides the parties toward restoration and away from further harm. In a restorative intervention, the victim's safety will be protected, offenders will also not be threatened, and the community's need for safety will be accommodated.

A particular area of concern for safety is when there is an imbalance of power between the victim and the offender. This may be due to differences in age, gender, economic or political status, or to the history of the relationship between the particular parties (e.g., where there has been domestic violence). These factors need to be considered carefully when making a determination of whether and how a restorative process might be used. There is evidence that in some of these situations, restorative justice can be beneficial if handled with skill.[4]

The UN's *Basic Principles* addresses this issue in two provisions:

9. Disparities leading to power imbalances, as well as cultural differences among the parties, should be taken into consideration in referring a case to, and in conducting, a restorative process.

10. The safety of the parties shall be considered in referring any case to, and in conducting, a restorative process.[5]

When the state of Virginia adopted legislation allowing crime victims to meet with incarcerated offenders, it explicitly provided that safety must be a consideration in arranging for such a visit:

The Department shall promulgate a policy to assist a person who was a victim of a crime committed by an offender incarcerated in any state correctional facility to visit with such offender. Such policy may include provisions necessary to preserve the safety and security of those at such visit and the good order of the facility, including consideration of the offender's security level, crime committed, and institutional behavior of the offender. The Department shall make whatever arrangements are necessary to effectuate such a visit. This subsection shall not apply to juvenile victims.[6]

Fundamental Rights

In building a restorative system, we do well to consider the strengths of nonrestorative approaches to crime and justice. These emerged over centuries of development and have important features that are frequently included in our understanding of justice. If we think of the best features of an effective criminal justice system, it is clear that there are elements worth preserving. For example, it identifies certain kinds of behavior that are not acceptable, and it establishes systems to determine whether those accused of those behaviors are indeed guilty. It is good at condemning criminal acts. In doing so, it provides an alternative to personal or collective vengeance, which could lead to cycles of vengeance and violence. Furthermore, as discussed in Chapter 1, it provides a police force, public prosecutors, governmentally operated prison systems, and other institutions rather than expecting individual victims to prosecute and punish individual offenders. It recognizes that those authorities should themselves act in accordance with the law and that persons accused of crimes should be afforded safeguards against the abuse of power of the government or the community. Finally, it aspires to overall fairness—working toward consistency of punishment for similar crimes, for example.

The strengths of restorative justice begin with its more holistic view of crime, recognizing the resulting harm and not just the lawbreaking. It measures success not by the amount of punishment imposed but, rather, by the amount of damage that has been repaired. Its focus on harm means that it should take the needs of victims seriously. It recognizes that there is a need for community participation in society's response to crime rather than leaving this to the government alone. Also, it offers considerably more flexibility in how particular cases are handled.

Blending the strengths of restorative justice with those of nonrestorative justice is the challenge today. With some notable exceptions, restorative justice is usually viewed as a supplement to conventional criminal justice rather than as its replacement. We consider various models for the incorporation of restorative justice into criminal justice systems in the next section. First, however, it is essential to recognize the importance of protection of fundamental rights in the development of any restorative system.

The UN's *Basic Principles on the Use of Restorative Justice Programmes in Criminal Matters* is an attempt to protect the fundamental rights of victims and accused and convicted defendants without losing the strengths of the admittedly informal approaches taken by restorative justice. It provides that countries should develop standards to govern the use of restorative approaches from referral of cases to them to rules of conduct of those operating them.[7] It requires that fundamental procedural safeguards be put in place to guarantee fairness to the victim and the offender, including the right to consult with attorneys, informed consent, and freedom from coercion.[8] Also, it provides that discussions that take place in restorative encounters should be kept confidential and that the results of those discussions should be judicially supervised.[9]

Five System Models and "Restorativeness"

How might we think systematically about the incorporation of restorative justice processes into contemporary criminal justice? Figure 9.1 offers a visual presentation of five possible models.

Most of the restorative justice programs mentioned in the previous section *augment* the contemporary criminal justice processes in their countries. That is, they are an alternative the parties may choose instead of proceeding with contemporary criminal justice processes. These alternatives may be available only at certain points in the justice process (e.g., by prosecutors), or they may be available throughout. If the parties do not choose a restorative alternative, then their matter is handled in familiar criminal justice fashion (courts, etc.). The results of the restorative process may or may not influence decisions made in the contemporary criminal justice process. Cases are filed, tracked, and monitored by the contemporary justice system and are sent to restorative programs only with the knowledge and consent of a decision maker in that system.

There are other alternatives for organizing restorative and contemporary criminal justice responses. In one, the assumption about the preferred approach to resolving crime would change so that the expectation would be that cases are handled restoratively; contemporary criminal justice would serve as a *safety net* when restorative approaches cannot or do not bring about resolution. For example, if one of the parties does not want to meet, or the parties do meet but are not able to come to an agreement, the matter would then be handled by contemporary criminal justice. Here one would expect a well-defined

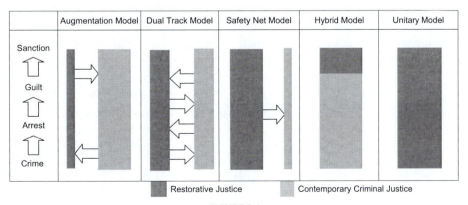

FIGURE 9.1

restorative justice structure, and cases would be processed through that structure unless sent to the contemporary justice system.

An intermediate option would be the *dual-track* approach, in which two separate systems are offered. One would be restorative in processes and values, and the other would be like the contemporary criminal justice system. The decision about which process to use would be made by the stakeholders—the parties with an interest in the case. Based on crime seriousness, assumptions might be established concerning the parties that must be included in the decision about which approach to use in handling the matter. For example, in the most serious crimes, the government would play a role in making this decision in addition to the victim, offender, and community.

A fourth model is one in which matters routinely proceed through courts and other agencies of contemporary criminal justice until a certain point in the process, at which time the matter is transferred to restorative programs. We might describe this as a *hybrid* model of justice, in which both restorative and contemporary criminal justice features make up part of the normative process. What makes this model different from the others is that restorative and contemporary criminal justice interventions operate consecutively and not as multiple alternatives at the same stages of the justice processes.

■ ■ ■ ▬▬▬▬▬▬▬▬▬▬▬▬▬▬▬▬▬▬▬▬▬▬▬▬▬▬▬▬▬▬▬▬▬▬▬▬

A system that seeks to be restorative will need strategies to maintain that over time and with large numbers of employees and volunteers.

▬▬▬▬▬▬▬▬▬▬▬▬▬▬▬▬▬▬▬▬▬▬▬▬▬▬▬▬▬▬▬▬▬ ■ ■ ■

The fifth model assumes a single, restorative process as the only alternative available. This *unitary* model must address all crimes, victims, and offenders in a restorative manner without relying on contemporary criminal justice for anything. Such a model would have to address situations in which the defendant denies guilt or raises a legal defense, such as self-defense. It would have to function when victims and offenders are unwilling to participate cooperatively. This is the most challenging model to consider, and it is a feasible model only within the *reparative* or *transformative* conceptions of restorative justice, not the *encounter* conception (see Chapter 3).

The feasibility of a unitary model is the subject of a research and design project conducted by Prison Fellowship International. The purpose of the project, called *RJ City*,[10] was to imagine a city of 1 million people that has decided to respond as restoratively as possible to all crimes, all victims, and all offenders and answer the following question: What would its restorative system look like? Such a system would face a number of practical realities and challenges to restorative justice thinking that are not necessary to address if restorative justice forms only part of a system's foundations. For example,

- How would it go about determining guilt or innocence for defendants who plead not guilty?
- What guidelines would there be for law enforcement concerning the use of force and incarceration?

- How would it respond to victims in the immediate aftermath of the crime and when no offender is apprehended?
- Does the emphasis on cooperative resolution affect how law enforcement investigates crimes?

In addition, any system that seeks to reflect restorative principles and values will need to consider how it will do this over time and with large numbers of employees and volunteers. For example,

- How does it determine whether victims, offenders, and community members are in fact experiencing restorative justice?
- How are staff hired, trained, and supervised so that they are likely to demonstrate restorative principles and values in their work?
- The justice system has many levels and interests. Is it possible for restorative justice to be the leading principle of the justice system and for its preeminence to be established restoratively?

In the Appendix, you will find a case study developed as part of the RJ City project. It illustrates what might happen after a burglary of an elderly woman's house by two offenders. It suggests how RJ City would respond to the woman, to the offender willing to accept responsibility, and to the other offender who denies that he was involved.

The unitary model is not the only one that raises difficult questions about how restorative a program or set of programs may be. For example, most large-scale attempts to initiate restorative justice are designed to divert offenders from the criminal justice system. This was the case, for example, with the Children, Young Persons and Their Families Act adopted by New Zealand in 1989. As a result, the family group conferences called for in the act may proceed even if the victim chooses not to participate. Although this—and, even more, the authority of the police to divert young people through cautions and so forth—has resulted in a significant reduction in the number of young people going through Youth Court and into custody, the focus of the act is on the offender (it is believed that conferences produce better results than court) and on the government (fewer court cases and young people in custody means lower costs).

Contrast this with the Crime (Restorative Justice) Act adopted for the Australian Capital Territory (ACT) in 2004. The statutory objectives of the act focus on giving crime victims options for participating in decisions about how the harm they have suffered should be repaired.[11] It does this by making restorative justice processes available at all stages of contemporary criminal justice, but it does not replace the criminal justice system. Judges or other decision makers in the justice system may or may not take agreements reached in the restorative process into consideration as they make those decisions. This act may or may not result in lower costs to the government, and offenders may or may not be diverted from the justice system.

Both of these schemes can fairly be called restorative in intention and as moving their jurisdiction toward embracing restorative justice as a fundamental part of their justice systems. The question that we must turn to is how to assess the "restorativeness" of those (and other) approaches.

Uses of Restorative Justice Processes in Contemporary Criminal Justice

Restorative justice processes were first used as part of presentence preparation. After guilt was determined by plea or trial, the judge or a probation officer responsible for the resentence investigation would refer the matter to the restorative program. If the parties were willing, they would meet in a restorative encounter, and any agreement reached as a result would be presented to the judge as a recommended sentence.

This use of restorative processes continues, as noted later. However, they are now also used in virtually every part of contemporary criminal justice with varying influence on decisions made in the justice system. In some instances, the agreement guides decision makers; in others, the process is independent of the justice system and has no effect on the outcome.

Use by Police

In a number of countries, police have begun using restorative processes in deciding what to do with juveniles and adults who come to their attention. This is, of course, only possible where police are given discretion to decide how to proceed with a matter. In some jurisdictions, the police conduct conferences themselves rather than referring the young people elsewhere. Thames Valley Police in England train police officers to conduct conferences that may involve the victim and offender, their family and friends, and, in some instances, members of the community. Other countries have adopted similar programs. Successful completion of a mediation agreement can result in the dismissal of charges (or in the decision not to charge), as in Norway.

In a growing number of countries, including New Zealand and England, these measures have been extended to adult offenders as well. In South Africa, Community Peace Committees were formed to assume responsibility for crime prevention and resolution in localities where there was little confidence in the justice system. Recently, however, a pilot project was initiated to form a partnership with the police. Although disputants may still go directly to the Community Peace Committee, they may also go to police, who will refer appropriate cases to the Community Peace Committee.

Use by Prosecutors

As a general rule, prosecutors are given more discretionary powers than police, and courts are given more than prosecutors. In common law countries, prosecutors have the authority to divert cases. Even in civil law countries, however, recent legislation allows prosecutors to refer certain cases to restorative processes. In Austria, for example, prosecutors may send matters to mediation (referred to as "out of court offense compensation") after they have received positive recommendations from the social worker/mediator. The German Juvenile Justice Act of 1990 allows prosecutors to dismiss criminal cases on their own authority if the juvenile has either reached a settlement with the victim or made efforts to do so.

Following the pattern noted previously in relation to police, countries that began with prosecutor-referred restorative processes for juveniles have since extended it to adults as well. An example of this is Austria, which in 2000 authorized prosecutorial diversion (including to victim–offender mediation) for adult defendants facing sentences of not more than 5 years' imprisonment. In some other countries, such as Colombia, legislation authorizing the use of mediation has applied first to adult cases, when the prosecutor agrees.

In general, the prosecutor's authority to divert a matter after charges have been filed appears to depend on the legal tradition of the country. In common law countries, the prosecutor may continue to divert until the trial (and withdraw charges in the event of a successful resolution) without the court's permission. In civil law countries, the power to divert is more likely to transfer to the judge once charges are laid.

Use by Courts

Judges use restorative processes both for pretrial diversion and as part of sentencing preparation. In those jurisdictions in which prosecutors have no authority to divert cases once charges are laid, judges may still have that authority. In Italy, for example, a judge may arrange for mediation between a juvenile offender and the victim, and following successful completion, a judge may enter an order suspending the trial and imposing probation. In the state of North Carolina, this approach has become so routine in some courts that at the beginning of hearings the prosecutor will invite any parties interested in mediation to identify themselves, and the judge will explain the benefits of mediation. Trained, volunteer court mediators are present to immediately help willing parties find a mutually acceptable resolution. In some jurisdictions, a judge may offer court-based mediation even after the trial has begun if it appears that the parties might benefit from it. However, as with other diversion programs, the decision by the parties not to participate will not influence the outcome of a trial.

■ ■ ■ ━━

Restorative justice processes are now used in virtually every phase of contemporary criminal justice.

━━ ■ ■ ■

In addition to pretrial diversion of cases to restorative processes, judges may also use restorative processes after conviction or a guilty plea and before sentencing. For example, in Finland, the judge may suspend the matter until an agreement is made and then carried out, at which point the sentence may be waived. Another example is the Restorative Resolutions Project in Canada, which focuses on adult offenders and their victims in cases of serious felonies. During its initial 18 months, judges accepted the plans in 80% of the cases.

Use by Probation Officers

Not all offenders and victims are willing or able to participate in a restorative process prior to disposition of the criminal case in court. In those instances, restorative processes may be used in the course of the offenders' sentences. In Japan, when the offender has been placed on probation, the probation officers may arrange meetings with the victim for the offender to apologize and make restitution. In fact, in 2001, a rehabilitation center was opened in order to arrange conferences between juvenile offenders and their victims. Participation is voluntary and may include family members and supporters of both parties. These conferences may be held prior to the court proceeding or while the juvenile is on probation. The agreement is then sent either to the judge or the probation officer for their use in working with the offender.

Use in Prison

There are several reasons for providing restorative processes in prison. One is to help prisoners develop an awareness of and empathy for victims. This may be done by bringing surrogate victims (i.e., victims of crimes committed by other offenders) to meet with groups of prisoners. An example is the Sycamore Tree Project, a program used by Prison Fellowship affiliates in a number of countries.

■ ■ ■ ▬▬▬▬▬▬▬▬▬▬▬▬▬▬▬▬▬▬▬▬▬▬▬▬▬▬▬▬

> One reason to use restorative justice processes in prison is to create a culture in which conflict is resolved peacefully.

▬▬▬▬▬▬▬▬▬▬▬▬▬▬▬▬▬▬▬▬▬▬▬▬▬▬▬▬ ■ ■ ■

Other programs provide an opportunity for prisoners to meet with their victims, their estranged families, or hostile communities. As noted previously, the state of Texas developed a program at the request of victims that facilitates meetings between crime victims or survivors and their offenders. Most of the offenders are serving very long sentences; some are on death row. The program does not affect the prisoners' sentence length; however, the victims' opinions are very influential in parole hearings, and some victims have decided not to contest parole after their meetings.

Many prisoners have alienated their families because of their involvement in crime, the embarrassment and harm they have caused their families, and in some cases because of crimes they have committed against family members. Furthermore, communities can be fearful and angry at the prospect of a prisoner returning. Consequently, it may be necessary for prisoners, family members, and community representatives to meet to discuss how to re-establish meaningful relationships together. Volunteers with the Prison Fellowship affiliate in Zimbabwe act as facilitators in conversations between prisoners' families, the head man of the prisoners' villages, and the prisoners about the conditions needed for a successful re-entry to their villages.

A final purpose for restorative justice processes in prison is to create a culture within prison in which conflict is resolved peacefully. This includes dispute resolution programs for conflict between prisoners. Imprisoned gang leaders in Bellavista prison in Medellin, Colombia, have created a peace table at which they meet to resolve disputes between gangs arising both inside and outside the prison. Other prisons have programs that address workplace conflict between correctional staff members, including senior management. Such programs have been used in the United States with success in Philadelphia City Prisons and the state of Ohio. The programs have not only helped staff address their own conflicts but also improved prison staff members' ability to deal with conflicts they may have with prisoners.

Use by Parole Officers

Restorative processes are used in parole in at least three ways. One is when, prior to the decision to parole an offender, the victim and offender have met in a restorative process and made agreements that could be considered in determining whether to parole the offender and what conditions to impose. These restorative processes might have taken place years before the parole hearing. The Parole Act 2002 in New Zealand provides that the dominant concern in deciding whether to release a prisoner on parole is the safety of the public. However, the board is also instructed to give "due weight" to restorative justice outcomes. On the other hand, there are those who oppose use of such agreements. The American Probation and Parole Association's manual on victim involvement in offender re-entry recommends that prisoners should not be offered, nor should they receive, any favorable treatment as the result of apologizing to the victim or attempting in some other way to make amends. The rationale is that victims will be able to trust the offenders' statements more if they know that the offenders have no ulterior motives.

A second use of restorative processes is at the time a release decision is to be made. The National Parole Board in Canada has created specialized hearings when the prisoner is an Aboriginal offender. An "elder-assisted hearing" is one in which an Aboriginal elder participates in the parole hearing in order to inform board members about Aboriginal culture, experiences, and traditions and their relevance to the decision facing the board members. The elder also participates in the deliberations. A "community-assisted hearing" takes place in an Aboriginal community, and all parties, including the victim and members of the community, are invited to participate in what is called a "releasing circle," which will consider the question of release.

A third use for restorative processes is immediately before parole to discuss what conditions of parole will be imposed on the parolee after release from prison. The New South Wales Department of Corrective Services uses "protective mediation" in situations in which it is likely that an offender will come into contact with the victim on release (e.g., they live in a small community or they are family members). The mediation is not "face to face" but is instead conducted by a trained staff person who acts as a "go-between" to clarify the needs and wishes of each party about contact with the other and helps them arrive at a practical agreement, when possible. The agreement may or may not be made part of the conditions of parole.

■ ■ ■ ━━

Restorative processes are used before release to prepare the prisoner, the victim, and the community for the prisoner's return.

━━ ■ ■ ■

A Framework for Assessing the "Restorativeness" of a System

It should be apparent by now that it is difficult to answer the question "Is this restorative or not?" because virtually all systems combine restorative and nonrestorative elements. A more helpful question would be "*How* restorative is this?" A fully restorative system would be one in which the principles and values of restorative justice prevail and, as a result, its processes and outcomes are experienced as restorative by their participants. Unless everyone who works within the justice system, including all volunteers and community members who have contact with the system, are restorative versions of the "Stepford wives," we can safely assume that no system will ever be fully restorative.

■ ■ ■ ▬▬▬▬▬▬▬▬▬▬▬▬▬▬▬▬▬▬▬▬▬▬▬▬▬▬

> It is not helpful to ask the question, "Is the system restorative or not?" A better question is, "How restorative is it?"

▬▬▬▬▬▬▬▬▬▬▬▬▬▬▬▬▬▬▬▬▬▬▬▬▬▬ ■ ■ ■

So how might we assess the degree of restorativeness of a system? An obvious point of departure is the principles and values of restorative justice. In Chapter 3, we outlined three key principles and the four "cornerpost" values of *inclusion, encounter, amends,* and *reintegration.* In Chapters 4–7, we identified a collection of important component elements for each cornerpost:

Inclusion: invitation, acknowledgment of interests, acceptance of alternative approaches
Encounter: meeting, narrative, emotion, understanding, agreement
Amends: apology, changed behavior, restitution, generosity
Reintegration: safety, respect, practical and material help, moral and spiritual guidance and care

Let us assume that a system that fully included all of these values and elements could be characterized as fully restorative. What if some of them are absent? How many could we go without and still characterize the resulting system as at least minimally restorative? Certainly more empirical data are needed before we can definitively answer this question, but here we make a few observations.

First, it is difficult to think of any system as restorative that does not fully exhibit the value of inclusion. One of the fundamental principles of restorative justice is that *victims, offenders, and communities should have the opportunity for active involvement in the justice process as early and as fully as they wish.* The system should not be considered restorative if victims, offenders, and affected community members are not invited to participate; if their interests are not acknowledged; and if alternative approaches are not created to permit their fuller participation in pursuit of those interests. It is not necessary that all parties participate, only that they be included if they choose to do so. Therefore, we suggest that all three elements of inclusion must be present to consider a system even minimally restorative.

Second, incorporation of the other three values will increase the restorative character of the system, but none of those other three are as indispensable to the system as the value of inclusion. To achieve a fully restorative system in which the processes and outcomes are primarily restorative, a system will need to include these three values. Their absence simply reduces the restorative character of the system; it does not eliminate it. For example, although a fundamental principle of restorative justice is that *justice requires that we work to heal victims, offenders, and communities that have been injured by crime*, it is not essential that the restoration be done by the offender. When the offender is not apprehended, for example, healing may take place through the material, moral, and spiritual assistance that comprises part of the value of reintegration. This would not be a fully restorative response, but it would be substantially restorative.

■ ■ ■ ━━

It is difficult to think of a system as restorative unless it is fully inclusive. It invites victims, offenders, and community members to participate, acknowledges their interests, and adjusts its processes as needed.

━━ ■ ■ ■

Likewise, it does not appear that encounter is essential because the two fundamental principles of opportunity to participate and restoration of the injured could be accomplished, at least to a significant degree, without an encounter. The example of a crime in which the offender is not identified will serve here as well. Significant restoration can still be accomplished through community or social service assistance.

Nor is successful reintegration of both parties essential because a victim and offender who meet and make amends will have accomplished a substantial degree of restoration even if they are not fully reintegrated into the community in the way that restorative justice anticipates.

Third, the included elements of those values do not have the same weight. For example, a meeting is undoubtedly more important to an encounter than the fact that emotion is expressed. Both often happen, but if only one does, the meeting would be the most essential. We suggest that some of the elements could be clustered, and that the following priority order within each value might be assigned:

Inclusion	(1) Invitation
	(3) Acknowledgment of interests
	(3) Acceptance of alternative approaches
Encounter	(1) Meeting
	(2) Communication (narrative, emotion, understanding)
	(3) Agreement

Amends	(1) Apology
	(2) Restitution
	(3) Change (changed behavior, generosity)
Reintegration	(1) Safety
	(2) Respect
	(3) Assistance (material assistance, moral and spiritual direction)

Figure 9.2 shows the range of responses to the value of inclusion. It involves an invitation, acknowledgment of the interests of the parties, and acceptance of alternative approaches (if needed) to allow the parties to participate. Lesser options are depicted in the lower cells. One involves an invitation to participate and acknowledges the parties' different interests, but it does not permit alternative approaches that would permit them to satisfy those interests more successfully. The least inclusive posture a system could take would be to coerce involvement in a process that serves the interests of the prosecution or defense.

It seems clear that an encounter that yields an agreement (e.g., through a form of shuttle diplomacy) will be less restorative than one that involves a meeting and an agreement. An encounter with a meeting and an agreement will have a more restorative character than an encounter that involves communication (e.g., by exchange of letters) but no meeting or agreement.

In fact, we could construct a series of options related to the value of encounter that would include not only these elements but also those elements of criminal justice that run counter to this value. These options are presented in Figure 9.3. The most complete encounter is one that involves all of the elements described in Chapter 4. The next most complete is one in which there is both a meeting and communication. This is a situation in which the parties are not able to agree on a response but in which each has been able to tell his or her story, express emotion, and come to understand one another. The third cell addresses situations in which there is a meeting but the discussion focuses

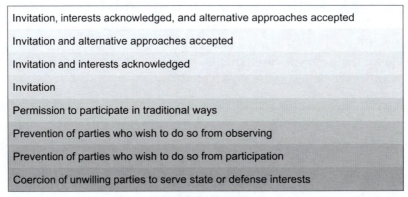

FIGURE 9.2 Inclusion

on negotiation of an agreement. This meeting will probably be relatively short, and the more relational effects of the crime will not be addressed. The fourth cell describes situations in which the parties do not meet directly but communicate indirectly their stories and emotions; as a result, they come to understanding and an agreement. In some cases of incest, for example, any interaction between the victim and the offender is conducted through writing rather than in person, due to the victim's vulnerability to the offender. The next cell describes such an indirect encounter that fails to reach an agreement but in which the parties are able to tell their stories, express emotion, and achieve a degree of understanding. The next cell covers the situation in which an agreement is reached but no other elements of encounter are reached. This possibility will arise in situations in which a probation officer or other person contacts both parties to negotiate an agreement. Little else about the crime and its effects will be exchanged. The next cell describes situations in which neither party has any contact (this is the most likely circumstance under contemporary criminal justice processes). The final category addresses situations in which the parties are kept apart, either for reasons of individual or public safety or to serve the trial interests of the prosecution or defense.

Figure 9.4 presents a similar range of options related to amends. The most expansive way of making amends will involve apology, restitution, and the constellation of changed behavior and generosity. The next most complete form involves an apology and restitution. In this situation, the offender is able to address the past but not the future. The next cell describes those situations in which the offender apologizes and changes. This might occur when there is no actual damage to the victim, when the victim's damages are covered in some other way (e.g., through insurance), or when the offender is unable to pay restitution. The fourth cell depicts a situation in which there is restitution and change. An example of this would be when the offender and victim negotiate both restitution payments and additional community service by the offender at an agency selected by the victim. The next cell describes those situations in which an apology is

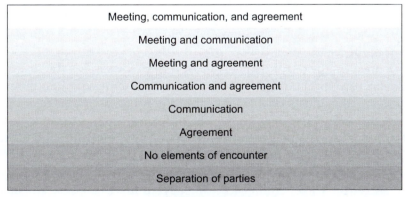

FIGURE 9.3 Encounter

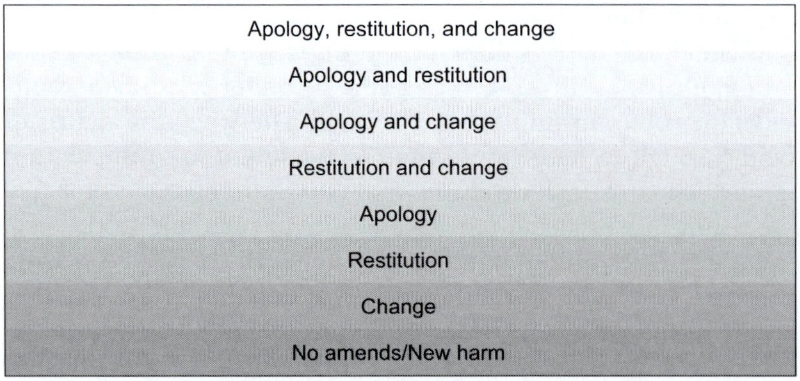

Apology, restitution, and change

Apology and restitution

Apology and change

Restitution and change

Apology

Restitution

Change

No amends/New harm

FIGURE 9.4 Amends

all that is offered by the offender. It may be all that the victim wants, or it could be that for some reason the offender is unable (or fails) to do more. The sixth cell describes the times when restitution is the only amends made. The seventh cell depicts situations in which the offender changes, but there is no apology or restitution. In the final cell, nothing related to amends takes place, or new harm is inflicted—a common result in contemporary criminal justice.

Figure 9.5 reviews different ways in which parties might be reintegrated into the community. The optimal response is for them to be shown respect; given the material, moral, and spiritual assistance they need; and kept safe. The next cell describes situations in which they are shown respect and are kept safe but do not receive assistance. The third cell describes a situation in which assistance is offered and the parties are kept safe, but the process may be degrading or dehumanizing to the individual. The fourth cell depicts the situation in which the parties are protected but not given assistance or respect. An example of this would be an offender who is imprisoned because of the threat of harm to or from community members. The fifth and sixth cells describe a community response of neglect—indifference to the needs of one or both of the parties. The seventh and eighth cells move to a community posture that stigmatizes or alienates one or both of the parties. This might be done through formal procedures or more likely through informal communication of shame.

These figures, when consolidated, suggest a way of assessing the restorative character of a particular case, program, or system. When evaluating the handling of a particular case or program, the question will be whether the response was as restorative as possible *under the circumstances*. It may be, for example, that the particular offender has never been identified. This means that a meeting is not possible, although it may be possible for the victim to meet with surrogate offenders and thereby tell his or her story, express emotion, and gain some understanding of the offender. Furthermore, the victim will not receive amends from the offender. However, a restorative response will ensure that there

Respect, assistance, and safety

Respect and safety

Assistance and safety

Safety

Indifference to either victim or offender

Indifference to both victim and offender

Stigmatization or isolation of either victim or offender

Stigmatization or isolation of both victim and offender

FIGURE 9.5 Reintegration

is sufficient material, moral, and spiritual support to help the victim recover his or her losses.

The restorative character of a system seems to reflect two features. The first has to do with its *aspirations* as reflected in programs and resources. How far up these charts does the system aspire to go? Or, to ask a somewhat different question, at what level is it willing to settle? The second evaluation criterion has to do with the *number of people given access* to the restorative system: Is this approach offered to every eligible person, or is it limited to a select few? The more people given access to the restorative approach, the more restorative the system will be.

The following three figures deal with the first factor, the level of restorativeness to which the system aspires. Figure 9.6 shows a fully restorative system in which all elements of each of the four values are available. Not all parties will avail themselves of these features because particular circumstances may make that unnecessary or unfeasible. All features are offered, however. If such a system makes this offer to all parties, it is easy to describe the system as fully restorative.

Figure 9.7 describes a system that aspires to something less. In this system, the relational elements of crime and justice are reflected in its commitment to offering parties the opportunity to communicate, the expectation that amends should include an apology, and the recognition that the parties deserve respect and safety as they reintegrate. This system would not accept, for example, a streamlined negotiation process conducted by probation officers to reach restitution agreements quickly without giving the victim and offender the chance to meet. Provided that these services are offered to all victims and offenders, we call this a moderately restorative system.

Figure 9.8 depicts the minimum to which we suggest a system could aspire and still claim to be restorative. In this approach, the relational elements of crime are not pursued, but material and financial costs of crime are taken seriously. This system is reparative in nature, but its respect for the value of inclusion moves it into the category of restorative justice.

Meeting, communication, and agreement	Apology, restitution, and change	Respect, assistance, and safety	Invitation, interests acknowledged, and alternative approaches accepted
Meeting and communication	Apology and restitution	Respect and safety	Invitation and alternative approaches accepted
Meeting and agreement	Apology and change	Assistance and safety	Invitation and interests acknowledged
Communication and agreement	Restitution and change	Safety	Invitation
Communication	Apology	Indifference to either victim or offender	Permission to participate in traditional ways
Agreement	Restitution	Indifference to both victim and offender	Prevention of parties who wish to do so from observing
No elements of encounter	Change	Stigmatization or isolation of either victim or offender	Prevention of parties who wish to do so from participation
Separation of parties	No amends/New harm	Stigmatization or isolation of both victim and offender	Coercion of unwilling parties to serve state or defense interests

FIGURE 9.6 Fully Restorative System

Meeting, communication, and agreement	Apology, restitution, and change	Respect, assistance, and safety	Invitation, interests acknowledged, and alternative approaches accepted
Meeting and communication	Apology and restitution	Respect and safety	Invitation and alternative approaches accepted
Meeting and agreement	Apology and change	Assistance and safety	Invitation and interests acknowledged
Communication and agreement	Restitution and change	Safety	Invitation
Communication	Apology	Indifference to either victim or offender	Permission to participate in traditional ways
Agreement	Restitution	Indifference to both victim and offender	Prevention of parties who wish to do so from observing
No elements of encounter	Change	Stigmatization or isolation of either victim or offender	Prevention of parties who wish to do so from participation
Separation of parties	No amends/New harm	Stigmatization or isolation of both victim and offender	Coercion of unwilling parties to serve state or defense interests

FIGURE 9.7 Moderately Restorative System

Conclusion

Restorative justice programs and thinking have now expanded throughout the world. This expansion shows no signs of letting up, and although there is always need for caution in making claims about a restorative future, there does seem to be evidence that restorative justice is becoming part of contemporary criminal justice. The extent to which it moves beyond augmenting that system remains to be seen.

One way of tracking the progress of restorative justice within a system is to use a framework such as the one we have proposed to assess the restorative character of the system. The availability of restorative programs is only one indicator; far more critical is the priority given to those programs in actual usage. In restorative systems, the values and principles of restorative justice are sufficiently predominant, and competing values and principles are sufficiently subordinate, that as a result the system's processes and outcomes can be deemed highly restorative.

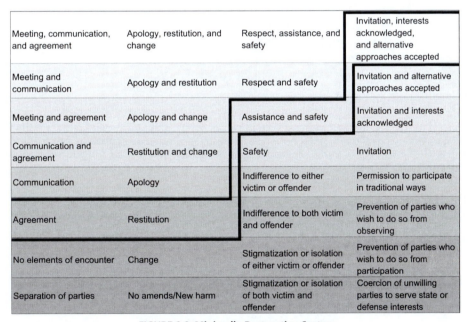

Meeting, communication, and agreement	Apology, restitution, and change	Respect, assistance, and safety	Invitation, interests acknowledged, and alternative approaches accepted
Meeting and communication	Apology and restitution	Respect and safety	Invitation and alternative approaches accepted
Meeting and agreement	Apology and change	Assistance and safety	Invitation and interests acknowledged
Communication and agreement	Restitution and change	Safety	Invitation
Communication	Apology	Indifference to either victim or offender	Permission to participate in traditional ways
Agreement	Restitution	Indifference to both victim and offender	Prevention of parties who wish to do so from observing
No elements of encounter	Change	Stigmatization or isolation of either victim or offender	Prevention of parties who wish to do so from participation
Separation of parties	No amends/New harm	Stigmatization or isolation of both victim and offender	Coercion of unwilling parties to serve state or defense interests

FIGURE 9.8 Minimally Restorative System

Review Questions

1. Why are consent, safety, and fundamental rights preconditions to constructing a restorative system?
2. What are the five models for a restorative system?
3. In what parts of contemporary criminal justice is restorative justice used?

4. Which four values are useful in measuring the restorativeness of a justice system?

5. Which of those values must be fully demonstrated to call a system "restorative"? Why?

Endnotes

1. The United Nations, *Basic Principles on the Use of Restorative Justice Programmes in Criminal Matters* (2002), paragraph 7.

2. Ibid., paragraph 13(c).

3. Alaska Code of Criminal Procedure, Sec. 12.55.011.

4. Julie Stubbs, "Relations of Domination and Subordination: Challenges for Restorative Justice in Responding to Domestic Violence," Sydney Law School Research Paper 10/61 (2010); Peggy Grauwiler, Nicole Peold, and Linda G. Mills, "Justice Is in the Design: Creating a Restorative Justice Treatment Model for Domestic Violence," in John Hamel and Tonia L. Nicholls, eds., *Family Interventions in Domestic Violence* (New York: Springer, 2007), 579–599.

5. The United Nations, *Basic Principles on the Use of Restorative Justice Programmes in Criminal Matters* (2002), paragraphs 9 and 10.

6. Virginia Acts of Assembly, Chapter 844, Sec. 53.1–30(B).

7. The United Nations, supra note 5, paragraph 12.

8. The United Nations, supra note 5, paragraph 13.

9. The United Nations, supra note 5, paragraphs 14 and 15.

10. For online information on this project, go to http://www.rjcity.org.

11. Crime (Restorative Justice) Act for the Australian Capital Territory (ACT), adopted in 2004 and implemented in 2005. Section 75 addresses a ministerial review and report that includes evaluation criteria such as victim satisfaction, reduction in recidivism, community satisfaction, reintegration of victims and offenders into the community, respect of everyone's rights, and a perception of fairness by victims and offenders.

10

Transformation

KEY CONCEPTS

- Transformation of perspective
- Transformation of structures
- Transformation of persons

In 1968, Herbert Packer wrote of two approaches to criminal justice, the crime control model and the due process model.[1] While acknowledging the limitations of such dichotomies, he suggested that examining criminal justice in this way would reveal "two separate value systems that compete for priority in the operation of the criminal process." Packer's dual models have been both widely admired and criticized. John Griffiths raised one of the more intriguing criticisms. He contended that rather than providing two models, Packer had really only offered one, which Griffiths called the battle model:

> *Packer consistently portrays the criminal process as a struggle—a stylized war—between two contending forces whose interests are implacably hostile: the individual (particularly, the accused individual) and the state. His two models are nothing more than alternative derivations from that conception of profound and irreconcilable disharmony of interest.[2]*

Griffiths was not particularly interested in advocating alternative approaches to Packer's adversarial paradigm of justice, but he did want to demonstrate that ideological preconceptions blind us to the possibilities that lie outside those conceptions. In order to do that, he posited what he called the "family" model.[3] Whereas Packer's adversarial models assumed disharmony and fundamentally irreconcilable interests amounting to a state of war, Griffiths proposed assuming "reconcilable—even mutually supportive—interests, a state of love." This would, he argued, significantly change our concepts of crime and the criminal. We would view crime as only one of a variety of relationships between the state and the accused, just as disobedience by children is only one dimension of their relationship with their parents. Furthermore, we would treat crime as normal behavior, expected even if not condoned. We would view criminals as people like us, not members of a special and deviant class of people. Furthermore, we would emphasize self-control rather than the imposition of external controls, and we would assign the criminal process an educational function, teaching those who observe it by what it does and how it does it. Although some of Griffiths' concepts may seem paternalistic or sentimental in view of the very real harms involved in crime, his family model is a personal model that assumes a kindred relationship between the offender and the community.

The adversarial model, by contrast, is impersonal and assumes an antagonistic relationship between the offender and the community—one that justifies (and indeed may require) declaring a war on criminals.

Whatever his purposes in outlining the family model, Griffiths did demonstrate the deep differences between it and the battle model. The parallels between restorative justice and the family model are obvious. Restorative justice recognizes the persons involved—not just the laws implicated. Such recognition is inherently transformational. That is, it transforms (rather than merely reforms) the nature of the justice process and our expectations concerning the outcome of that process. To use Howard Zehr's analogy, things look different when we view them through a new lens. Old problems, issues, and solutions fade in importance as new ones come into perspective. Structures that once made sense are now recognized as inadequate; formulations that once seemed to be the essence of wisdom are transparently foolish. Over time, we begin to see new implications, to ask new questions, to uncover new inadequacies with the status quo, and to qualify and deepen our initial impressions. A hallmark of restorative justice, then, should be transformation.

■ ■ ■ ▬▬▬▬▬▬▬▬▬▬▬▬▬▬▬▬▬▬▬▬▬▬▬▬▬▬▬▬▬▬▬▬

A hallmark of restorative justice is transformation.

▬▬▬▬▬▬▬▬▬▬▬▬▬▬▬▬▬▬▬▬▬▬▬▬▬▬▬▬▬▬▬▬ ■ ■ ■

In previous chapters, we discussed the concepts of restorative justice, its cornerstone values, and the challenge to take the incremental steps needed to put it into practice. In this chapter, we step back slightly and explore the elements of transformation—the metamorphosis needed to bring into reality a restorative system—at three levels: (1) transformation of perspective, (2) transformation of structures, and (3) transformation of persons.

Transformation of Perspective

Patterns of thinking shape what we know to be true, as we discussed in Chapter 1. Our thought patterns help us order what we experience, hear, and receive so we can function more easily in our daily lives, but they also make our perception selective and can blind us to conflicting or challenging data. Once we recognize that limitation—often when we are forced to admit the inadequacy of the existing pattern—we are faced with the need to move to an alternative. Whether we know it or not, in such instances, we may be on our way to a transformed perspective.

But how can we find viable alternatives when we are so entrenched that we can neither see nor evaluate them? Edward de Bono observed that it can actually be misleading to seek insight by looking to previous situations in which our pattern of thinking changed dramatically. This is because every "creative thought must always be logical in hindsight."[4] It is necessary to connect a creative insight with current reality in order to make use of it. As soon as we have cut the path from the creative idea to our present situation, we discover that the path moves both ways. We now can understand the logic of the new idea, and we may conclude that what we needed all along was better logic. When confronted with the need for more creativity, we remember our past experience and attempt to improve our logic. However, he argues, it was not logic that produced the insight; it was creativity.

Creativity, then, is an important element in transformation of perspective. It entails risk. We attempt something because it makes intuitive sense, or because the circumstances seem to leave us no other choice, but not because we know it will work. Victim–offender mediation, conferencing, and circles did not begin with a theory and move from there to programmatic expression; in fact, the opposite happened. As early program staff and observers began to ask themselves why restorative results were so different from what they had anticipated, they began to understand the psychological, theological, criminological, and philosophical implications of what they observed in practice.

A second element in transformation of perspective is openness to learning how to order our thoughts in a different pattern. This is the approach offered by the Alternatives to Violence Project. This project helps prisoners, accustomed to dealing with conflict through violence, learn nonviolent responses instead. In the course of two 3-day workshops, participants first discover, then learn through presentation, discussion, and experience, that violence need not be a given. It is possible to convert hostility, destructiveness, aggression, and violence into cooperation and community. Participants are taught conflict resolution skills and are given opportunities to practice these. The effect of these workshops, however, is more fundamental than simply skill enhancement:

> *It is enlivening to observe, much less experience, the process at work: affirmation, love, openness, honesty, laughter, respect, diligence, genuineness. At the outset of a workshop, participants seem wary and guarded. Some feign nonchalance with nervous laughter and chatter; others sit cautiously expressionless, arms crossed, registering everything; others engage in conversation, filling this unfamiliar space with something, anything; still others feign aloofness, exuding an air of superiority. By workshop's end, however, there is a deeply abiding sense of goodwill that permeates the atmosphere. People look at one another rather than through one another or at the floor. Laughter and joking fill the air. Faces are soft. Eyes sparkle. Smiles abound. Ancient doors have creaked open. Tears spill down radiant cheeks. Heads are on straight; bodies erect. Voices are clear and strong. People approach rather than avoid each other; they connect.[5]*

Third, we can look to other places, times, or traditions to find new ways of looking at familiar problems. One of the hallmarks of restorative justice has been the interest of its advocates in looking outside their own present cultures for inspiration and ideas. Considering how crime has been handled in the past or how it is resolved in other cultures helps pull us out of the troughs of our current patterns of thinking about crime.

Although what we see in the past or in other cultures cannot be transferred directly to our contemporary situations, it may spur us to new ideas and possibilities.

Fourth, we can reflect on alternatives to approaches that we have taken for granted. For example, the adversarial paradigm of crime has significant implications in our thinking about criminal justice. A statue of the goddess Justicia stands above the Old Bailey law courts in London; she is blindfolded as she holds the scales of justice. This reminds us that justice must not be skewed by the status of, relationship to, or hope of reward from one of the parties to a dispute. Impartial justice has become equated with mechanically (and sometimes mechanistically) applying rules to determine an outcome. Dispassionate justice has come to mean indifference concerning that outcome. We are preoccupied with what Jonathan Burnside called "an antiseptic construal of justice," one that values "objectivity, impartiality and the fair application of rules." That, he argues, must be balanced by "a passionate construal of justice [that] would emphasize love, compassion and the vindication of the weak."[6]

■ ■ ■ ━━━

Transformation of perspective has four elements: creativity, openness to learning, looking at familiar problems in new ways, and considering new alternatives.

━━━ ■ ■ ■

Under such a "passionate construal" of justice, the goddess might throw off her blindfold and draw her sword in righteous anger or open her arms in a merciful embrace. A law court with that sort of statue on its roof would dispense justice differently, but in what ways? What outcomes would we expect? How would its processes be different? How would the architecture of the building change? Would the demeanor of those who staff it be different? Reflection on this sort of question can prepare us for a transformation of perspective.

Another example is the premise that criminal law expresses in a symbolic way the norms of a society. One alternative premise worth exploring is that criminal law, because it is maintained by force, expresses in a symbolic way the *lack* of consensus concerning the norms of a society. We might ask why it is that so many of us are disinclined to embrace lawful behavior, causing governments to spend billions of dollars to investigate, punish, and attempt to deter. This could lead into extended and important political, sociological, and theological discussions.

An alternative hypothesis concerning criminal law and societal norms might be the following: Society's norms are best revealed in the course of conversation. Under this perspective, law might be considered the conclusion of a kind of conversation (the lobbying and deliberative process that precedes its adoption), but there are other forms of conversation as well. We might look at the nature of discourse in the media, in entertainment, or in art for clues concerning what is important to our society. We might conclude that because those sorts of discourse are carried on by representatives (e.g., elected representatives who pass laws, columnists or talk-show hosts who find topics that will interest their audiences, and artists and producers who need to make money), they give us skewed and inaccurate perceptions of norms and values. For a more accurate picture, we would need to look at more intimate discussions carried on by the participants themselves, not by representatives. Out of those conversations, we may discern a different set (or a different formulation of the same set) of norms. This certainly carries with it important implications for the criminal justice process and in particular spurs our interest in comparing justice dispensed by professionals with justice arrived at by the participants themselves.[7]

Transformation of Structures

Transformed perspectives lead to the recognition that some of the structures that are interwoven with criminal justice also need transformation. For instance, imbalances of power among the parties in a criminal justice proceeding can exist at many levels and tip the process toward certain outcomes, even if the procedural intent is otherwise. One such imbalance that has received official recognition is the disproportionate power of civil government over individual defendants. A panoply of procedural protections designed to protect defendants' human rights has been devised to help offset this imbalance.

There are, however, other imbalances as well, such as those that result from poverty. Accused defendants with abundant financial resources receive substantially better representation than do indigent defendants who are assigned overworked, underpaid public defenders. The pithy title of Jeffrey Reiman's book, *The Rich Get Richer and the Poor Get Prison*,[8] underscores this point. Poverty creates imbalances among victims as well, the majority of whom are as poor and powerless as their offenders. Although there has been a steady growth of services to victims during the past 20 years, disenfranchised crime victims—especially those who are members of racial minority groups—are not benefiting from them as much as wealthier, more powerful victims.

A third example of a power imbalance is the disparity that may exist between victims and offenders caused by social, economic, and political inequities and by a preexisting relationship between the two (a particular problem in domestic violence cases). As negotiation and mediation become more accepted in resolving disputes, these imbalances become increasingly important for restorative justice practitioners to recognize and address.

■ ■ ■ ━━━━━━━━━━━━━━━━━━━━━━━━━━━━━━━━━━━

It is essential to monitor justice structures—including restorative justice structures—to identify problems that result in less justice for some, and then to remedy and even transform those structures.

━━━━━━━━━━━━━━━━━━━━━━━━━━━━━━━━━━━ ■ ■ ■

The existence of social, political, and economic inequities challenges any society that values justice and fairness. Under the restorative justice model, it poses a special challenge to communities, which are responsible for creating peace, and to governments, which are charged with providing order that protects the disenfranchised. There has been long and heated debate about the extent to which these inequities either cause crime (by reducing the honorable choices available to the offender) or produce unfairness in the criminal justice system. Because the discussion has been linked to issues of offender responsibility and accountability, it has become highly polarized. Although a society may determine that such inequities do not reduce or nullify individual responsibility, their existence creates a moral obligation for that society. Just as individuals must accept responsibility for their acts, so societies must assume some responsibility for the inequalities that plague them. It is an essential task to monitor the structures whose interplay affects criminal justice—including so-called restorative justice structures (and perhaps especially these)—to discern imbalances, inequities, or disparities that result in less justice for some and to seek remediation and even transformation of those structures.

Transformation of Persons

In this book, we have used words not usually heard in contemporary debate over criminal justice policy: healing, reconciliation, negotiation, vindication, and transformation. They are words that mingle uneasily with much common parlance on how to handle crime. In this book, we have attempted to show that these words and concepts actually resonate within our legal and social traditions, that they are professed by major segments of our societies, and that they are being demonstrated in programs throughout the world. They are catalytic words, reminding us of the passionate side of justice, which appears to be largely neglected in these early years of the twenty-first century.

They are also convicting words. It is easier to hypothesize the "family model" of justice, with its assumption of a state of love, than to live it. It is more orderly to design systems than to encounter living, breathing people. It is simpler to edit this chapter into its final form than to deal with the contradictions and complexities of human relationships.

It is not surprising that encounter has been a hallmark of the restorative justice movement. In victim–offender mediation, conferences, and circles, real people confronting specific crimes meet to understand the dimensions of the injustice done, the harm that resulted, and the steps that must be taken to make things right. Those meetings permit participants to deal with the relational and passionate dimensions of crime as well as the material and factual aspects, and they create the opportunity to seek more satisfying responses than can be offered by antiseptic justice.

Crime and injustice are moral problems at their root. A criminal act's nature as wrongdoing is important to the participants and to their communities. Its nature as lawbreaking answers a jurisdictional question: Will this case be heard in criminal courts? It also represents a violation of legal norms designed (in theory) to uphold the common good. Its nature as wrongdoing has personal and social consequences that surpass questions of procedure but still go to the heart of "common good."

A danger, however, in recognizing that crime has moral roots is that it can lead us into hypocrisy. "Crime has moral roots; therefore criminals are immoral. I am not a criminal;

therefore...." Our glib assertions lead us into another "us/them" dichotomy and intensify, often without our realizing it, the existing state of war against criminals. Charles Colson remarked that there are two kinds of criminals: those who get caught and the rest of us.[9] Jerome Miller said that there are two kinds of criminologists: those who view criminals as different from themselves and those who do not.[10]

Hypocrisy, injustice, and indifference are moral problems. The ancient rebuke (made to "good" people) warned that when we are angry with others without cause, we have committed murder in our hearts, and that when we think of them as fools, we have condemned ourselves.[11] When we fail to respond to crime victims as our neighbors[12] and offenders as our brothers and sisters,[13] we ignore the injustice they experience or cause and escape our own responsibility. Where, then, shall we find the resources for transformation of ourselves and of the world? This, Richard Quinney reminds us, is a spiritual issue:

> *All of this is to say, to us as criminologists, that crime is suffering and that the ending of crime is possible only with the ending of suffering. And the ending both of suffering and of crime, which is the establishing of justice, can come only out of peace, out of a peace that is spiritually grounded in our very being. To eliminate crime—to end the construction and perpetuation of an existence that makes crime possible—requires a transformation of our human being.... When our hearts are filled with love and our minds with willingness to serve, we will know what has to be done and how it is to be done.[14]*

Where can we go to have our hearts and minds so filled? This is a question each person must answer for himself or herself. Many find this place within the reintegrating community we spoke of in Chapter 6: faith communities. That has been our experience. We have encountered within our churches the living presence of the One who preached the gospel to the poor, healed the brokenhearted, brought deliverance to captives and recovery of sight to the blind, liberated the oppressed, and proclaimed the year of the Lord's favor.[15] One who continues to speak to our own brokenness, "I have loved you with an everlasting love; I have drawn you with loving-kindness. I will build you up again and you will be rebuilt."[16] One who calls us to "let justice roll on like a river, righteousness like a never-failing stream."[17]

■ ■ ■ ▬▬▬▬▬▬▬▬▬▬▬▬▬▬▬▬▬▬▬▬▬▬▬▬▬▬▬▬▬▬▬▬▬▬▬▬▬▬

Restorative justice can produce ongoing transformation. However, the transformation must begin with ourselves, for we too have recompense to pay, reconciliation to seek, forgiveness to ask, and healing to receive.

▬▬▬▬▬▬▬▬▬▬▬▬▬▬▬▬▬▬▬▬▬▬▬▬▬▬▬▬▬▬▬▬▬▬▬▬▬▬ ■ ■ ■

A hallmark of restorative justice must be ongoing transformation: transformation of perspective, transformation of structures, and transformation of people. It begins with transformation of ourselves, for we too have recompense to pay, reconciliation to seek, forgiveness to ask, and healing to receive. We not only look for justice "out there" but also must turn the lens on ourselves—on our daily patterns of life and on our treatment of and attitudes toward others. Restorative justice is an invitation to reflection and renewal in communities and individuals as well as procedures and programs. Transformation of the world begins with transformation of ourselves—our own values, behavior, mind-set, and character. Without this personal transformation, we risk a hollow victory in trying to transform the wider world.

Review Questions

1. How do thought patterns either positively or negatively affect our perspective about reality?
2. What are the four elements of transformation of perspective?
3. What are some examples of structural "power imbalances," and what are their consequences?
4. What pitfalls are inherent in personalizing the moral dimension of crime?
5. What personal obligations does the moral dimension of justice and injustice place on people who aspire to a just society?

Endnotes

1. Herbert L. Packer, *The Limits of the Criminal Sanction* (Stanford, CA: Stanford University Press, 1968), 153.

2. John Griffiths, "Ideology in Criminal Procedure or a Third 'Model' of the Criminal Process," *Yale Law Journal* 79 (1970): 359, at 367.

3. Ibid., 371ff.

4. Edward de Bono, *Conflicts: A Better Way to Resolve Them* (New York: Penguin, 1991), 14.

5. Lila Rucker, "Peacemaking in Prisons," in Harold E. Pepinsky and Richard Quinney, eds., *Criminology as Peacemaking* (Bloomington: Indiana University Press, 1991), 177–178.

6. Jonathan Burnside and Nicola Baker, eds., "Tension and Tradition in the Pursuit of Justice," in *Relational Justice: Repairing the Breach* (Winchester, UK: Waterside Press, 1994), 43.

7. Francis J. Schweigert, "Learning the Common Good: Principles of Community-Based Moral Education in Restorative Justice," *Journal of Moral Education* 28(2) (June 1999): 163.

8. Jeffrey H. Reiman, *The Rich Get Richer and the Poor Get Prison: Ideology, Class, and Criminal Justice* (New York: Wiley, 1979).

9. Colson used this line regularly in speeches and conversations, although to our knowledge it has not been included in any of his publications.

10. Quoted in Pepinsky and Quinney, eds., *Criminology as Peacemaking* (Bloomington: Indiana University Press, 1991), 303.

11. Matthew 5:21–22.

12. See Luke 10:25–37.

13. See Luke 19:1–10.

14. Pepinsky and Quinney, supra note 10, at 11, 12.

15. Luke 4:18–19.

16. Jeremiah 31:3–4.

17. Amos 5:24.

Appendix

RJ City℠

Case Study

When Ed and David Broke into Mildred's House and Took Things

A Story about RJ City's Response to Crime, Victims and Offenders

One afternoon two young men broke into a house, ransacked it and took small valuables they could easily sell.

This is the story of those two men, the woman who lived in the house, and how RJ City responded to all of them. RJ City℠ is creating a system that will allow it to respond as restoratively as possible to all crimes, all victims and all offenders.

In the course of this story you will meet family members and friends of all three. You will see how the crime had effects that went beyond the harm to the immediate victim.

And you will observe how RJ City's℠ response is different from contemporary criminal justice.

Features

Some of the unique features that you will notice in this Case Study include:

Victim support is offered from the moment a crime takes place.

Restorative processes such as circles are routinely used.

When cases go to Adversarial Court, victims have the right to have lawyers present evidence and to make arguments during proceedings.

Contents

The Break-In 178

Mildred Returns Home 178

Victim Support for Mildred 179

The Arrest 180

David and the Justice System 181

Ed and the Justice System 181

Mildred and the Justice System 182

The Circle 182

Adversarial Court 185

How Things Worked Out for Mildred .. 186

How Things Worked Out for David 187

How Things Worked Out for Ed 187

Notes

1. This story has happy endings. This is not because that always happens in restorative processes, although there are more happy endings than in contemporary criminal justice. This story has happy endings because RJ City℠ does not give up on people. The story is never considered complete until the ending is satisfying, if not happy.

2. This story is fictional and not based on any particular crime or people. However, it reflects only one set of facts and individuals. Other scenarios for use in simulations are available for classroom and other use. These encourage creative application of restorative principles to difficult issues. You can find those, and other RJ City℠ materials, at www.rjcity.org.

3. RJ City℠ is a work in progress, which means that this Case Study is as well. For more information about the features of RJ City's℠ response to crime that are reflected in this example, please refer to RJ City℠: Phase 1 Final Report [http://rjcity.org/the-project/1_Final]. If you have comments, criticisms or suggestions, please offer them. As we learn more, we may modify this story.

4. This is the October 2009 version.

The Break-In

One afternoon, two young men knocked on the door of a home. Getting no answer, they broke in. They moved quickly through the house, looking for small items they could carry easily.

They found what they were looking for in the back bedroom. They ransacked the room, grabbing things they could fence.

"Let's get out of here," one of them said, stuffing the last of the loot in his pocket.

"All right," said the other, pulling a watch out of a drawer. They hurried out of the house and ran down the street.

They never thought about who lived in the house, or how those people would feel when they got back home.

Mildred Returns Home

Mildred owns the house and has lived alone for two years since her husband died.

The day of the burglary she was visiting her daughter, Betty. When Betty drove her home, they saw the door was broken and called 911.

Officer Randy, who works for the Investigating Magistrate, arrived soon. He went through the house to make sure no one was still inside.

While Officer Randy was in the house, John, the Victim Support Coordinator for Mildred's neighborhood, arrived.

He gave Mildred and Betty a booklet with information about how RJ City responds to crime. It included these provisions:

We are very sorry this happened.

Our commitment to you:

- To protect you .
- To keep you informed.
- To include you, if you wish.
- To allow you to *not* participate, if you prefer.
- To help you find assistance.
- To help you get restitution.
- To treat you with respect.

What we ask of you:

- Treat others with respect.
- Do not retaliate.
- Allow others to participate.

Victims are central in our response to crime.

We will work with you to make it less likely that this will happen again to you or to anyone.

When Officer Randy was sure no one was inside, Mildred, Betty, John and he went through the house together.

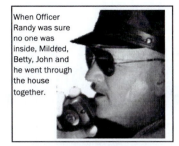

Mildred was horrified when she saw her bedroom. Someone had emptied every drawer and ransacked the place.

Just as she had feared, the anniversary watch was missing, along with jewelry and some money.

Victim Support for Mildred

"Who can help me clean up," Mildred worried. "My door is kicked in; I won't be safe."

John told her about a group of volunteers from a nearby church that helps with crime scene clean-up and repair.

Mildred asked him to contact the group, and two hours later Jo and Bill arrived to help straighten up and to repair the door.

Betty insisted that Mildred stay with her for a few nights. She, her husband, and their two children live in RJ City, too.

John told Mildred that a volunteer from his office would call her at Betty's house that night to see how she was doing.

Sure enough, Helen called later that evening. Mildred told her she was worried about returning home.

"I'm so upset I don't feel like eating," she said. "I don't know my neighbors anymore — so many people have moved in."

Helen told her that a community group called Caring Neighbors could bring meals for a week or so once she returned home. Mildred liked that idea.

These volunteers help people facing tough times. They are trained to be good listeners, so Mildred found it easy to talk with them.

Helen agreed to visit Mildred each evening to see how she was doing. Each night she and Mildred went through the house to make sure it was secure.

After a couple of weeks, Mildred felt safe enough that it was enough for Helen to just call.

So this is Mildred's support team: her daughter Betty, Victim Support Coordinator John, and Helen the volunteer.

The Arrest

Two weeks later the police received a tip about who had done the burglary, and both young men were arrested.

This is Ed. He has a previous conviction for burglary. He was 19 years old when arrested and not employed or going to school.

Ed denied having anything to do with the break-in, or even being with David.

This is David. He's never been in trouble before. He was 18 and in his final year of high school.

After an initial denial, David soon broke down and confessed. He was ashamed, and worried about how his folks would respond.

He told the police where some of the stolen property was, but some of it had already been sold, including the anniversary watch.

Officer Randy gave both Ed and David a brochure with information about the justice process in RJ City. It included these provisions:

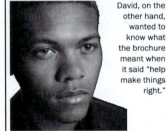

We are sorry that this crime took place in RJ City. We believe that you were responsible.

- You may require us to prove our charges against you in court.
- You may accept responsibility.
- If you were responsible, you have an obligation to help make things right.

Crime is what a person does; it does not define who they are unless they let it.

Our commitment to you:

- To include you.
- To help you make amends and to return to the community.
- To help you meet with the victims (if they wish) to decide how to do this.
- To treat you with respect.

What we ask from you:

- Treat others with respect.
- Do not retaliate
- Allow others to participate.

Ed continued to deny he had done anything wrong, so his case was sent to Adversarial Court.

David, on the other hand, wanted to know what the brochure meant when it said "help make things right."

Both were allowed to meet with attorneys who reviewed their options with them.

 **David and the Justice System**

 David wanted to "make things right," so he met with Brenda, an Offender Support officer. She told him about making amends in RJ City: he would apologize to Mildred, answer her questions, pay restitution and/or do any community service they agreed on.

 David wanted to know how he could do that. "There are two options," Brenda said. "Which one we take depends on what you and Mildred want."

 "Soon Judge Veronica, the Investigating Magistrate will be issuing a report about the burglary. This will include a recommended amount of restitution," Brenda continued.

 "If you and Mildred agree with the report, the Magistrate will enter an order requiring you to pay restitution. You can also send Mildred a written apology, if you wish."

"The alternative is to meet with Mildred, answer questions she may have, and together decide what needs to be done to make amends."

 Brenda made sure that David had the opportunity to talk with Santiago, a lawyer, about these choices.

 After learning more about restorative circles, David decided that he would like to participate in one, if he could bring his parents and some other supporters.

Brenda said that she would find out whether Mildred was also interested in participating in a circle.

 **Ed and the Justice System**

 Ed told the police that he had nothing to do with the burglary. He was given the opportunity to talk with Priscilla, a lawyer, about the options available to him.

Cases go to Adversarial Court if the suspect denies responsibility or denies legal guilt. Suspects have the right to counsel in an Adversarial Court proceeding.

Victims also have the right to appear with a lawyer concerning the charge, restitution and protection, if necessary. So there could be three attorneys in these trials.

Suspects are also told about cooperative processes, such as restorative circles. These are used only when the suspect admits responsibility.

Mildred and the Justice System

John kept Mildred informed about the progress of the investigation, including the arrests of David and Ed.

Once it was clear that David accepted responsibility but Ed didn't, John explained the alternatives before Mildred.

She could ask the Investigating Magistrate to order David to pay restitution.

John described how restorative circles worked, and explained that David was willing to participate in one. Mildred decided that she wanted to as well, as long as Betty and John could be there, too.

Ed's situation was different. Because Ed denied he was involved, his case would go to Adversarial Court for trial.

The prosecution would try to prove that Ed was guilty. Mildred could have a lawyer, if she wished, to protect her interests in the charge, in reparation, and in protection.

Mildred was given the chance to talk with Miriam, a Victim Advocate. These lawyers or para-legals advise victims about their options, including hiring a lawyer for the Adversarial Court trial. Mildred chose not to do that.

The Circle

Mildred and David agreed to hold the circle at the Community Centre because it had a room large enough to hold everyone who would come, and because its central location made it easy for people to get here.

Mildred invited Betty and her husband to come.

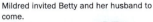

She also asked John and Officer Randy to participate.

David's parents attended.

So did his uncle, with whom he got along well in part because of their mutual interest in fishing.

And he invited his baseball coach, even though he had recently been kicked off the team for disciplinary problems.

Brenda attended as well.

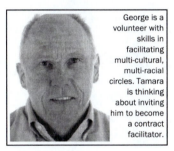

Barbara, one of the people who recently moved into Mildred's neighborhood, heard about the circle and decided to come to present concerns about the effects of crime on community members' lives.

Because of the nature of the crime, two people facilitated the meeting. Tamara is an experienced facilitator and works for RJ City.

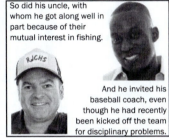

George is a volunteer with skills in facilitating multi-cultural, multi-racial circles. Tamara is thinking about inviting him to become a contract facilitator.

David began with an apology. Mildred asked why he had broken into her house and what had happened to the property.

David said they had sold some of it, including the watch. The rest he had turned over to the police.

Mildred explained to David how the burglary had affected her. She was afraid. She had lost important mementos of her marriage — particularly the watch. She felt like a stranger in her neighborhood. She worried about how much time Betty had to give to her since the burglary.

Betty and her husband spoke about the increased demands this placed on them at a time they were especially busy with heir kids. Her husband was involved in Little League and both children had other activities as well. This had already meant a lot of driving for Betty. Now they wanted to support Mildred as well, and that required taking extra trips across town.

David's coach said he was surprised David invited him to the circle. He had recently kicked David off the baseball team after he started a fight with a teammate. David was a good player, but had recently become disruptive and angry. He wouldn't talk about what was going on, and after the fight the coach felt he had to remove him from the team.

David's parents disclosed that his Dad had lost his job six months ago. The financial anxiety had strained everyone's relationships. His Dad had recently gotten a job,  but his shift was at night, which meant he slept in the afternoon. He and David had gotten into arguments about how much noise David made when he came home from school.

David's Mom said that David seemed to be angry all the time, and that he had started spending time with young men like Ed whom they were worried would get him in trouble.

 David's uncle said that he and David shared a love for fishing. This had often given them a chance to talk, and they seemed to get along well. Lately he hadn't been around as much because his brother, David's Dad, was out of work and stressed out. They always got into pointless arguments, so the uncle just stayed away.

Barbara told the group how worried the neighbors were. Most have recently moved into the area, and many families are either single-parent or dual-income. They feel particularly vulnerable during the days when no one is home. They had called a public meeting to talk with RJ City officials about how to improve safety.

She said that her young son had asked her the other day if the bad people were going to come to their house and take his toys.

 Once again David apologized, saying he had no idea the number of people affected by the break-in. He wished he could undo things. Since he couldn't, he hoped there was some way he could help repair some of the damage he had caused.

Mildred said it had been very helpful to hear from David and his parents and supporters. She thought David had done a bad thing, but was not a bad person. She accepted his apology and said she hoped he would learn from this.

The discussion then moved to what kinds of things might help make things right.

First, David agreed to pay restitution for half the value of the stolen property that was not recovered.

This led to a discussion about how David could make payments without a job. The coach offered to help David get work at a batting cage near school, and said he would stop by regularly to make sure David didn't lose his good swing.

Third, David's parents were interested to learn that the local community college offers courses on  communicating with teenagers. They decided that they would attend.

In addition, David's uncle agreed to get together with David every other weekend to do some fishing. That would give them a chance to talk about things David might not feel comfortable raising with his parents.

The coach said that David could rejoin the baseball team as long as he was current in completing his part of the agreement.

David agreed to come to the neighborhood meeting Barbara was organizing, if Barbara introduced him by describing the circle. David's Mom said she would come, too.

Mildred said she would also attend so she could meet her neighbors and say how satisfied she was that David had taken responsibility.

Barbara assured Mildred that she would make sure that people in the community kept an eye on her house. She invited Mildred to visit her and her son at their home. Mildred accepted the invitation gratefully and said that she loved children and perhaps could care for Barbara's son from time to time.

So this is David's support team: his uncle, Offender Support officer Brenda, and his baseball coach.

Adversarial Court

Because Ed denied having anything to do with the burglary, his matter was sent to the Adversarial Court for trial. He was told, however, that at any point in the process he could still request that the matter be returned for cooperative resolution.

When cases go to Adversarial Court, the victim has the right to hire an attorney to offer evidence and make arguments on three issues: first, the charges against the suspect; second, any decision that could affect the victim's likelihood of receiving restitution; and third, any decision that could affect the victim's safety.

Mildred decided that she did not want to do that, but she did want to file a victim impact statement and submit a claim for restitution. Helen helped her prepare the statement in the form required by the courts.

Ed was represented by Priscilla. The trial focused on the issues of whether a crime had occurred and whether Ed had been involved in the crime.

Mildred was called to testify; Helen attended court with her that day.

David was also called as a witness. During his testimony he spoke about his agreement.

At the conclusion of the trial, Ed was found guilty. Judge Bernard ordered a pre-sentence investigation into Ed's background, the impact of the crime on Mildred, and the impact on the community.

At the sentencing hearing, the prosecutor, defense attorney (and victim's lawyer, had there been one) were invited to present evidence and make arguments.

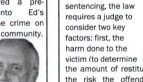

When it comes to sentencing, the law requires a judge to consider two key factors: first, the harm done to the victim (to determine the amount of restitution), and second, the risk the offender poses to the community or victim (to determine incapacitative or reintegrative measures).

Thomas, the Offender Support officer assigned to Ed, prepared the pre-sentence report. It showed Ed's prior burglary conviction, that he had lived with a girlfriend for the past nine months, that he

had no job, used marijuana regularly and also abused alcohol.

Ed had dropped out of school when he turned 16. Frank, his woodshop teacher, told Thomas that it was unfortunate that Ed had not developed his interest in woodworking. That was something he had excelled in, and when he quit school it was to take a job as a carpenter. But he had gotten into an argument with his supervisor and was fired.

Ed's sentence had three parts:

First, he was ordered to pay restitution for half the value of the stolen property that was not recovered.

Second, he was assigned to live for 12 months in a closed workshop that manufactures furniture. "Closed" meant that he would be confined there.

Third, he was ordered to follow a reintegration plan that included substance abuse treatment, anger management, and participation in a victim empathy program. If his behavior was good, he could start graduated release after eight months.

This is Ed's support team: Offender Support officer Thomas; Delbert, director of the closed workshop; and Frank, his former teacher.

How Things Worked Out for Mildred

Mildred's fear was significantly reduced after the restorative circle with David.

Barbara made sure that her neighbors who attended the public meeting were introduced to Mildred.

She also invited Mildred to her house where Mildred met Barbara's young son, Aklilu. Mildred began doing occasional childcare for Aklilu.

Over time, Betty noticed that Mildred was less depressed and dependent than she had been even before the burglary.

Several years later, as Mildred's health began to deteriorate, she moved to a nursing home. Barbara, Aklilu, and several other neighbors visited her on a regular basis.

How Things Worked Out for David

David successfully completed his agreement. His relationship with his parents improved significantly in part because of the course they took and because of the time he spent with his uncle.

He rejoined his baseball team and played well. He was the team's leadoff batter during the second half of the season.

He entered RJ City Community College and began to coach Little League. Sometimes his team played Betty's husband's team (David's team usually won).

About a year after the circle, David noticed an anniversary clock in the front window of an antique shop. It was in good working order, and he bought it.

David asked Barbara to arrange for him to visit Mildred to talk about how their lives were.

David told Mildred that he continued to be sorry about her husband's watch. He hoped that she would accept the anniversary clock as a gift, even though it could not replace the watch.

Mildred appreciated the gift and displayed the clock on her mantle.

Eventually, David became a restorative circles facilitator.

He was an excellent volunteer recruiter for the program.

How Things Worked Out for Ed

Ed did reasonably well while he was in the closed workshop. He was a very good carpenter.

In fact, he surprised Delbert, the director of the workshop, by designing a new piece of furniture that ended up being a top seller.

Ed had noticed that wall-mounted flat screen TVs looked great when they were on, but

unattractive when turned off.

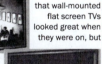

So he designed framed mirrors that covered the screen. He used a special glass for the mirror that allowed the screen o be visible when the TV was turned on, but invisible behind a normal-looking mirror when it was off.

However, when he was released he fell in with old friends and began to abuse substances again. He got his money by breaking into houses (but now, after David's testimony against him, he only worked alone).

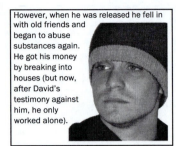

During one burglary, he was stunned to see that the owners had covered their flat screen TV with one of his mirrors.

This happened shortly after his girlfriend had told him she was pregnant, and he began to think about what was happening in his life.

He got in touch with Frank for advice.

Frank challenged him to deal with his substance abuse problem and promised that if he did, Frank would be there when he was released from treatment.

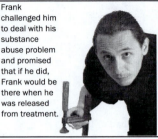

So Ed checked himself into a House of Refuge with substance abuse programming. When he finished treatment he was sober.

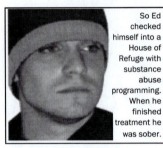

Frank helped him find a part-time job with a cabinetry maker. The owner was impressed with Ed's work and after six months made the position full time.

For outpatient treatment, Ed joined a twelve step programme. After awhile, he began thinking about how he could make amends to those he had harmed during his burglaries.

He visited Community Restorative Services, a public agency offering conflict resolution services. They contacted the people he had robbed. Most victims were not interested in meeting, but did submit claims for restitution.

He met with several victims in restorative circles, and sent messages of apology to several others who were willing to receive them.

Judge Veronica, the Investigating Magistrate determined that there was evidence to charge Ed with 6 more counts of burglary, but agreed that they would not have been solved without Ed's coming forward.

So she consolidated the charges and sentenced Ed to probation.

The conditions of probation included completing the restitution agreements he had reached with his victims, and continuing his twelve step program.

Ed settled down, married his girlfriend and raised several children. He continued to improve as a woodworker and volunteered at the closed workshop from time to time.

This Case Study, "When Ed and David Broke into Mildred's House and Took Things," was written by Dan Van Ness and is based on the description of RJ City contained in **RJ City℠ Phase 1 Final Report.**

This is the October 2009 version.

Select Bibliography

A comprehensive library of restorative justice resources is found online at http://www.rjonline.org. This online library contains citations and abstracts (and in some cases full text) of books, articles, theses, video programs, etc., dating from the current date back to 1970.

Abel, Charles F., & Marsh, Frank A. (1984). *Punishment and Restitution: A Restitutionary Approach to Crime and the Criminal.* Westport, CT: Greenwood.

Achilles, Mary (2004). Can Restorative Justice Live Up to Its Promise to Victims. In Howard Zehr & Barb Toews (Eds.), *Critical Issues in Restorative Justice* (pp. 65–74). Monsey, NY: Criminal Justice Press.

Acorn, Analise (2004). *Compulsory Compassion: A Critique of Restorative Justice.* Vancouver: UBC Press.

Aertsen, Ivo (2000). Victim–Offender Mediation in Belgium. In *The European Forum for Victim–Offender Mediation and Restorative Justice, Victim–Offender Mediation in Europe: Making Restorative Justice Work* (pp. 153–192). Leuven, Belgium: Leuven University Press.

Aertsen, Ivo, Arsovska, Jana, Rohne, Holger-C., Valiñas, Marta, & Vanspauwen, Kris (Eds.). (2012). *Restoring Justice after Large-Scale Violent Conflicts.* London: Routledge.

Aertsen, Ivo, & Beyens, Kristel (2005). Restorative Justice and the Morality of Law: A Reply to Brochu. In Erik Claes, René Foqué & Tony Peters (Eds.), *Punishment, Restorative Justice and the Morality of Law* (pp. 101–118). Oxford, UK: Intersentia.

Aertsen, Ivo, Daems, Tom, & Luc, Robert (Eds.). (2006). *Institutionalizing Restorative Justice.* Cullompton, UK: Willan.

Aertsen, Ivo, Mackay, Robert, Pelikan, Christa, Willemsens, Jolien, & Wright, Martin (2004). *Rebuilding Community Connections—Mediation and Restorative Justice in Europe.* Strasbourg: Council of Europe Publishing/Editions du Conseil de l'Europe.

Aertsen, Ivo, & Vanfraechem, Inge (2014, forthcoming). *Victims and Restorative Justice.* London: Routledge.

Aertsen, Ivo, Vanspauwen, Kris, Arsovska, Jana, Rohne, Holger-C., & Valinas, Marta (2008). *Restoring Justice after Large-Scale Violent Conflict.* Cullompton, UK: Willan.

Aertsen, Ivo, & Willemsens, Jolien (2001). The European Forum for Victim–Offender Mediation and Restorative Justice. *European Journal on Criminal Policy and Research, 9*(3), 291–300.

American Bar Association. (1994). Victim–Offender Mediation/Dialogue Program Requirements. *Resolution adopted by the American Bar Association House of Delegates.*

American Bar Association Criminal Justice Section. (1998). *Guidelines Governing Restitution to Victims of Criminal Conduct (including commentary on the guidelines).* Chicago: American Bar Association.

Anand, Sanjeev (2003). Crafting Youth Sentences: The Roles of Rehabilitation, Proportionality, Restraint, Restorative Justice, and Race under the Youth Criminal Justice Act. *Alberta Law Review, 40*, 943 ff.

Andrews, Arlene (1990). Crisis and Recovery Services for Family Violence Survivors. In L. Arthur, Lurigio, Wesley G. Skogan & Robert C. Davis (Eds.), *Victims of Crime: Problems, Policies, and Programs.* Newbury Park, CA: Sage.

Auerbach, Jerold S. (1983). *Justice without Law?* New York: Oxford University Press.

Bacon, G. Richard, et al. (1971). *Struggle for Justice: A Report on Crime and Punishment in America.* New York: Hill & Wang.

Balahur, Doina, Littlechild, Brian, & Smith, Roger (2007). *Restorative Justice Developments in Romania and Great Britain: Sociological–Juridical Enquires and Applied Studies of Social Work*. Romania: Editura Universitatii Alexandru Ioan Cuza.

Bard, Morton, & Sangrey, Dawn (1986). *The Crime Victim's Book* (2nd ed.). Secaucus, NJ: Citadel Press.

Barnett, Randy E., & Hagel, John, (Eds.), (1977). *Assessing the Criminal: Restitution, Retribution, and the Legal Process*. Cambridge, MA: Ballinger.

Barton, Charles (2000). Empowerment and Retribution in Criminal and Restorative Justice. In Heather Strang & John Braithwaite (Eds.), *Restorative Justice: From Philosophy to Practice* (pp. 55–76). Aldershot, UK: Dartmouth.

Bazemore, Gordon (2005). Reaction Essay: Whom and How Do We Reintegrate? Finding Community in Restorative Justice. *Criminology & Public Policy, 4*(1), 131–148.

Bazemore, Gordon (2002). Three Paradigms for Juvenile Justice. In Burt Galaway & Joe Hudson (Eds.), *Restorative Justice: International Perspectives*. Monsey, NY: Criminal Justice Press.

Bazemore, Gordon, Elis, Lori, & Green, Diane L. (2007). The Independent Variable in Restorative Justice: Theory-Based Standards for Evaluating the Impact and Integrity of Victim Sensitive Process (Part II). *Victims & Offenders, 2*(4), 351–373.

Bazemore, Gordon, & Erbe, Carsten (2004). Reintegration and Restorative Justice: Towards a Theory and Practice of Informal Social Control and Support. In Maruna Shadd & Russ Immarigeon (Eds.), *After Crime and Punishment: Pathways to Offender Reintegration* (pp. 27–56). Cullompton, UK: Willan.

Bazemore, Gordon, & Green, Diane L. (2007). Yardsticks' for Victim Sensitive Process: Principle-Based Standards for Gauging the Integrity of Restorative Justice Process. *Victims and Offenders, 2*(3), 289–301.

Bazemore, Gordon, & Schiff, Mara F. (2005). *Juvenile Justice Reform and Restorative Justice: Building Theory and Policy from Practice*. Cullompton, UK: Willan.

Bazemore, Gordon, & Umbreit, Mark S. (2004). Balanced and Restorative Justice: Prospects for Juvenile Justice in the 21st Century. In Albert R. Roberts (Ed.), *Juvenile Justice Sourcebook: Past, Present, and Future* (pp. 467–507). New York: Oxford University Press.

Bazemore, Gordon, & Umbreit, Mark (1999). *Conferences, Circles, Boards, and Mediations: Restorative Justice and Citizen Involvement in the Response to Youth Crime*. Washington, DC: Office of Juvenile Justice and Delinquency Prevention, U.S. Department of Justice.

Bazemore, Gordon, Zaslaw, Jay G., & Riester, Danielle (2005). Behind the Walls and Beyond: Restorative Justice, Instrumental Communities, and Effective Residential Treatment. *Juvenile and Family Court Journal (Winter)*, 53–73.

Beattie, J. M. (1986). *Crime and the Courts in England: 1660–1800*. Princeton, NJ: Princeton University Press.

Beck, Elizabeth, Britto, Sarah, & Andrews, Arlene (2007). *In the Shadow of Death: Restorative Justice and Death Row Families*. New York: Oxford University Press.

Borer, & Anne, Tristan (2006). *Telling the Truths: Truth Telling and Peace Building in Post-Conflict Societies*. Notre Dame, IN: University of Notre Dame Press.

Bottoms, Anthony (2003). Some Sociological Reflections on Restorative Justice. In Andrew von Hirsch et al., (Ed.), *Restorative Justice and Criminal Justice: Competing or Reconcilable Paradigms?* (pp. 79–114). Hart: Oxford.

Bottoms, Anthony, & Dignan, James (2004). Youth Justice in Great Britain. *Crime and Justice, 31*, 21–183.

Bowen, Helen, Marshall, Chris, & Boyack, Jim (2004). How Does Restorative Justice Ensure Good Practice? In Howard Zehr & Barb Toews (Eds.), *Critical Issues in Restorative Justice* (pp. 265–271). Monsey, NY/ Cullompton, UK: Criminal Justice Press/Willan.

Braithwaite, John (2007). Encourage Restorative Justice. *Criminology & Public Policy, 6*(4), 689–696.

Braithwaite, John (2005). Between Proportionality and Impunity: Confrontation → Truth → Prevention. *Criminology, 43*(2), 283–306.

Braithwaite, John (2004a). The Evolution of Restorative Justice. Visiting Experts' Papers, 123rd International Senior Seminar, Resource Material Series No. 63, pp. 37–47. Tokyo: United Nations Asia and Far East Institute for the Prevention of Crime and the Treatment of Offenders.

Braithwaite, John (2004b). Restorative Justice and De-Professionalization. *The Good Society, 13*(1), 28–31.

Braithwaite, John, et al. (2003a). Principles of Restorative Justice. In Andrew von Hirsch (Ed.), *Restorative Justice and Criminal Justice: Competing or Reconcilable Paradigms?* (pp. 9–13). Hart: Oxford.

Braithwaite, John (2003b). Holism, Justice, and Atonement. *Utah Law Review* (1), 389–412.

Braithwaite, John (1994). Thinking Harder about Democratising Social Control. In C. Alder & J. Wundersitz (Eds.), *Family Conferencing and Juvenile Justice: The Way Forward or Misplaced Optimism?* (pp. 199–216). Canberra: Australian Institute of Criminology.

Braithwaite, John (1989). *Crime, Shame and Reintegration.* Cambridge, UK: Cambridge University Press.

Braithwaite, John, & Roche, Declan (2001). Responsibility and Restorative Justice. In Gordon Bazemore & Mara Schiff (Eds.), *Restorative Community Justice: Repairing Harm and Transforming Communities* (pp. 63–84). Cincinnati, OH: Anderson.

Braithwaite, Valerie, Morrison, Brenda, Ahmed, Brenda, & Reinhart, Monika (2003). Researching the Prospects for Restorative Justice Practice in Schools: The Life at School Survey 1996–99. In Lode Walgrave (Ed.), *Repositioning Restorative Justice* (pp. 169–190). Cullompton, UK: Willan.

Brunk, Conrad G. (2001). Restorative Justice and the Philosophical Theories of Punishment. In Michael L. Hadley (Ed.), *The Spiritual Roots of Restorative Justice* (pp. 39). Albany: State University of New York Press.

Burford, Gale, & Pennell, Joan (1995). *Family Group Decision Making: New Roles for "Old" Partners in Resolving Family Violence: Implementation Report Summary.* St. Johns: Memorial University of Newfoundland.

Burnside, Jonathan, Adler, Joanna, Rose, Gerry, & Loucks, Nancy (2005). *My Brother's Keeper: Faith-Based Units in Prisons.* Cullompton, UK: Willan.

Burnside, Jonathan, & Baker, Nicola (1994a). Tension and Tradition in the Pursuit of Justice. In Jonathan Burnside & Nicola Baker (Eds.), *Relational Justice: Repairing the Breach.* Winchester, UK: Waterside Press.

Burnside, Jonathan, & Baker, Nicola (Eds.), (1994b). *Relational Justice: Repairing the Breach.* Winchester, UK: Waterside Press.

Bushie, & Berma (n.d.). (Community Holistic Circle Healing: A Community Approach. Posted online at the International Institute for Restorative Practices. http://www.iirp.org/library/vt/vt_bushie.html#top, downloaded October 2005.

Cardenas, Juan (1986). The Crime Victim in the Prosecutorial Process. *Harvard Journal of Law and Public Policy, 9,* 371.

Carey, Mark (2001). Infancy, Adolescence, and Restorative Justice: Strategies for Promoting Organizational Reform. In Gordon Bazemore & Maria Schiff (Eds.), *Restorative Community Justice: Repairing Harm and Transforming Communities* (pp. 151–169). Cincinnati, OH: Anderson.

Carey, Mark (1997). *Taking Down the Walls: Measures to Integrate the Objectives of the Justice System with the Community's.* Originally published in *Community Corrections Report, 1997.* (Available at http://www.ojp.usdoj.gov/nij/rest-just/ch6/takingdown.html. as of August 22, 2000).

Carr, Lloyd G. (1980). Shalom. In R. L. Harris, et al., (Ed.), *Theological Wordbook of the Old Testament* (pp. 931). Chicago: Moody Press.

Chankova, Dobrinka (2003). *Mediation—An Innovation in Criminal Justice*. Sofia, Bulgaria: Feneya Press.

Chankova, Dobrinka (2001). Applicability of Mediation in Bulgaria: The View of Law Enforcement Professionals. *Law, Administration, and Politics n.2.*

Christie, Nils (1977). Conflict as Property. *British Journal of Criminology, 17*(1), 1 ff.

Christie, Nils (1981). *Limits to Pain*. Oslo-Bergen-Tromsø: Universitetsforlaget.

Claassen, Ron (2004). Two Useful Models for Implementing Restorative Justice. *ACResolution, 3*(4), 34–35.

Claassen, Ron (2003). *A Peacemaking Model: A Biblical Perspective*. Fresno, CA: Center for Peacemaking and Conflict Studies.

Claassen, Ron (2002). Building Peace: The Victim–Offender Reconciliation Program Approach and Its Growing Role in Communities. In John G. Perry (Ed.), *Repairing Communities through Restorative Justice* (pp. 141–152). Lanham, MD: American Correctional Association.

Claassen, Ron, & Zehr, Howard (1989). *VORP Organizing: A Foundation in the Church*. Elkhart, IN: Mennonite Central Committee, U.S. Office of Criminal Justice.

Claassen, Roxanne (2004). New Approaches to Classroom Discipline. *ACResolution, 3*(4), 35–36.

Clamp, Kerry (2013). *Restorative Justice in Transition*. London: Routledge.

Clark, Janine Natalya (2008). The Three Rs: Retributive Justice, Restorative Justice, and Reconciliation. *Contemporary Justice Review, 11*(4), 331–350.

Clear, Todd R. (2004). Thoughts about Action and Ideology in Criminal Justice Reform. *Contemporary Justice Review, 7*(1), 69–73.

Clear, Todd R., & Karp, David R. (1999). *The Community Justice Ideal: Preventing Crime and Achieving Justice*. Boulder, CO: Westview.

Cnaan, Ram A., Wineburg, Robert J., & Boddie, Stephanie C. (1999). *The Newer Deal: Social Work and Religion in Partnership*. New York: Columbia University Press.

Coates, Robert, & Gehm, John (1989). An Empirical Assessment. In Martin Wright & Burt Galaway (Eds.), *Mediation and Criminal Justice*. Newbury Park, CA: Sage.

Colson, Charles W. (2001). *Justice That Restores*. Wheaton, IL: Tyndale House.

Colson, Charles W. (1980a). Towards an Understanding of the Origins of Crime. In John Stott & Nick Miller (Eds.), *Crime and the Responsible Community: A Christian Contribution to the Debate about Criminal Justice*. London: Hodder & Stoughton.

Colson, Charles W. (1980b). Towards an Understanding of Imprisonment and Rehabilitation. In John Stott & Nick Miller (Eds.), *Crime and the Responsible Community: A Christian Contribution to the Debate about Criminal Justice*. London: Hodder & Stoughton.

Colson, Charles W., & Benson, Daniel H. (1980). Restitution as an Alternative to Imprisonment. *Detroit College of Law Review* (2), 523–598.

Colson, Charles W., & Nolan, Pat (2004). Prescription for Safer Communities. *Notre Dame Journal of Law, Ethics and Public Policy, 18*, 387–399.

Colson, Charles W., & Van Ness, Daniel W. (1989). *Convicted: New Hope for Ending America's Crime Crisis*. Westchester, IL: Crossway Books.

Consedine, Jim (1995). *Restorative Justice: Healing the Effects of Crime*. Lyttelton, NZ: Ploughshares.

Cornwell, David J. (2007). *Doing Justice Better: The Politics of Restorative Justice*. Winchester, UK: Waterside Press.

Cornwell, David J. (2006). *Criminal Punishment and Restorative Justice: Past, Present and Future Perspectives*. Winchester, UK: Waterside Press.

Coyle, Andrew (1994). My Brother's Keeper: Relationships in Prison. In Jonathan Burnside & Nicola Baker (Eds.), *Relational Justice: Repairing the Breach*. Winchester, UK: Waterside Press.

Cragg, Wesley (1992). *The Practice of Punishment: Towards a Theory of Restorative Justice*. New York: Routledge.

Crawford, Adam, & Newburn, Tim (2003). *Youth Offending and Restorative Justice: Implementing Reform in Youth Justice*. Cullompton, UK: Willan.

Crime and Justice Research Centre, and Sue Triggs. (2005). *New Zealand Couri-Referred Restorative Justice Pilot: Evaluation*. Wellington, NZ: Ministry of Justice.

Cunneen, Chris (2004). What Are the Implications of Restorative Justice's Use of Indigenous Traditions? In Howard Zehr & Barb Toews (Eds.), *Critical Issues in Restorative Justice*. Monsey (pp. 341–349). NY/Cullompton, UK: Criminal Justice Press/Willan.

Cunneen, Chris (2003). Thinking Critically about Restorative Justice. In Eugene McLaughlin, Ross Fergusson, Gordon Hughes & Louise Westmarland (Eds.), *Restorative Justice: Critical Issues* (pp. 182–194). London: Sage, in association with The Open University.

Cunneen, Chris (2002). Restorative Justice and the Politics of Decolonization. In Elmar G. M. Weitekamp & Hans-Jürgen Kerner (Eds.), *Restorative Justice: Theoretical Foundations* (pp. 32–49). Cullompton, UK: Willan.

Cunneen, Chris, & Hoyle, Carolyn (2010). *Debating Restorative Justice*. Portland, OR: Hart.

Dagger, Richard (1980). Restitution, Punishment, and Debts to Society. In Joe Hudson & Burt Galaway (Eds.), *Victims, Offenders and Alternative Sanctions*. Lexington, MA: Lexington Books.

Daly, Kathleen (2008). Setting the Record Straight and a Call for Radical Change: A Reply to Annie Cossins on Restorative Justice and Child Sex Offences. *British Journal of Criminology, 48*(4), 557–566.

Daly, Kathleen (2005). A Tale of Two Studies: Restorative Justice from a Victims' Perspective. In Elizabeth Elliott & Robert M. Gordon (Eds.), *New Directions in Restorative Justice: Issues, Practice, Evaluation* (pp. 153–174). Cullompton, UK: Willan.

Daly, Kathleen (2003). Mind the Gap: Restorative Justice in Theory and Practice. In Andrew von Hirsch, et al. (Eds.), *Restorative Justice and Criminal Justice: Competing or Reconcilable Paradigms?* (pp. 219–236). Oxford: Hart.

Daly, Kathleen (2001). Revisiting the Relationship between Retributive and Restorative Justice. In Heather Strang & John Braithwaite (Eds.), *Restorative Justice: Philosophy to Practice*. Burlington, VT: Ashgate.

Daly, Kathleen, & Nancarrow, Heather (2009). *Restorative Justice and Youth Violence Toward Parent*. New York: Oxford University Press.

Daly, Kathleen, & Stubbs, Julie (2006). Feminist Engagement with Restorative Justice. *Theoretical Criminology, 10*(1), 9–28.

Dandurand, Yvon, & Griffiths, Curt Taylor (2006). *Handbook on Restorative Justice Programmes. Criminal Justice Handbook Series*. Vienna: United Nations Office on Drugs and Crime.

Danieli, Yael (1999). Healing Components: The Right to Restitution for Victims of Gross Violations of Human Rights and Humanitarian Law. In M. Hayse, D. Pollefeyt, G. J. Colijn & M. S. Littell (Eds.), *Hearing the Voices: Teaching the Holocaust to Future Generations*. Merion Station, PA: Merion Westfield Press International.

Davis, Robert C., Lurigio, Arthur J., & Herman, Susan (2013). *Victims of Crime* (4th ed.). Thousand Oaks, CA: Sage.

de Bono, Edward (1991). *Conflicts: A Better Way to Resolve Them*. New York: Penguin.

Pablo, De Greiff (2006). *The Handbook of Reparations*. New York: Oxford University Press.

Dickens, Charles (1976). *The Annotated Christmas Carol, with Introduction and Notes by Michael Patrick Eran*. New York: Clarkson N. Potter.

Dignan, James (2005). *Understanding Victims and Restorative Justice*. Maidenhead, UK: Open University Press.

Dignan, Jim, (2003). Towards a Systemic Model of Restorative Justice. In Andrew von Hirsch et al. (Eds.), *Restorative Justice and Criminal Justice: Competing or Reconcilable Paradigms?* (pp. 135–156). Oxford: Hart.

Dignan, Jim (2002). Restorative Justice and the Law: The Case for an Integrated, Systemic Approach. In Lode Walgrave (Ed.), *Restorative Justice and the Law* (pp. 168–190). Cullompton, UK: Willan.

Doak, Jonathan (2005). Victims' Rights in Criminal Trials: Prospects for Participation. *Journal of Law and Society, 32*(2), 294–316.

Doolin, Katherine (2007). But What Does It Mean? Seeking Definitional Clarity in Restorative Justice. *Journal of Criminal Law, 71*(5), 427–440.

Duff, Antony (2005a). Punishment and the Morality of Law. In Erik Claes, René Foqué & Tony Peters (Eds.), *Punishment, Restorative Justice and the Morality of Law* (pp. 121–144). Oxford, UK: Intersentia.

Duff, Antony (2005b). A Response to Walgrave, Van Stokkom, and Burms. In Erik Claes, René Foqué & Tony Peters (Eds.), *Punishment, Restorative Justice and the Morality of Law* (pp. 179–182). Oxford, UK: Intersentia.

Duff, Antony, et al. (2003). Restoration and Retribution. In von Hirsch Andrew (Ed.), *Restorative Justice and Criminal Justice: Competing or Reconcilable Paradigms?* (pp. 43–60). Hart: Oxford.

Dünkel, Frieder (2001). The Victim in Criminal Law—On the Way from an Offender-Related to a Victim-Related Criminal Justice? In E. Fattah & S. Parmentier (Eds.), *Victim Policies and Criminal Justice on the Road to Restorative Justice* (pp. 167–209). Essays in Honour of Tony Peters.

Dünkel, Frieder, & Rössner, Dieter (1989). Law and Practice of Victim/Offender Agreements. In Martin Wright & Burt Galaway (Eds.), *Mediation and Criminal Justice: Victims, Offenders and Community*. London: Sage.

Dussich, John P. J., & Schellenberg, Jill (Eds.), (2010). *The Promise of Restorative Justice: New Approaches for Criminal Justice and Beyond*. London: Lynne Reiner.

Edgar, Kimmett, & Newell, Tim (2006). *Restorative Justice in Prisons. A Guide to Making It Happen*. Winchester, UK: Waterside Press.

Eglash, Albert (1977). Beyond Restitution: Creative Restitution. In Joe Hudson & Burt Galaway (Eds.), *Restitution in Criminal Justice*. Lexington, MA: D. C. Heath.

Eglash, Albert (1958a). Creative Restitution: A Broader Meaning for an Old Term. *Journal of Criminal Law, Criminology and Police Science, 48*, 619–622.

Eglash, Albert (1958b). Creative Restitution: Offenders' Comments. *Journal of Social Therapy, 4*, 32–40.

Eglash, Albert (1958c). Creative Restitution: Some Suggestions for Prison Rehabilitation Programs. *American Journal of Corrections, 20*, 20–34.

Eglash, Albert, & Papanek, E. (1959). Creative Restitution: A Correctional Technique and Theory. *Journal of Individual Psychology, 15*, 226–232.

Elechi, O. Oko (2006). *Doing Justice without the State: The Afikpo (Ehugbo) Nigeria Model*. New York: Routledge.

Eriksson, Anna (2009). *Justice in Transition: Community Restorative Justice in Ireland*. Portland, OR: Willan.

Evans, T. D., et al. (1995). Religion and Crime Reexamined: The Impact of Religion, Secular Controls, and Social Ecology on Adult Criminality. *Criminology, 33*, 195–217.

European Forum for Victim–Offender Mediation and Restorative Justice. (2000). *Victim–Offender Mediation in Europe: Making Restorative Justice Work*. Leuven, Belgium: Leuven University Press.

Faget, Jaques (2000). Mediation, Criminal Justice and Community Involvement: A European Perspective. In the European Forum for Victim–Offender Mediation and Restorative Justice (Ed.), *Victim–Offender Mediation in Europe: Making Restorative Justice Work*. Leuven, Belgium: Leuven University Press.

Fortune, Marie M. (1989). *Domestic Violence and Its Aftermath*. Elkhart, IN: Mennonite Central Committee, U.S. Office of Criminal Justice.

Freiberg, Arie, King, Michael S., Batagol, Becky, & Hyams, Ross (2009). *Non-Adversarial Justice*. Sydney: The Federation Press.

Gal, Tali (2011). *Child Victims and Restorative Justice. A Needs–Rights Model*. New York: Oxford University Press.

Galaway, Burt, & Hudson, Joe (Eds.), (1996). *Restorative Justice: International Perspectives*. Monsey, NY: Criminal Justice Press.

Galaway, Burt, & Hudson, Joe (Eds.), (1990). *Criminal Justice, Restitution and Reconciliation*. Monsey, NY: Criminal Justice Press.

Garfinkel, Harold (1956). Conditions of Successful Degradation Ceremonies. *American Journal of Sociology, 61*(5), 420–424.

Gartner, J., Larson, D. B., & Allen, G. D. (1991). Religious Commitment and Mental Health: A Review of the Empirical Literature. *Journal of Psychology and Theology, 2*, 1115–1123.

Garvey, Stephen P. (2003). Restorative Justice, Punishment, and Atonement. *Utah Law Review, 303*(1), 303–317.

Gavrielides, Theo (2008). Restorative Justice—The Perplexing Concept: Conceptual Fault-Lines and Power Battles within the Restorative Justice Movement. *Criminology and Criminal Justice, 8*(2), 165–183.

Gavrielides, Theo (2007). *Restorative Justice Theory and Practice: Addressing the Discrepancy*. Helsinki: European Institute for Crime Prevention and Control affiliated with the United Nations.

Gerkin, Patrick M. (2009). Participation in Victim–Offender Mediation: Lessons Learned from Observations. *Criminal Justice Review, 34*(2), 226–247.

Gilman, Eric (2004). Victim–Offender Meetings: A Restorative Focus for Victims *.RJ Online*, (online journal), December. Available at http://www.restorativejustice.org/editions/2004/December.

Gittler, Josephine (1984). Expanding the Role of the Victim in a Criminal Action: An Overview of Issues and Problems. *Pepperdine Law Review, 11*, 117–182.

Goodwin, Catharine M. (2000). Imposition and Enforcement of Restitution. *Federal Probation, 64*(1), 62–72.

Goolsby, Deborah Gatske (1990). Using Mediation in Cases of Simple Rape. *Washington and Lee Law Review, 47*(4), 1183–1214.

Gorringe, Timothy J. (2005). *Crime: Changing Society and the Churches*. London: SPCK.

Gottfredson, Don M., & Gottfredson, Stephen D. (1988). Stakes and Risks in the Prediction of Violent Criminal Behavior. *Violence and Victims: Special Issue on the Prediction of Violent Criminal Behavior, 3*(4), 247–262.

Green, Ross Gordon (1998). *Justice in Aboriginal Communities: Sentencing Alternatives*. Saskatoon: Saskatchewan, Canada: Purich.

Griffiths, Curt T., & Hamilton, Ron (1996). Sanctioning and Healing: Restorative Justice in Canadian Aboriginal Communities. In Burt Galaway & Joe Hudson (Eds.), *Restorative Justice: International Perspectives*. Monsey, NY: Criminal Justice Press.

Griffiths, John (1970). Ideology in Criminal Procedure or a Third Model of the Criminal Process. *Yale Law Journal, 79*, 359.

Gumz, Edward J., & Grant, Cynthia L. (2009). Restorative Justice: A Systematic Review of the Social Work Literature. *Families in Society: The Journal of Contemporary Social Services, 90*(1), 119–126.

Hadley, Michael L. (Ed.), (2001). *The Spiritual Roots of Restorative Justice*. Albany: State University of New York Press.

Haley, John O. (1989). Confession, Repentance and Absolution. In Martin Wright & Burt Galaway (Eds.), *Mediation and Criminal Justice*. Newbury Park, CA: Sage.

Handbook on Justice for Victims: On the Use and Application of the Declaration of Basic Principles of Justice for Victims of Crime and Abuse of Power (1999). New York: United Nations Office for Drug Control and Crime Prevention, Centre for International Crime Prevention.

Harding, John (1989). Reconciling Mediation with Criminal Justice. In Martin Wright & Burt Galaway (Eds.), *Mediation and Criminal Justice: Victims, Offenders and Community*. London: Sage.

Harland, Alan T., & Rosen, Cathryn J. (1990). Impediments to the Recovery of Restitution by Crime Victims. *Violence and Victims, 5*(2), 127–140.

Harrman, Margaret S. (Ed.), (2006). *Handbook of Mediation: Bridging Theory, Research, and Practice*. Oxford, UK: Blackwell.

Kay, Harris, M. (1987). Moving into the New Millennium: Toward a Feminist Vision of Justice. *Prison Journal, 67*(2), 27–38.

Hay, Douglas, & Snyder, Francis (Eds.), (1989). *Using the Criminal Law, 1750–1850: Policing, Private Prosecution, and the State. In Policing and Prosecution in Britain 1750–1850*. Oxford, UK: Clarendon.

Hayes, Hennessey (2005). Assessing Reoffending in Restorative Justice Conferences. *Australian and New Zealand Journal of Criminology, 38*(1), 77–102.

Hayes, Hennessey (2003). Youth Justice Conferencing and Re-Offending in Queensland. *Final report submitted to Queensland Department of Families*, February 2003.

Hayes, Hennessey (1998). Restorative Justice and the Notion of Success. *Ethics and Justice, 1*(1).

Hayes, Hennessey, & Daly, Kathleen (2004). Conferencing and Re-Offending in Queensland. *Australian and New Zealand Journal of Criminology, 37*(2), 167–191.

Hayes, Hennessey, Tim, Prenzler, & Richard, Wortley (1998). *Making Amends: Final Evaluation of the Queensland Community Conferencing Pilot*. Brisbane: Queensland Department of Justice, Juvenile Justice Branch.

Herman, Susan (2004). Is Restorative Justice Possible without a Parallel System for Victims? In Howard Zehr & Barb Toews (Eds.), *Critical Issues in Restorative Justice* (pp. 75–84). Monsey, NY: Criminal Justice Press.

Hoyle, Carolyn, & Young, Richard (2002). *New Visions of Crime Victims*. Oxford, UK: Hart.

Hoyle, Carolyn, Young, Richard, & Hill, Roderick (2002). *Proceed with Caution: An Evaluation of the Thames Valley Police Initiative in Restorative Cautioning*. York, UK: Joseph Rowntree Foundation.

Huculak, Bria (2005). From the Power to Punish to the Power to Heal. In Wanda D. McCaslin (Ed.), *Justice as Healing: Indigenous Ways*. St. Paul, MN: Living Justice Press.

Hudson, Joe, & Galaway, Burt (1989). Financial Restitution: Toward an Evaluable Program Model. *Canadian Journal of Criminology, 31*, 1–8.

Hudson, Joe, & Galaway, Burt (Eds.), (1977). *Restitution in Criminal Justice*. Lexington, MA: D. C. Heath.

Hudson, Joe, & Galaway, Burt (Eds.), (1975). *Considering the Victim*. Springfield, IL: Charles C Thomas.

Hudson, Joe, Morris, Allison, Maxwell, Gabrielle, & Galaway, Burt (1996). *Family Group Conferences: Perspectives on Policy and Practice*. Annandale, Australia: Federation Press.

Hugo, Victor (1992). Les Misérables, Charles E. Wilbour, trans. New York: The Modern Library.

Hydle, Ida, & Dale, Geir (2008). Challenging the Evaluation of Norwegian Restorative Justice Experiences. *British Journal of Community Justice, 6*(2), 69–76.

Idler, E. L., & Kasl, S. V. (1992). Religion, Disability, Depression, and the Timing of Death. *American Journal of Sociology, 97*, 1052–1079.

Ilivari, Juhani (2000). Mediation in Finland. In Tony Peters (Ed.), *Victim–Offender Mediation in Europe: Making Restorative Justice Work*. Leuven, Belgium: Leuven University Press.

Johnston, Barbara Rose, & Slyomovics, Susan (2009). *Waging War, Making Peace: Reparations and Human Rights*. Walnut Creek, CA: Left Coast Press.

Johnstone, Gerry (Ed.), (2012). *A Restorative Justice Reader* (2nd ed.). Portland, OR: Willan.

Johnstone, Gerry (2011). *Restorative Justice: Ideas, Values, Debates* (2nd ed.). London: Routledge.

Johnstone, Gerry (2007). Restorative Justice and the Practice of Imprisonment. *Prison Service Journal, 174*, 15–20.

Johnstone, Gerry (2004). How, and in What Terms, Should Restorative Justice Be Conceived? In Howard Zehr & Barb Toews (Eds.), *Critical Issues in Restorative Justice* (pp. 5–15). Monsey, NY/Cullompton, UK: Criminal Justice Press/Willan.

Johnstone, Gerry (1999). Restorative Justice, Shame and Forgiveness. *Liverpool Law Review, 21*(2/3), 197–216.

Johnstone, Gerry, & Van Ness, Daniel W. (Eds.), (2007). *Handbook of Restorative Justice*. Cullompton, UK: Willan.

Johnstone, Gerry, & Van Ness, Daniel W. (2006). The Meaning of Restorative Justice. In Gerry Johnstone & Daniel W. Van Ness (Eds.), *Handbook of Restorative Justice*. Cullompton, UK: Willan.

Joutsen, Matti (1987). Listening to the Victim: The Victim's Role in European Criminal Justice Systems. *Wayne Law Review, 34*(1), 95–124.

Karp, David R., Bazemore, Gordon, Sweet, Matthew, & Kirshenbaum, Andrew (2004). Reluctant Participants in Restorative Justice? Youthful Offenders and Their Parents. *Contemporary Justice Review, 7*(2), 199–216.

Kaptein, Hendrik, & Malsch, Marijke (2004). *Crime, Victims, and Justice: Essays on Principles and Practice*. Burlington, VT: Ashgate.

Kilpatrick, Dean G. (1996). The Mental Health Impact of Crime: Fundamentals in Counseling and Advocacy. In *materials for the National Victim Assistance Academy, sponsored by the U.S. Department of Justice*. Office for Victims of Crime.

Lampman, & Barnes, Lisa (Eds.), (1997). *Helping a Neighbor in Crisis: How to Encourage When You Don't Know What to Say*. Wheaton, IL: Tyndale House.

Lampman, Lisa Barnes, & Shattuck, Michelle (Eds.), (1999). *God and the Victim: Theological Reflections on Evil, Victimization, Justice, and Forgiveness*. Grand Rapids, MI: William B. Eerdmans.

Lane, Roger (1987). *Policing the City: Boston 1822–1885*. Cambridge, MA: Harvard University Press.

Leges Henrici Primi 109 (1972). L. J. Downer, ed. & trans.

Laufer, William S., & Strudler, Alan (2007). Corporate Crime and Making Amends. *American Criminal, 44*(4), 1307–1319.

Liebmann, Marian (2007). *Restorative Justice, How It Works*. London: Kingsley.

Liebmann, Marian, & Braithwaite, Stephanie (1999). *Restorative Justice in Custodial Settings: Report for the Restorative Justice Working Group in Northern Ireland*. Restorative Justice Ireland Network.

Liebrich, Julie (1996). The Role of Shame in Going Straight: A Study of Former Offenders. In Burt Galaway & Joe Hudson (Eds.), *Restorative Justice: International Perspectives*. Monsey, NY: Criminal Justice Press.

Liebrich, Julie (1993). *Straight to the Point: Angles on Giving Up Crime*. Dunedin, NZ: University of Otago Press.

Lerner, Michael J. (1980). *The Belief in a Just World: A Fundamental Delusion*. New York: Plenum.

Llewellyn, Jennifer J. (2002). Dealing with the Legacy of Native Residential School Abuse in Canada: Litigation, ADR, and Restorative Justice. *University of Toronto Law Review, 52*, 253–300.

Llewellyn, Jennifer J., & Howse, Robert (1999a). *Restorative Justice—A Conceptual Framework*. Paper for the Law Commission of Canada.

Llewellyn, Jennifer J., & Howse, Robert (1999b). Institutions for Restorative Justice: The South African Truth and Reconciliation Commission. *University of Toronto Law Journal, 49*(3), 355 ff.

London, Ross (2011). *Crime, Punishment and Restorative Justice: From the Margins to the Mainstream*. Boulder, CO: First Forum Press.

Lord, Janice Harris (1990). Victim Impact Panels: A Creative Sentencing Opportunity. *Mothers Against Drunk Driving*.

Lurigio, Arthur J., & Resick, Patricia A. (1990). Healing the Psychological Wounds of Criminal Victimization: Predicting Postcrime Distress and Recovery. In Arthur J. Lurigio, Wesley G. Skogan & Robert C. Davis (Eds.), *Victims of Crime: Problems, Policies, and Programs*. Newbury Park, CA: Sage.

Machiavelli, Niccolò (1984). The Prince. In Peter Boudanella & Mark Musa (Eds.), *trans*. New York: Oxford University Press.

Mackay, Robert, Bosnjak, Marko, Deklerck, John, Pelikan, Christa, Stokkom, Bas van, & Wright, Martin (Eds.), (2007). *Images of Restorative Justice Theory*. Frankfurt: Verlag fur Polizeiwissenschaft.

Mackey, Virginia (1992). *Restorative Justice: Toward Nonviolence*. Louisville, KY: Presbyterian Justice Program.

Mackey, Virginia (1981). *Punishment: In the Scripture and Tradition of Judaism, Christianity and Islam*. Claremont, CA: Paper presented to the National Religious Leaders Consultation of Criminal Justice, September 1981.

Maruna, Shadd, & Immarigeon, Russ (Eds.), (2004). *After Crime and Punishment: Pathways to Offender Reintegration*. Portland OR: Willan.

Marshall, Chris (2005). *The Little Book of Biblical Justice*. Intercourse, PA: Good Books.

Marshall, Christopher D. (2012). *Compassionate Justice: An Interdisciplinary Dialogue with Two Gospel Parables on Law, Crime, and Restorative Justice*. Eugene, OR: Cascade Books.

Marshall, Christopher D. (2003). Christian Care for the Victim. *Stimulus, 11*(3), 11–15.

Marshall, Christopher D. (2002). Grounding Justice in Reality: Theological Reflections on Overcoming Violence in the Criminal Justice System. In J. Roberts (Ed.), *Overcoming Violence in New Zealand* (pp. 81–95). Wellington, NZ: Philip Garside.

Marshall, Christopher D. (2001). *Beyond Retribution: A New Testament Vision for Justice, Crime, and Punishment*. Grand Rapids, MI: Wm. B. Eerdman.

Massaro, Toni (1991). Shame, Culture, and American Criminal Law. *Michigan Law Review, 89*, 1880–1944.

Masters, Guy (2004). What Happens When Restorative Justice Is Encouraged, Enabled and/or Guided by Legislation? In Howard Zehr & Barb Toews (Eds.), *Critical Issues in Restorative Justice* (pp. 227–238). Monsey, NY/Cullompton, UK: Criminal Justice Press/Willan.

Masters, Guy (1998). The Importance of Shame to Restorative Justice. In Lode Walgrave (Ed.), *Restorative Justice for Juveniles: Potentialities, Risks and Problems for Research* (pp. 123–136). Leuven, Belgium: Leuven University Press.

Masters, Guy, & Smith, David (1998). Portia and Persephone Revisited: Thinking about Feeling in Criminal Justice. *Theoretical Criminology, 2*(1), 5–27.

Masters, Guy, & Roberts, Ann Warner (2000). Family Group Conferencing for Victims, Offenders and Communities. In Marian Liebmann (Ed.), *Mediation in Context. With an introduction by Marian Liebmann* (pp. 140–154). London: Jessica Kingsley.

Matthews, Roger (1988). Reassessing Informal Justice. In Roger Matthews (Ed.), *Informal Justice?.* Newbury Park, CA: Sage.

Maxwell, Gabrielle (2005). Achieving Effective Outcomes in Youth Justice: Implications of New Research for Principles, Policy and Practice. In Elizabeth Elliott & Robert M. Gordon (Eds.), *New Directions in Restorative Justice: Issues, Practice, Evaluation* (pp. 53–74). Cullompton, UK: Willan.

Maxwell, Gabrielle, & Liu, James H. (Eds.), (2007). *Restorative Justice and Practices in New Zealand: Towards a Restorative Society* (pp. 5–28). Wellington, NZ: Institute of Policy Studies.

Maxwell, Gabrielle, & Morris, Allison (2004). What Is the Place of Shame in Restorative Justice? In Howard Zehr & Barb Toews (Eds.), *Critical Issues in Restorative Justice.* Monsey (pp. 133–141). NY/Cullompton, UK: Criminal Justice Press/Willan.

Maxwell, Gabrielle, & Morris, Allison (2002). Restorative Justice and Reconviction. *Contemporary Justice Review, 5*(2), 133–146.

Maxwell, Gabrielle, Morris, Allison, Robertson, Jeremy, Anderson, Tracy, & Kingi, Venezia (2003). Differences in How Girls and Boys Respond to Family Group Conferences: Preliminary Research Results. In Lode Walgrave (Ed.), *Repositioning Restorative Justice* (pp. 136–148). Cullompton, UK: Willan.

McCold, Paul (2008). Protocols for Evaluating Restorative Justice Programmes. *British Journal of Community Justice, 6*(2), 9–28.

McCold, Paul (2004a). Dangers and Opportunities of Setting Standards for RJ Practices. Paper presented at the Third Conference of the European Forum for Victim–Offender Mediation and Restorative Justice, Restorative Justice in Europe: Where Are We Heading? *Budapest, Hungary*, October 14–16, 2004.

McCold, Paul (2004b). Paradigm Muddle: The Threat to Restorative Justice Posed by Its Merger with Community Justice. *Contemporary Justice Review, 7*(1), 13–35.

McCold, Paul (2004c). What Is the Role of Community in Restorative Justice Theory and Practice? In Howard Zehr & Barb Toews (Eds.), *Critical Issues in Restorative Justice.* Monsey (pp. 155–171). NY/Cullompton, UK: Criminal Justice Press/Willan.

McCold, Paul (2003a). A Survey Assessment Research on Mediation and Conferencing. In Lode Walgrave (Ed.), *Repositioning Restorative Justice* (pp. 67–120). Cullompton, UK: Willan.

McCold, Paul (2003b). An Experiment in Police-Based Restorative Justice: The Bethlehem (PA) Project. *Police Practice and Research: An International Journal, 4*(4), 379–390.

McCold, Paul (1999a). *Toward a Holistic Vision of Restorative Juvenile Justice: A Reply to Walgrave. Paper presented to the Third International Conference on Restorative Justice for Juveniles.* Leuven, Belgium: International Network for Research on Restorative Justice for Juveniles, October 24–27, 1999.

McCold, Paul (1999b). *Restorative Justice Practice—The State of the Field 1999. Paper presented at the Building Strong Partnerships for Restorative Practices Conference, August 5–7, 1999.* Burlington: Vermont. Available at http://www.realjustice.org/Pages/vt99papers/vt_mccold.html as of August 21, 2000.

McCold, Paul (1997). *Restorative Justice: An Annotated Bibliography 1997.* Monsey, NY: Criminal Justice Press.

McCold, Paul, & Wachtel, Benjamin (2002a). Community Is Not a Place: A New Look at Community Justice Initiatives. In John G. Perry (Ed.), *Repairing Communities through Restorative Justice* (pp. 39–53). Lanham, MD: American Correctional Association.

McCold, Paul, & Wachtel, Ted (2002b). Restorative Justice Theory Validation. In G. M. Elmar (Ed.), *Weitekamp and Hans-Jürgen Kerner, Restorative Justice: Theoretical Foundations* (pp. 110–142). Cullompton, UK: Willan.

McDonald, William F. (Ed.), (1976). *Criminal Justice and the Victim*. Beverly Hills, CA: Sage.

McElrea, Fred (1994). Justice in the Community: The New Zealand Experience. In Jonathan Burnside & Nicola Baker (Eds.), *Relational Justice: Repairing the Breach*. Winchester, UK: Waterside Press.

McEvoy, Kieran (2003). Beyond the Metaphor: Political Violence, Human Rights and New Peacemaking Criminology. *Theoretical Criminology, 7*(3), 319–346.

McEvoy, Kieran, & Mika, Harry (2013). *Restorative Justice: Theory, Practice and Critique*. Thousand Oaks, CA: Sage.

McEvoy, Kieran, & Mika, Harry (2002). Restorative Justice and the Critique of Informalism in Northern Ireland. *British Journal of Criminology, 42*, 534–562.

McEvoy, Kieran, & Newburn, Tim (2003). *Criminology, Conflict Resolution and Restorative Justice*. New York: Palgrave MacMillan.

McHugh, Gerald A. (1978). *Christian Faith and Criminal Justice: Toward a Christian Response to Crime and Punishment*. New York: Paulist Press.

McKelvey, Blake (1977). *American Prisons: A History of Good Intentions*. Montclair, NJ: Patterson Smith.

McLaughlin, Eugene, Fergusson, Ross, Hughes, Gordon, & Westmarland, Louise (Eds.), (2013). *Restorative Justice: Critical Issues*. Thousand Oaks, CA: Sage.

McWhinnie, Andrew (2003). *Circles of Support and Accountability: Guide to Project Development: Project Guide 2003*. Ottawa, Ontario, Canada: Correctional Service Canada.

Menkel-Meadow, Carrie J. (2007). Restorative Justice: What Is It and Does It Work? *Annual Review of Law and Social Science, 3* 10.1–10.27.

Messmer, Heinz, & Otto, Hans-Uwe (Eds.), (1992). *Restorative Justice on Trial: Pitfalls and Potentials of Victim–Offender Mediation: International Research Perspectives*. Dordrecht, The Netherlands: Kluwer.

Miers, David (2004). Situating and Researching Restorative Justice in Great Britain. *Punishment and Society, 6*(1), 23–46.

Miers, David (2001). *International Review of Restorative Justice*. London: Home Office Research, Development and Statistics Directorate.

Miers, David, & Willemsens, Jolien (2004). *Mapping Restorative Justice: Developments in 25 European Countries*. Leuven, Belgium: European Forum for Victim–Offender Mediation and Restorative Justice.

Mika, Harry, Achilles, Mary, Halbert, Ellen, Zehr, Howard, & Amstutz, Lorraine Stutzman (2005). *Taking Victims and Their Advocates Seriously: A Listening Project*. Harrisonburg, VA: Institute for Justice and Peacebuilding at Eastern Mennonite University.

Mika, Harry, Achilles, Mary, Halbert, Ellen, Zehr, Howard, & Amstutz, Lorraine Stutzman (2004). Listening to Victims—A Critique of Restorative Justice Policy and Practice in the United States. *Federal Probation, 68*(1), 32–38.

Mika, Harry, & McEvoy, Kieran (2001). Restorative Justice in Conflict: Paramilitarism, Community, and the Construction of Legitimacy in Northern Ireland. *Contemporary Justice Review, 4*(3–4), 291–319.

Mika, Harry, & Zehr, Howard (2003). A Restorative Framework for Community Justice Practice. In Kieran McEvoy & Tim Newburn (Eds.), *Criminology, Conflict Resolution and Restorative Justice* (pp. 135–152). New York: Palgrave MacMillan.

Miller, Holly Ventura (Ed.), (2008). *Restorative Justice: From Theory to Practice*. Bingley, UK: Emerald Group.

Miller, Susan L. (2011). *After the Crime: The Power of Restorative Justice Dialogues between Victims and Violent Offenders*. New York: New York University Press.

Mills, Linda G., Shy, Yael, & Maley, Mary Helen (2009). Circulos de Paz and the Promise of Peace: Restorative Justice Meets Intimate Violence. *New York University Review of Law & Social Change, 33*(1), 127 ff.

Moore, David (1994). Evaluating Family Group Conferences. In David Biles & Sandra McKillop (Eds.), *Criminal Justice Planning and Coordination: Proceedings of a Conference Held 19–21—April 1993*. Canberra: Australian Institute of Criminology.

Moore, David (1993). Shame, Forgiveness, and Juvenile Justice. *Criminal Justice Ethics (Winter/Spring)*, 3.

Moriarty, Laura J. (Ed.), (2008). *Controversies in Victimology* (2nd ed). Newark, NJ: LexisNexis Matthew Bender.

Morris, Allison, Maxwell, Gabrielle, et al. (2003). Restorative Justice in New Zealand. In Andrew von Hirsch (Ed.), *Restorative Justice and Criminal Justice: Competing or Reconcilable Paradigms?* (pp. 257–272). Oxford: Hart.

Morris, Norval, & Rothman, David (Eds.), (1995). *The Oxford History of the Prison: The Practice of Punishment in Western Society*. New York: Oxford University Press.

Morris, Ruth (2000). *Stories of Transformative Justice*. Toronto: Canadian Scholars Press.

Morris, Ruth (1994). *A Practical Path to Transformative Justice*. Toronto: Rittenhouse.

Morrison, Brenda (2005). Restorative Justice in Schools. In Elizabeth Elliott & Robert M. Gordon (Eds.), *New Directions in Restorative Justice: Issues, Practice, Evaluation* (pp. 26–52). Cullompton, UK: Willan.

Morrison, Brenda (2003). Regulating Safe School Communities: Being Responsive and Restorative. *Journal of Educational Administration, 41*(6), 689–704.

Morrison, Brenda (2002). *Bullying and Victimisation in Schools: A Restorative Justice Approach. Trends and Issues in Crime and Criminal Justice*, No. 219, February 2002: Australian Institute of Criminology.

Morrison, Brenda (2001). The School System: Developing Its Capacity in the Regulation of a Civil Society. In Heather Strang & John Braithwaite (Eds.), *Restorative Justice and Civil Society* (pp. 195–210). Cambridge, UK: Cambridge University Press.

Morrison, Brenda, & Ahmed, Eliza (2006). Restorative Justice and Civil Society: Emerging Practice, Theory and Evidence. *Journal of Social Issues, 62*(2), 209–215 (special issue).

Mukherjee, Stayanshu, & Reichel, Philip (1999). Bringing to Justice. In Graeme Newman (Ed.), *Global Report on Crime and Justice*. New York: Oxford University Press.

Murphy, Jeffrie G. (1988). Retributive Hatred: An Essay on Criminal Liability and the Emotions. Paper presented at a conference on Liability in Law and Morals, Bowling Green State University, Bowling Green, OH, April 15–17.

National Victim Assistance Academy. (2002). *Foundations in Victimology and Victims' Rights and Services*. Washington, DC: U.S. Department of Justice, Office for Victims of Crime. Entire textbook available online at https://www.ncjrs.gov/ovc_archives/nvaa2002/welcome.html.

Neiderbach, Shelley (1989). *Invisible Wounds: Crime Victims Speak*. New York: Harrington Park Press.

Nicholl, Caroline G. (2000). *Toolbox for Implementing Restorative Justice and Advancing Community Policing*. Washington, DC: U.S. Department of Justice, Office of Community Oriented Policing Services.

Nicholl, Caroline G. (1999). *Community Policing, Community Justice, and Restorative Justice: Exploring the Links for the Delivery of a Balanced Approach to Public Safety*. Washington, DC: U.S. Department of Justice, Office of Community Oriented Policing Services.

Nielsen, Marianne O. (1996). A Comparison of Developmental Ideologies: Navajo Peacemaker Courts and Canadian Native Justice Committees. In Burt Galaway & Joe Hudson (Eds.), *Restorative Justice: International Perspectives*. Monsey, NY: Criminal Justice Press.

Nolan, Pat (2004). *When Prisoners Return: Why We Should Care and How You and Your Church Can Help*. Washington, DC: Prison Fellowship.

Noll, Douglas E., & Harvey, Linda (2008). Restorative Mediation: The Application of Restorative Justice Practice and Philosophy to Clergy Sexual Abuse Cases. *Journal of Child Sexual Abuse, 17*(3–4), 377–396.

O'Connell, Terry, & McCold, Paul (2004). *Beyond the Journey, Not Much Else Matters: Avoiding the Expert Model with Explicit Restorative Practice. Paper presented at New Frontiers in Restorative Justice: Advancing Theory and Practice, Centre for Justice and Peace Development.* New Zealand: Massey University at Albany, December 2–5.

O'Connell, Terry, Wachtel, Ben, & Wachtel, Ted (1999). *Conferencing Handbook: The New Real Justice Training Manual.* Pipersville, PA: The Piper's Press.

Packer, Herbert L. (1968). *The Limits of the Criminal Sanction.* Stanford, CA: Stanford University Press.

Pavlich, George (2005). *Governing Paradoxes of Restorative Justice.* London: GlassHouse Press.

Pavlich, George (2004). What Are the Dangers as Well as the Promises of Community Involvement? In Howard Zehr & Barb Toews (Eds.), *Critical Issues in Restorative Justice.* Monsey (pp. 173–184). NY/Cullompton, UK: Criminal Justice Press/Willan.

Pavlich, George (2002a). Towards an Ethics of Restorative Justice. In Lode Walgrave (Ed.), *Restorative Justice and the Law* (pp. 1–18). Cullompton, UK: Willan.

Pavlich, George (2002b). Deconstructing Restoration: The Promise of Restorative Justice. In Elmar G. M. Weitekamp & Hans-Jürgen Kerner (Eds.), *Restorative Justice: Theoretical Foundations* (pp. 90–109). Cullompton, UK: Willan.

Pavlich, George (2001). The Force of Community. In Heather Strang & John Braithwaite (Eds.), *Restorative Justice and Civil Society.* Cambridge, UK: Cambridge University Press.

Pelikan, Christa (2000). *Victim–Offender Mediation in Domestic Violence Cases: A Research Report.* Austria: Paper presented at the United Nations Crime Congress Ancillary Meetings, Vienna August 2000.

Pelikan, Christa (1991). Conflict Resolution between Victims and Offenders in Austria and the Federal Republic of Germany. In Frances Heidensohn & Martin Farrell (Eds.), *Crime in Europe.* New York: Routledge.

Pepinsky, Hal (2000a). Making Peace with Shame. *Red Feather Journal of Postmodern Criminology, 8.*

Pepinsky, Hal (2000b). Distilling Love and Inclusion. *Contemporary Justice Review, 3*(4), 479.

Pepinsky, Hal (1999). Empathy Works, Obedience Doesn't. *Criminal Justice Policy Review, 9*(2), 141–167.

Pepinsky, Harold E., & Quinney, Richard (Eds.), (1991). *Criminology as Peacemaking.* Bloomington: Indiana University Press.

Peter C. Hart Research Associates, Inc. (2002). *Changing Public Attitudes Toward the Criminal Justice System.* New York: Open Society Institute.

Peters, Tony, Aertsen, Ivo, Robert, Luc, & Lauwaert, Katrien (2003). *From Community Sanctions to Restorative Justice: The Belgian Example.* Tokyo: United Nations Asia and Far East Institute for the Prevention of Crime and Treatment of Offenders, 180–211.

Pollock, Frederick (1898). English Law before the Norman Conquest. *Law Quarterly Review, 14,* 291 ff.

Pranis, Kay (2009). *Restorative Justice: Implications for Women Offenders.* St. Paul: Minnesota Department of Corrections.

Pranis, Kay (2000). *Building Community Support for Restorative Justice.* Available at http://www.restorativejustice.org/10fulltext/pranis-kay.-building-support-for-community-justice-principles-and-strategies.

Pranis, Kay, Bazemore, Gordon, Umbreit, Mark, & Lipkin, Rachel (1998). *Guide for Implementing the Balanced and Restorative Justice Model.* Washington, DC: Office of Juvenile Justice and Delinquency Prevention.

Pranis, Kay, Stuart, Barry, & Wedge, Mark (2003). *Peacemaking Circles: From Crime to Community.* St. Paul, MN: Living Justice Press.

Presser, Lois, Gaarder, Emily, & Hesselton, Denise (2007). Imagining Restorative Justice Beyond Recidivism. *Journal of Offender Rehabilitation, 46*(1–2), 163–176.

Quinney, R. (1996). Life of Crime: Criminology and Public Policy as Peacemaking. In Barry W. Hancock & Paul M. Sharp (Eds.), *Criminal Justice in America: Theory, Practice, and Policy* (pp. 410–415). Upper Saddle River, NJ: Prentice Hall.

Radzik, Linda (2009). *Making Amends: Atonement in Morality, Law, and Politics.* New York: Oxford University Press.

Radzik, Linda (2003). Do Wrongdoers Have a Right to Make Amends? *Social Theory and Practice, 29*(2), 325–341.

Raye, Barbara (2004). How Do Culture, Class and Gender Affect the Practice of Restorative Justice? (Part 2). In Howard Zehr & Barb Toews (Eds.), *Critical Issues in Restorative Justice* (pp. 325–336). Monsey, NY/Cullompton, UK: Criminal Justice Press/Willan.

Raye, Barbara, Wiese, Sue, & Roberts, Annie Warner (2003). VOMA Assists Romanian Efforts to Establish Mediation Services. *VOMA Connections Fall* (15), 4.

Redekop, Paul (2007). *Changing Paradigms.* Scottdale, PA: Herald Press.

Restorative Justice Consortium. (2002). *Statement of Restorative Justice Principles.* London: Restorative Justice Consortium.

Richards, Kelly (2004). *Exploring the History of the Restorative Justice Movement.* Vancouver, Canada: Paper presented at the Fifth International Conference on Conferencing and Circles, organized by the International Institute for Restorative Practices, August 5–7.

Roberts, Albert R. (1990). *Helping Crime Victims: Research, Policy, and Practice.* Newbury Park, CA: Sage.

Roberts, Paul, et al. (2003). Restoration and Retribution in International Criminal Justice: An Exploratory Analysis. In Andrew von Hirsch (Ed.), *Restorative Justice and Criminal Justice: Competing or Reconcilable Paradigms?* (pp. 115–134). Hart: Oxford.

Roche, Declan (2003). *Accountability in Restorative Justice.* Oxford, UK: Oxford University Press.

Rodriguez, Nancy (2007). Restorative Justice at Work: Examining the Impact of Restorative Justice Resolutions on Juvenile Recidivism. *Crime & Delinquency, 53*(3), 355–379.

Roht-Arriaza, Naomi, & Mariezcurrena, Javier (Eds.), (2006). *Transitional Justice in the Twenty-First Century, Beyond Truth Versus Justice.* New York: Cambridge University Press.

Ross, Ian, Jeffrey, & Gould, Larry (2006). *Native Americans and the Criminal Justice System.* Boulder, CO: Paradigm.

Rossi, & Alexandra, Rachel (2008). Meet Me on Death-Row: Post-Sentence Victim–Offender Mediation in Capital Cases. *Pepperdine Dispute Resolution Law Journal, 9*(10), 185–210.

Rossner, D. (1996). Situation, Ethical Grounds and Criminal Political Perspective of Victim–Offender Reconciliation in Community. In B. Galaway & J. Hudson (Eds.), *Restorative Justice: International Perspectives* (pp. 403–416). Monsey, NY: Criminal Justice Press.

Rowland, Judith A. (1987). Representation of Victims' Interests within the Criminal Justice System. In *The Attorney's Victim Assistance Manual: A Guide to the Legal Issues Confronting Victims of Crime and Victim Service Providers,* prepared for the Sunny von Bulow National Victim Advocacy Center in cooperation with the Attorney's Victim Assistance Project of the American Bar Association, Criminal Justice Section.

Rucker, Lila (1991). Peacemaking in Prisons. In E. Harold, Pepinsky & Quinney Richard (Eds.), *Criminology as Peacemaking.* Bloomington: Indiana University Press.

Ruth-Heffelbower, Duane (2002). Local Capacities for Peace Meets Conflict Resolution Practice. *Journal of Peacebuilding and Development, 1*(1), 85–97.

Ruth-Heffelbower, Duane (2001). *Restorative Justice or Impunity: The Choice for East Timor (paper).* Fresno, CA: Center for Peacemaking and Conflict Studies, Fresno Pacific University.

Ruth-Heffelbower, Duane (1989). What Does It Mean to Be Church-Based? In Ron Claassen & Howard Zehr (Eds.), *VORP Organizing: A Foundation in the Church.* Elkhart, IN: Mennonite Central Committee, U.S. Office of Criminal Justice.

Schafer, Stephen (1977). *Victimology: The Victim and His Criminal.* Reston, VA: Reston.

Schafer, Stephen (1975). The Restitutive Concept of Punishment. In Joe Hudson & Burt Galaway (Eds.), *Considering the Victim.* Springfield, IL: Charles C Thomas.

Schafer, Stephen (1970a). Victim Compensation and Responsibility. *Southern California Law Review, 43,* 55.

Schafer, Stephen (1970b). *Compensation and Restitution to Victims of Crime.* Montclair, NJ: Patterson Smith.

Schiff, Mara F., et al. (2003). Models, Challenges and the Promise of Restorative Conferencing Strategies. In Andrew von Hirsch (Ed.), *Restorative Justice and Criminal Justice: Competing or Reconcilable Paradigms?* (pp. 315–338). Oxford: Hart.

Schiff, Mara F. (1999). The Impact of Restorative Interventions on Juvenile Offenders. In Gordon Bazemore & Lode Walgrave (Eds.), *Restorative Juvenile Justice: Repairing the Harm of Youth Crime* (pp. 327–356). Monsey, NY: Criminal Justice Press.

Schiff, Mara F. (1998). Restorative Justice Interventions for Juvenile Offenders: A Research Agenda for the Next Decade. *Western Criminology Review, 1*(1), 1–22.

Schiff, Mara F., & Bazemore, Gordon (2002a). Restorative Conferencing for Juveniles in the United States: Prevalence, Process, and Practice. In G. M. Elmar (Ed.), *Weitekamp and Hans-Jürgen Kerner, Restorative Justice: Theoretical Foundations* (pp. 177–203). Cullompton, UK: Willan.

Schiff, Mara F., and Gordon Bazemore (2002b). *Understanding Restorative Conferencing: A Case Study in Informal Decisionmaking in the Response to Youth Crime.* National Institute of Justice Grant 1999-IJ-CK-0060. Ft. Lauderdale: Balanced and Restorative Justice Project, Florida Atlantic University.

Schluter, Michael, & Lee, David (1993). *The R Factor.* London: Hodder & Stoughton.

Schneider, Carl D. (2000). What It Means to Be Sorry: The Power of Apology in Mediation. *Mediation Quarterly, 17*(3).

Schrey, H., Walz, H., & Whitehouse, W. (1955). *The Biblical Doctrine of Justice and Law.* London: SCM Press.

Schweigert, Francis J. (2002). Moral and Philosophical Foundations of Restorative Justice. In John G. Perry (Ed.), *Repairing Communities through Restorative Justice* (pp. 19–37). Lanham, MD: American Correctional Association.

Schweigert, Francis J. (1999). Learning the Common Good: Principles of Community-Based Moral Education in Restorative Justice. *Journal of Moral Education, 28*(2), 163–184.

Seymour, Anne (2004). Victims of Juvenile Offenders: An Important Component of the Juvenile Justice Equation. *Corrections Today, 6*(1), 32–35.

Seymour, Anne (2001). *A Community Response Manual: The Victim's Role in Offender Reentry.* Lexington, KY: American Probation and Parole Association.

Shapland, Joanna (2008). *Justice, Community and Civil Society: A Contested Terrain.* Devon, UK: Willan.

Shapland, Joanna (2007). *Restorative Justice: The Views of Victims and Offenders.* London: Ministry of Justice.

Shapland, Joanna, Robinson, Gwen, & Sorsby, Angela (2011). *Restorative Justice in Practice: Evaluating What Works for Victims and Offenders.* Oxford, UK: Taylor & Francis.

Sharpe, Susan (2004). How Large Should the Restorative Justice Tent Be? In Howard Zehr & Barb Toews (Eds.), *Critical Issues in Restorative Justice.* Monsey (pp. 17–31). NY/Cullompton, UK: Criminal Justice Press/Willan.

Sharpe, Susan (2003). *Beyond the Comfort Zone: A Guide to the Practice of Community Conferencing.* Calgary: Alberta, Canada: Calgary Community Conferencing.

Sharpe, Susan (1998). *Restorative Justice: A Vision for Healing and Change.* Edmonton, Alberta, Canada: Edmonton Victim Offender Mediation Society.

Shearing, Clifford (2001). Transforming Security: A South African Experiment. In Heather Strang & John Braithwaite (Eds.), *Restorative Justice and Civil Society* (pp. 14–34). Cambridge, UK: Cambridge University Press.

Sherman, Lawrence W. (2003). Reason for Emotion: Reinventing Justice with Theories, Innovations, and Research: The American Society of Criminology 2002 Presidential Address. *Criminology, 41*(1), 7–37.

Sherman, Lawrence W. (2001). Two Protestant Ethics and the Spirit of Restoration. In Heather Strang & John Braithwaite (Eds.), *Restorative Justice and Civil Society* (pp. 35–55). Cambridge, UK: Cambridge University Press.

Sherman, Lawrence W., Barnes, Geoffrey, Strang, Heather, Woods, Daniel, Inkpen, Nova, Bennett, Sarah, et al. (2005). Effects of Face-to-Face Restorative Justice on Victims of Crime in Four Randomized, Controlled Trials. *Journal of Experimental Criminology, 1,* 367–395.

Sherman, Lawrence W., & Strang, Heather (2007). *Restorative Justice: The Evidence.* London: Smith Institute.

Sherman, Lawrence W., Strang, Heather, & Woods, Daniel (2003). Captains of Restorative Justice: Experience, Legitimacy and Recidivism by Type of Offence. In Elmar G. M. Weitekamp & Hans-Jürgen Kerner (Eds.), *Restorative Justice in Context: International Practice and Directions* (pp. 229–256). Portland, OR: Willan.

Shoham, Shlomo Giora, Beck, Ori, & Kett, Martin (Eds.), (2008). *International Handbook of Penology and Criminal Justice.* Boca Raton, FL: CRC Press.

Skelton, Ann (2005). The Child Justice Bill from a Restorative Justice Perspective. In Traggy Maepa (Ed.), *Beyond Retribution: Prospects for Restorative Justice in South Africa.* Monograph No. 111, February. Pretoria, South Africa: Institute for Security Studies, with the Restorative Justice Centre.

Skelton, Ann (2002). Restorative Justice as a Framework for Juvenile Justice Reform: A South African Perspective. *British Journal of Criminology, 42,* 496–513.

Skelton, Ann, & Frank, Cheryl (2007). *Practice Standards for Restorative Justice: A Practitioner's Toolkit.* Pretoria, South Africa: The Restorative Justice Initiative.

Skelton, Ann, & Frank, Cheryl (2004). How Does Restorative Justice Address Human Rights and Due Process Issues? In Howard Zehr & Barb Toews (Eds.), *Critical Issues in Restorative Justice* (pp. 203–213). Monsey, NY/Cullompton, UK: Criminal Justice Press/Willan.

Skelton, Ann, & Frank, Cheryl (2001). Conferencing in South Africa: Returning to Our Future. In Allison Morris & Gabrielle Maxwell (Eds.), *Restorative Justice for Juveniles: Conferencing, Mediation and Circles. With a foreword by D. J. Carruthers* (pp. 103–119). Oxford: Hart.

Skelton, Ann Marie (2005). *The Influence of the Theory and Practice of Restorative Justice in South Africa with Special Reference to Child Justice.* Dissertation submitted in partial fulfillment of the degree Doctor Legum in the Faculty of Law. University of Pretoria.

Steinberg, Allen (1989). *The Transformation of Criminal Justice: Philadelphia, 1800–1880.* Chapel Hill: University of North Carolina Press.

Stephen, James F. (1883). *A History of the Criminal Law of England.* London: Macmillan.

Stern, Vivien (1998). *A Sin against the Future: Imprisonment in the World.* London: Penguin.

Strang, Heather (2004). Is Restorative Justice Imposing Its Agenda on Victims? In Howard Zehr & Barb Toews (Eds.), *Critical Issues in Restorative Justice* (pp. 95–105). Monsey, NY; Cullompton, UK: Criminal Justice Press and Willan.

Strang, Heather (2002). *Repair or Revenge: Victims and Restorative Justice.* Clarendon Studies in Criminology. Oxford: Oxford University Press.

Strang, Heather, & Braithwaite, John (Eds.), (2001). *Restorative Justice: Philosophy to Practice*. Burlington, VT: Ashgate.

Strang, Heather, & Sherman, Lawrence W. (2003). Repairing the Harm: Victims and Restorative Justice. *Utah Law Review, 2003*(1), 15–42.

Stuart, Barry (1997). *Building Community Justice Partnerships: Community Peacemaking Circles*. Ottawa, Ontario, Canada: Aboriginal Justice Directorate, Department of Justice of Canada.

Stuart, Barry (1996). Circle Sentencing: Turning Swords into Ploughshares. In Burt Galaway & Joe Hudson (Eds.), *Restorative Justice: International Perspectives*. Monsey, NY: Criminal Justice Press.

Stubbs, Julie (2007). Beyond Apology? Domestic Violence and Critical Questions for Restorative Justice. *Criminology and Criminal Justice, 7*(2), 169–187.

Sullivan, Dennis (2002). Navajo Peacemaking History, Development, and Possibilities for Adjudication-Based Systems of Justice: An Interview with James Zion. *Contemporary Justice Review, 5*(2), 167–188.

Sullivan, Dennis, & Tifft, Larry (Eds.), (2006). *Handbook of Restorative Justice: A Global Perspective*. London: Routledge.

Sullivan, Dennis, & Tifft, Larry (2004). What Are the Implications of Restorative Justice for Society and Our Lives? In Howard Zehr & Barb Toews (Eds.), *Critical Issues in Restorative Justice* (pp. 387–400). Monsey, NY/Cullompton, UK: Criminal Justice Press/Willan.

Sullivan, Dennis, & Tifft, Larry (2001). *Restorative Justice: Healing the Foundations of Our Everyday Lives*. Foreword by Harry Mika. Monsey, NY: Willow Tree Press.

Sullivan, Dennis, & Tifft, Larry (2000). *Restorative Justice as a Transformative Process: The Application of Restorative Justice Principles to Our Everyday Lives*. Voorheesville, NY: Mutual Aid Press.

Swanson, Cheryl (2009). *Restorative Justice in a Prison Community: Or Everything I Didn't Learn in Kindergarten I Learned in Prison*. Lanham, MD: Lexington Books.

Sylvester, Douglas J. (2003). Myth in Restorative Justice History. *Utah Law Review* (1), 471–522.

Taylor, Anthony J. W. (2006). *Justice as a Basic Human Need*. New York: Nova Science.

Tifft, Larry (2002). Crime and Peace: A Walk with Richard Quinney. *Crime & Delinquency, 48*(2), 243–262.

Toews, Barb (2006). *The Little Book of Restorative Justice for People in Prison: Rebuilding the Web of Relationships*. Intercourse, PA: Good Books.

Trenczek, Thomas (1990). A Review and Assessment of Victim–Offender Reconciliation Programming in West Germany. In Burt Galaway & Joe Hudson (Eds.), *Criminal Justice, Restitution, and Reconciliation*. Monsey, NY: Criminal Justice Press.

Tutu, Desmond (1999). *No Future without Forgiveness*. New York: Doubleday.

Umbreit, Mark S. (2001). *The Handbook of Victim Offender Mediation: An Essential Guide to Practice and Research*. San Francisco: Jossey-Bass.

Umbreit, Mark S. (1999). Avoiding the Marginalization and McDonaldization of Victim–Offender Mediation: A Case Study in Moving Toward the Mainstream. In Gordon Bazemore & Lode Walgrave (Eds.), *Restorative Juvenile Justice: Repairing the Harm of Youth Crime* (pp. 213–234). Monsey, NY: Criminal Justice Press.

Umbreit, Mark S. (1990). The Meaning of Fairness to Burglary Victims. In Burt Galaway & Joe Hudson (Eds.), *Criminal Justice, Restitution, and Reconciliation*. Monsey, NY: Criminal Justice Press.

Umbreit, Mark S. (1988). Mediation of Victim–Offender Conflict. *Missouri Journal of Dispute Resolution (Fall)*, 85, 87.

Umbreit, Mark S., Coates, Robert B., & Kalanj, Boris (1994). *Victim Meets Offender: The Impact of Restorative Justice and Mediation*. Monsey, NY: Criminal Justice Press.

Umbreit, Mark S., & Armour, Marilyn Peterson (2011). *Restorative Justice Dialogue: An Essential Guide for Research and Practice*. New York: Springer.

Umbreit, Mark S., Vos, Betty, Coates, Robert B., & Brown, Katherine A. (2003). *Facing Violence: The Path of Restorative Justice and Dialogue*. Monsey, NY: Criminal Justice Press.

Umbreit, Mark S., Vos, Betty, Coates, Robert B., & Brown, Kathy (2004a). Victim–Offender Dialogue in Violent Cases: The Texas and Ohio Experience, Part One. *Crime Victims Report, 7*(6), 81–82, 90–94.

Umbreit, Mark S., Vos, Betty, Coates, Robert B., & Brown, Kathy (2004b). Victim–Offender Dialogue in Violent Cases: The Texas and Ohio Experience, Part Two. *Crime Victims Report, 8*(1), 1–2, 14.

Umbreit, Mark S., Vos, Betty, Coates, Robert B., & Lightfoot, Elizabeth (2005). Restorative Justice in the Twenty-First Century: A Social Movement Full of Opportunities and Pitfalls. *Marquette Law Review, 89*, 251–304.

Van Camp, Tinneke (2014, forthcoming). *Victims of Violence and Restorative Practices*. London: Routledge.

van Dijk, Jan J. M. (1999). The Experience of Crime and Justice. In Graeme Newman (Ed.), *Global Report on Crime and Justice*. Oxford: Oxford University Press.

Vanfraechem, Inge, Pemberton, Anthony, & Felix, Ndahinda (Eds.), (2014, forthcoming). *Routledge International Handbook of Victimology*. London: Routledge.

Vanfraechem, Inge, & Walgrave, Lode (2004). Restorative Conferencing in Belgium: Can It Decrease the Confinement of Young Offenders? *Corrections Today, (*December*)*, 72–75.

Van Ness, Daniel W. (2004). Justice That Restores: From Impersonal to Personal Justice. *Journal of Religion & Spirituality in Social Work, 23*(1–2), 93–109.

Van Ness, Daniel W., et al. (2003). Proposed Basic Principles on the Use of Restorative Justice: Recognising the Aims and Limits of Restorative Justice. In Andrew von Hirsch (Ed.), *Restorative Justice and Criminal Justice: Competing or Reconcilable Paradigms?* (pp. 157–176). Hart: Oxford.

Van Ness, Daniel W. (2002a). Creating Restorative Justice Systems. In Lode Walgrave (Ed.), *Restorative Justice and the Law* (pp. 130–149). Cullompton, UK: Willan.

Van Ness, Daniel W. (2002b). The Shape of Things to Come: A Framework for Thinking About a Restorative Justice System. In Elmar G. M. Weitekamp & Hans-Jürgen Kerner (Eds.), *Restorative Justice: Theoretical Foundations*. Cullompton, UK: Willan.

Van Ness, Daniel W. (1999). Legal Issues of Restorative Justice. In Gordon Bazemore & Lode Walgrave (Eds.), *Restorative Juvenile Justice: Repairing the Harm of Youth Crime*. Monsey, NY: Criminal Justice Press.

Van Ness, Daniel W. (1996). Restorative Justice and International Human Rights. In Burt Galaway & Joe Hudson (Eds.), *Restorative Justice: International Perspectives*. Monsey, NY: Criminal Justice Press.

Van Ness, Daniel W. (1995). Anchoring Just Deserts. *Criminal Law Forum, 6*(3), 507–517.

Van Ness, Daniel W. (1994). Preserving a Community Voice: The Case for Half-and-Half Juries in Racially-Charged Criminal Cases. *John Marshall Law Review, 28*(1), 1–56.

Van Ness, Daniel W. (1993). New Wine in Old Wineskins: Four Challenges of Restorative Justice. *Criminal Law Forum, 4*(2), 251–276.

Van Ness, Daniel W. (1990a). Christians and Prison Reform. In Daniel Reid, Robert D. Linder, Bruce L. Shelley & Harry S. Stout (Eds.), *Dictionary of Christianity in America*. Downers Grove, IL: InterVarsity Press.

Van Ness, Daniel W. (1990b). Restorative Justice. In Burt Galaway & Joe Hudson (Eds.), *Criminal Justice, Restitution, and Reconciliation*. Monsey, NY: Criminal Justice Press.

Van Ness, Daniel W. (1986). *Crime and Its Victims: What We Can Do*. Downers Grove, IL: InterVarsity Press.

Van Ness, Daniel W., & Nolan, Pat (1998). Legislating for Restorative Justice. *Regent University Law Review, 10*(Spring), 53–110.

Van Ness, Daniel W., & Schiff, Mara (2001). Satisfaction Guaranteed? The Meaning of Satisfaction in Restorative Justice. In Gordon Bazemore & Mara Schiff (Eds.), *Restorative Community Justice: Repairing Harm and Transforming Communities.* Anderson: Cincinnati, OH.

Van Wormer, Katherine (2008). *Restorative Justice across the East and the West.* Manchester, UK: Casa Verde.

Van Wormer, Katherine S., & Walker, Lorenn (Eds.), (2012). *Restorative Justice Today: Practical Applications.* Thousand Oaks, CA: Sage.

Villmoare, Edwin, & Neto, Virginia V. (1992). *Victim Appearances at Sentencing Hearings under the California Bill of Rights: Executive Summary.* Washington, DC: U.S. Department of Justice, National Institute of Justice.

von Hirsch, Andrew (1993). *Censure and Sanctions.* Oxford: Clarendon.

von Hirsch, Andrew, Julian Roberts, Bottoms, Anthony E., Roach, Kent, & Schiff, Mara (Eds.), (2005). *Restorative Justice and Criminal Justice: Competing or Reconcilable Paradigms?.* Hart: Oxford.

von Hirsch, Andrew, Shearing, Clifford, & Ashworth, Andrew (2003). Specifying Aims and Limits for Restorative Justice: A Making Amends Model? In Andrew von Hirsch, et al. (Ed.), *Restorative Justice and Criminal Justice: Competing or Reconcilable Paradigms?* (pp. 21–42). Hart: Oxford.

Wachtel, Ted (2003). Restorative Practices in Schools: An Antidote to Zero Tolerance. *VOMA Connections, 13*(1), 4.

Wachtel, Ted (2000). Restorative Practices with High-Risk Youth. In Gale Buford & Joe Hudson (Eds.), *Family Group Conferencing: New Directions in Community Centered Child & Family Practice* (pp. 86–92). Hawthorne, NY: Aldine de Gruyter.

Wachtel, Ted (1997). *Real Justice: How We Can Revolutionize Our Response to Wrongdoing.* Pipersville, PA: The Piper's Press.

Wachtel, Ted (1995). Family Group Conferencing: Restorative Justice in Practice. *Juvenile Justice Update, 1*(4), 1–2, 13–14.

Wachtel, Ted, & McCold, Paul (2001). Restorative Justice in Everyday Life. In Heather Strang & John Braithwaite (Eds.), *Restorative Justice and Civil Society* (pp. 114–129). Cambridge, UK: Cambridge University Press.

Walgrave, Lode (2008). *Restorative Justice, Self-Interest and Responsible Citizenship.* Cullompton, UK: Willan.

Walgrave, Lode (2005a). Towards Restoration as the Mainstream in Youth Justice. In Elizabeth Elliott & Robert M. Gordon (Eds.), *New Directions in Restorative Justice: Issues, Practice, Evaluation* (pp. 3–25). Cullompton, UK: Willan.

Walgrave, Lode (2005b). Retributivism and the Quality of Social Life: A Reply to Duff. In Erik Claes, René Foqué & Tony Peters (Eds.), *Punishment, Restorative Justice and the Morality of Law* (pp. 145–156). Oxford: Intersentia.

Walgrave, Lode (2004). Has Restorative Justice Appropriately Responded to Retribution Theory and Impulses? In Howard Zehr & Barb Toews (Eds.), *Critical Issues in Restorative Justice.* Monsey (pp. 47–60). NY/Cullompton, UK: Criminal Justice Press/Willan.

Walgrave, Lode (2003a). Imposing Restoration Instead of Inflicting Pain. In Andrew von Hirsch, et al. (Eds.), *Restorative Justice and Criminal Justice: Competing or Reconcilable Paradigms?* (pp. 61–78). Hart: Oxford.

Walgrave, Lode (Ed.), (2003b). *Repositioning Restorative Justice.* Cullompton, UK: Willan.

Walgrave, Lode (Ed.), (1998). *Restorative Justice for Juveniles: Potentialities, Risks and Problems*. Leuven, Belgium: Leuven University Press.

Walgrave, Lode, & Geudens, H. (1996). The Restorative Proportionality of Community Service for Juveniles. *European Journal of Crime, Criminal Law and Criminal Justice, 4*(4), 361–380.

Walker, Lorenn (2010). Huikahi Restorative Circles: Group Process for Self-Directed Reentry Planning and Family Healing. *European Journal of Probation, 2*(2), 76–95.

Walklate, Sandra (Ed.), (2007). *Handbook of Victims and Victimology*. Cullompton, UK: Willan.

Wallis, Pete, & Tudor, Barbara (2007). *The Pocket Guide to Restorative Justice*. London: Jessica Kingsley.

Warner, Kate (1994). Family Group Conferences and the Rights of the Offender. In C. Alder & J. Wundersitz (Eds.), *Family Conferencing and Juvenile Justice: The Way Forward or Misplaced Optimism?* (pp. 141–152). Canberra: Australian Institute of Criminology.

Warner Roberts, Annie (2004). Is Restorative Justice Tied to Specific Models of Practice? In Howard Zehr & Barb Toews (Eds.), *Critical Issues in Restorative Justice*. Monsey (pp. 241–251). NY/Cullompton, UK: Criminal Justice Press/Willan.

Weitekamp, Elmar G. M. (2001). Mediation in Europe: Paradoxes, Problems and Promises. In Allison Morris & Gabrielle Maxwell (Eds.), *Restorative Justice for Juveniles: Conferencing, Mediation and Circles*. With a foreword by D. J. Carruthers (pp. 145–160). Oxford: Hart.

Weitekamp, Elmar G. M. (1992). Can Restitution Serve as a Reasonable Alternative to Imprisonment? An Assessment of the Situation in the USA. In Heinz Messmer & Hans-Uwe Otto (Eds.), *Restorative Justice on Trial*. Dordrecht, The Netherlands: Kluwer.

Weitekamp, Elmar G. M., & Kerner, Hans-Jürgen (Eds.), (2003). *Restorative Justice in Context: International Practice and Directions*. Cullompton, UK: Willan.

Weitekamp, Elmar G. M., & Kerner, Hans-Jürgen (Eds.), (2002). *Restorative Justice: Theoretical Foundations*. Cullompton, UK: Willan.

Welsh, Brandon C., & Farrington, David P. (2006). *Preventing Crime: What Works for Children Offenders, Victims, and Places*. New York: Springer.

Wemmers, Jo Anne, & Van Camp, Tinneke (2011). The Offer of Restorative Justice to Victims of Violent Crime: Should It Be Protective or Proactive? *Montreal: International Centre for Comparative Criminology*.

White, Linda L. (1999). A Journey to Restoration. *The Crime Victims Report* (March/April):8–9.

Wilcox, Aidan, & Hoyle, Carolyn (2004). *The National Evaluation of the Youth Justice Board's Restorative Justice Projects*. London: Youth Justice Board for England and Wales.

Wilcox, Aidan, Young, Richard, & Hoyle, Carolyn (2004). *An Evaluation of the Impact of Restorative Cautioning: Findings from a Reconviction Study*. Findings 255. London Research: Development and Statistics Directorate, Home Office.

Willemsens, Jolien (2003). Restorative Justice: A Discussion of Punishment? In Lode Walgrave (Ed.), *Repositioning Restorative Justice* (pp. 24–42). Cullompton, UK: Willan.

Wing Lo, T., Maxwell, Gabrielle, & Wong, Dennis (2005). *Alternatives to Prosecution: Rehabilitative and Restorative Models of Youth Justice*. Singapore: Marshall Cavendish Academic.

Woolford, Andrew (2010). *The Politics of Restorative Justice: A Critical Introduction*. Canada: Fernwood: Winnipeg, Ontario.

Workman, Kim (2008). *Restorative Reintegration: A New Approach to Prisoner Aftercare in New Zealand*. Auckland, NZ: Prison Fellowship New Zealand.

Worth, Dave (1989). Mediation and Values. *Accord, A Mennonite Central Committee Canada Publication for Victim Offender Ministries, 8*(3), 11–12.

Wozniak, John F., Braswell, Michael C., Blevins, Kristie R., & Vogel, Ronald E. (2008). *Transformative Justice: Critical and Peacemaking Themes Influenced by Richard Quinney*. Lanham, MD: Lexington Books.

Wright, Fran, & Humphreys, Rob (2008). *Restorative Justice: Reconciliation for a Hurt Generation*. Cambridge, UK: Grove.

Wright, Martin (2000). Restorative Justice: For Whose Benefit? In The European Forum for Victim–Offender Mediation and Restorative Justice (Ed.), *Victim–Offender Mediation in Europe: Making Restorative Justice Work*. Leuven, Belgium: Leuven University Press.

Wright, Martin (1999). *Restoring Respect for Justice: A Symposium*. Winchester, UK: Waterside Press.

Wright, Martin (1991). *Justice for Victims and Offenders*. Philadelphia: Open University Press.

Wright, Martin (1982). *Making Good: Prisons, Punishment, and Beyond*. London: Burnett.

Wright, Martin, & Foucault, Orlane (2005). Community Involvement in Restorative Justice. *VOMA Connections 19*(Winter), 1, 11–16.

Wright, Martin, & Galaway, Burt (Eds.), (1989). *Mediation and Criminal Justice: Victims, Offenders, and Community*. Newbury Park, CA: Sage.

Wright, Martin, & Masters, Guy (2002). Justified Criticism, Misunderstanding, or Important Steps on the Road to Acceptance? In Elmar G. M. Weitekamp & Hans-Jürgen Kerner (Eds.), *Restorative Justice: Theoretical Foundations* (pp. 50–70). Cullompton, UK: Willan.

Yantzi, Mark (1998). *Sexual Offending and Restoration*. Scottdale, PA: Herald Press.

Yazzie, Robert (1994). Life Comes from It: Navajo Justice Concepts. *New Mexico Law Review, 24*(2), 175–190.

Yazzie, Robert, & Zion, James W. (1996). Navajo Restorative Justice: The Law of Equality and Justice. In Burt Galaway & Joe Hudson (Eds.), *Restorative Justice: International Perspectives*. Monsey, NY: Criminal Justice Press.

Young, Marlene A. (1995). *Restorative Community Justice: A Call to Action*. Washington, DC: National Organization for Victim Assistance.

Young, Richard, & Hoyle, Carolyn (2003a). New Improved Police-Led Restorative Justice. In Andrew von Hirsch, et al. (Eds.), *Restorative Justice and Criminal Justice: Competing or Reconcilable Paradigms?* (pp. 273–292). Hart: Oxford.

Young, Richard, & Hoyle, Carolyn (2003b). Restorative Justice and Punishment. In Sean McConville (Ed.), *Use of Punishment* (pp. 199–234). Cullompton, UK: Willan.

Young, Richard, Hoyle, Carolyn, Hill, Roderick, & Cooper, Karen (2005). Informal Resolution of Complaints against the Police: A Quasi-Experimental Test of Restorative Justice. *Criminal Justice, 5*(3), 279–317.

Zehr, Howard (2002). *The Little Book of Restorative Justice*. Intercourse, PA: Good Books.

Zehr, Howard (2001). *Transcending: Reflections of Crime Victims*. New York: Good Books.

Zehr, Howard (1990). *Changing Lenses: A New Focus for Crime and Justice*. Scottdale, PA: Herald Press.

Zehr, Howard (1989). VORP Dangers. *Accord: A Mennonite Central Committee Canada Publication for Victim Offender Ministries, 8*(3), 13.

Zehr, Howard, & Toews, Barb (Eds.), (2004). *Critical Issues in Restorative Justice* (pp. 133–142). Monsey, NY: Criminal Justice Press.

Zernova, Margarita (2007). *Restorative Justice: Ideals and Realities*. Burlington, VT: Ashgate.

Index

Note: Page numbers with "*b*" denote boxes; "*f*" figures; "*t*" tables.

A

Abel, Charles F., 17, 20
Abolition movement, for prisons, 14–15
Aboriginal peoples
    circles (community/healing/sentencing),
        29–30, 85
    conferencing and, 29
    elder-assisted hearings for (Canada), 159
Absolution, 7
Absurd information, patterns of thinking and, 4
Accountability
    for conduct and outcomes of encounter,
        94–95
    in criminal cases, 94–95
    deliberative, 94
    informal, 94
    offender injuries and, 46–47
    for reparations, 140
    as restorative justice principle, 51, 51b
Acknowledgment, in apology, 101
Acorn, Analise, 96
Active information systems, of the brain, 4
Active responsibility, 49, 104
Adversarial court, 177, 185
Adversarial justice systems, 172
Adversarial paradigm of justice/crime,
        169–170, 172
Aertsen, Ivo, 59
Affect, in apology, 101
Affinity groups (support groups, for victim/
        offender reintegration), 122–124. *See
        also* Faith communities
Africa
    compensation in pre-colonial societies, 7
    investment in restorative justice programs,
        31. *See also* individual nations
African-Americans, civil rights movement
        and, 48

Agreement, in encounter, 88–89, 88b, 160
Alaska Code of Criminal Procedure, 168
Aldermen, 11
Allen, G.D., 131
Alternative approaches
    in inclusion, 65, 72, 160
    transformation of perspective and, 171–172
Alternatives to Violence Project, 171
Amends, 161t–162t
    apology, 101–102
    in assessment framework, 163–164, 164f
    changed behavior, 100b, 101–103
    defined, 110
    in fully restorative system, 160
    generosity, 100b, 101, 104
    as cornerpost value in restorative process, 50
    restitution, 100–101, 100b, 103–109. *See also*
        Victim-offender mediation programs
        (VOMs)
American Bar Association (ABA)
    Criminal Justice Section, 107
    Guidelines Governing Restitution to Victims
        of Criminal Conduct, 70–71, 107–108
    on restitution, 107
    Standards Relating to the Prosecution
        Function, 70–71
American Bible Society, 124
American civil rights movement, 48
American Friends Service Committee, 14
American Probation and Parole Association,
        159
Andrews, Arlene Bowers, 115–116, 129
Antiseptic construal of justice, 172
Apology
    amends and, 101–102, 160
    in conferencing, 101
    defined, 101
    exchange of shame and power, 101

Apology (*Continued*)
following victim-offender mediation, 83
genuineness, 102
of government, 102
limited, 83
no favorable treatment following, 159
restitution and, 102
Appeal element, in inclusion, 64–65
Arbitration, victim-offender mediation
distinguished from, 82
Argentina, restorative justice principles and
practices in, 33t–38t
Armour, Marilyn Peterson, 137–138
Arraignment, victim inclusion in, 73
Ashworth, Andrew, 26
Asia, restorative justice principles and
practices in, 31
Assessing the Criminal (Barnett and Hagel), 17
Assessment. *See* Evaluation
Assessment framework, for restorative justice
system, 160–165
Assistance groups, for victim/offender
reintegration, 122–124
Assumption of responsibility, 47
Auburn System of corrections, 124
Auerbach, Jerold S., 15, 20
Augmentation model, of restorative justice,
153
Australia, 7
apology, changed behavior, restitution,
generosity, and, 101
conferencing in, 84, 101
encounter participants in, 94–95
juvenile justice bills, 31
restorative justice principles and practices
in, 33t–38t
Wagga Wagga family group conferences
in, 26, 29. *See also* Family group
conferencing (FGC)
Australian Capital Territory (ACT), Crimes
(Restorative Justice) Act, 155
Austria
mediation referrals by prosecutors, 156–157
prosecutorial diversion in, 156–157
restorative justice principles and practices
in, 33t–38t

B
Bacon, G. Richard, 20
Bail proceedings, victim inclusion in, 73
Baker, Nicola, 24, 26, 40, 176
Balanced and Restorative Justice Project
(BARJ), 30, 33t–38t
Barangay Justice System (Philippines),
33t–38t
Bard, Morton, 13, 20, 116, 129, 131
Barnes, Lisa (Lampman), 131
Barnett, Randy E., 17, 20
Barton, Charles, 66, 78
Basic Principles on the Use of Restorative
Justice Programmes in Criminal Matters
(United Nations), 31, 33t–38t, 95
Battle model, of criminal justice, 169–170
Bazemore, Gordon, 30, 51, 59, 86, 97, 111
Behavior. *See* Changed behavior
Belgium
encounter participants in, 94–95
restitution in, 108
restorative justice principles and practices in,
33t–38t
Bellavista prison (Medellin, Colombia), peace
table in, 158–159
Bentham, Jeremy, 8, 10, 103
Best practices, 48–49
"Beyond Restitution: Creative Restitution"
(Eglash), 39
Bianchi, Herman, 14–15
Biblical Doctrine of Justice and Law, The
(Schrey, Walz, and Whitehouse), 39
Biblical justice, 17, 19, 25, 39
Biblical tradition, in faith communities, 126
Biles, David, 40, 97
Black, M., 59
Boddie, Stephanie C., 130
Bottoms, Anthony, 59, 111
Braithwaite, John, 26, 40, 46, 49, 59, 119,
121, 130
Brazil, restorative justice principles and
practices in, 33t–38t
Breach of the king's peace, 7
Brunk, Conrad G., 51, 59
Bulgaria, restorative justice principles and
practices in, 33t–38t

Burford, Gale, 29, 40
Burnside, Jonathan, 24, 26, 40, 172, 176
Bushie, Berma, 30, 40

C

California, victims' right to speak at felony
    sentencing, 74
California Prison Moratorium Project, 14–15
Canada
    circles in, 16, 29–30
    Circles of Support and Accountability,
        33t–38t, 120–121
    Correctional Service of Canada, 120–121
    early victim-offender mediation in, 27
    First Nations people in, 16, 29–30
    incorporation of restorative justice in
        sentencing principles, 30–31
    investment in restorative justice programs,
        30–31
    Mennonite Central Committee, 27, 120–121
    National Parole Board, 159
    Parliamentary Standing Committee
        (Daubney Committee), 32–33, 33t–38t
    parole hearings for Aboriginal offenders, 159
    prisoner ministry in, 130
    restorative justice principles and practices
        in, 33t–38t
    R. v. Moses (sentencing circle case; 1992),
        33t–38t
    Restorative Resolutions Project, 157
    sentencing law changes, 32–33
    victim-offender mediation started in, 27
    victim-offender reconciliation programs in,
        32
    Youth Criminal Justice Act, 31
Cardenas, Juan, 20
Care, 114, 117, 119, 125–127, 129, 160
    community of, 6, 84, 93
Caregivers, of victims, 127
Carey, Mark, 138, 148
Caring response, 17–18
Carr, G. Lloyd, 19
Casey, Louise, 115
Catholic Charities, 130
Center for Alternative Dispute Resolution
    (Chile), 33t–38t

Centre for Justice and Reconciliation (Prison
    Fellowship International), 145, 154
Centre for Restorative Justice (China), 33t–38t
Changed behavior
    amends and, 100b, 101–103, 160
    strategies for, 103
Changed values, 103, 103b
Changing Lenses (Zehr), 24–25, 148
Child Justice Act
    South Africa (2009), 33t–38t
    Uganda (1996), 33t–38t
Children, Young Persons and their Families
    Act (New Zealand; 1989), 28, 31,
    33t–38t, 155
Chile, restorative justice principles and
    practices in, 33t–38t
China, restorative justice principles and
    practices in, 33t–38t
Christian Faith and Criminal Justice
    (McHugh), 17, 125
Christian organizations, 130. *See also* Faith
    communities
Christianity
    alignment of justice and love, 39
    criminal justice and values of, 17
    idea of imprisonment from, 8–9
    Judeo-Christian tradition, in reintegration,
        125
    on justice, 39
    on punishment and mercy, 17b
    restorative justice elements of, 17. *See also*
        Faith communities
Christie, Nils, 15–16, 20, 28
Christmas Carol, A (Dickens), amends in,
    99–101, 103–104
Churches
    -based programs, 27
    presence in community, 126–128
    volunteers from, 126. *See also* Faith
        communities
Circles
    Aboriginal peoples and, 29–30, 85
    community, 85
    defined, 85
    as encounter, 85–86
    facilitators in, 85, 91

Circles (*Continued*)
  First Nations people (Canada), 16, 29–30
  government representatives in, 93–94
  healing, 29
  inclusion of offenders, 75–76
  inclusion of community members, 76
  initiation of process, 86
  meeting element of, 88
  model, 85
  participants in, 85, 91–94
  process of, 85–86, 86b
  R. v. Moses (Canada; 1992), 33t–38t
  releasing, 159
  as restorative process program, 29–30
  sentencing, 29–30, 33t–38t, 85–86
  support persons/community members in, 93
  traditional rituals, 85
  transformation and, 174
  victims and offenders and, 85–86
Circles of Support and Accountability
  (Canada), 33t–38t, 120–121
Civil claims, by victims, in criminal cases, 75
Civil law of torts, restorative justice, criminal
  law, and, 17
Civil rights movement (United States), 48
Civil society, 46
Claassen, Ron, 6, 27, 40, 89, 97–98
Clark County Juvenile Court (Vancouver,
  Washington), 90
Cnaan, Ram, 123–124, 130
Coalition development, in restorative justice,
  138–139
Coalition of Prison Evangelists (COPE), 130
Coates, Robert, 98
Code of Eshnunna, 6
Code of Hammurabi, 6
Code of Lipit-Ishtar, 6
Code of Ur-Nammu, 6
Coercion, 149–150
  minimizing, as encounter strategy, 90–91
Colijn, G.J., 111
Colombia
  mediation legislation, 156–157
  peace table, in Bellavista Prison, 158–159
  prisons and restorative justice processes in,
    158–159

restorative justice principles and practices
  in, 33t–38t
Sycamore Tree Project, 87
Colson, Charles, 17, 20, 125, 174–176
Committee of Ministers of the Council of
  Europe, 31
Common law, 97
Communication. *See* Encounter
Community
  -assisted hearings, for Aboriginal offenders
    (Canada), 159
  -based programs, 27, 32
  of care, 6, 84, 93
  circles and, 85–86
  corrections, 26–27
  courts, 26–27
  crime as damage to peace of, 6–7
  definition, 45–46
  fair and humane, in response to crime, 18
  geographic community, 6
  healing of, 45
  inclusion of, 76–78
  injuries to and needs of, 45–47
  of interest, 6, 93
  involvement in the justice process, 47
  meaningful, 18
  members of, and encounter, 93
  peace as responsibility of, 47, 94, 173–174
  in place of prison, 14
  policing, 24–27
  prosecution, 26–27
  as provider of safety need, 115
  reintegration and, 119
  responsibility of, 47, 93, 173–174
  in restorative justice support, 135–136
  service
    in Belgian prisons, 108
    offender's ability to pay restitution,
      108–109
    as restitution, 104, 106
  stigmatization of victims and offenders by,
    114–115
  types of, 6
  victim distinguished from, 59
  in visual model of restorative justice,
    54, 56

"we-they" attitude, with justice system,
    138. *See also* Faith communities;
    Reintegrating communities;
    Reintegration
Community circles, 29
Community group conferences, 84
Community Justice Initiatives (Canada), 33t–38t
Community Mediation and Safety Center
    (Romania), 33t–38t
Community Peace Committees (South Africa),
    156
Community Safety/Restorative Model
    (Mackey), 25
Commutative justice, 39
Compassion, 6, 25–26
Compensation
    in place of prison, 14
    prisoners' opportunity to provide, 17
    restitution distinguished from, 111
    victim participation and, 25
*Compulsory Compassion: A Critique of
    Restorative Justice* (Acorn), 96
Conferencing, 16, 77
    apology in, 101
    emotion in, 88
    facilitators in, 91
    government representatives in, 93–94
    meeting element of, 88
    participants in, 90–91
    reintegrative shaming and, 26
    as restorative process program, 28–29
    support persons/community members in,
        93
    transformation and, 174
    victim-offender mediation distinguished
        from, 29
    victim-offender panels (VOPs)
        distinguished from, 86. *See also* Family
        group conferencing (FGC)
Confession, 87
    confession, repentance and absolution
        process, 7
Conflict
    resolution, 82
        Alternatives to Violence Project and, 171
        as focus of peacemaking, 18

among the Maori people, 28
    citizen-government, 31. *See also* Victim-
        offender mediation programs (VOMs)
    between government and victim, for
        ownership of victimization experience,
        66
    of victim and offender, 15, 28
    between victim and prosecutor, 70–71
"Conflict as Property" (Christie), 15
Connolly, William, 59
Consent, as a restorative system condition,
    149–150
Contemporary criminal justice
    coerciveness of, 90–91
    failure of, 139
    restorative justice compared to, 53–54, 58
    restorative justice models and, 153–155
    restorative justice processes in, 156–160
    RJ City project (case study) and, 177, 178,
        179, 180, 181, 182, 183, 184, 185, 186,
        187, 188
    usage of term, 53
    visual model, 54–57
Contributing injuries, of offenders, 46–47
Conversation, norms of society and,
    172–173
Cook, Bruce, 130
Cooperation, 18
Copernicus, 4
Cornerpost values. *See* Amends; Encounter;
    Inclusion; Reintegration
Corporal punishment, 8
Correctional officials, 10–11
Correctional Service of Canada, 120–121
"Correction of the mind", 8
Corrections, community, 26–27
Costa Rica, restorative justice principles and
    practices in, 33t–38t
Costs, of victimization, 13–14
Council of Europe, endorsement of restorative
    justice, 33–39
Courts
    community, 26–27
    consideration of restorative justice by, 30
    mediators, 157
    use of restorative justice processes, 157

Courts (*Continued*)
  victim-offender mediation vs., 82
  victim's right to presence in, inclusion, 67–69
Co-victims, restitution and, 105
Cragg, Wesley, 25–26, 40
Creative restitution, 39, 104
Creativity, in transformation of perspective,
    171
Crime
  as damage to community peace, 6–7
  as defining moment for victims and
    offenders, 114
  injured parties of, 3–4
  as lawbreaking, 3–5, 16b, 25
  macro response to, 54, 56
  micro dimension of, 54, 56
  as moral problem, 174–175
  as offense against victims, their families,
    the community, society, and the
    government, 6
  -related psychological trauma, 115–116
  restitution's preferred definition of, 17
  royal jurisdiction over offenses, 7–8
  victims. *See* Victims
  Zehr's definition, 24
Crime and Disorder Act (England; 1998),
    33t–38t
Crime and Its Victims (Van Ness), 17
Crime control model, of criminal justice, 169
Crime (Restorative Justice) Act (Australian
    Capital Territory), 155, 168
Crime Victims Advocacy Council (CVAC), 130
Crime Victim's Book, The (Bard and Sangrey),
    13, 116
Crime Victims Equality Act (New Hampshire;
    2009), 71
Criminal behavior, failure to address reasons
    for, 5
Criminal justice
  ancient approach to, 6–7
  battle model, 169–170
  crime control model, 169
  defined, 51, 53
  due process model, 169
  family model, 169–170, 174
  as healing mechanism, 3

modern thinking about, 7–10
nagging questions, 5
personal responsibility and, 17
rehabilitation model, 3–4
shift in patterns of thinking, 4–5, 7–10
unachievable in unjust society, 14
victims' dissatisfaction with, 5
Criminal Justice and the Victim (McDonald), 14
Criminal Justice Program, of the Presbyterian
    Church (USA), 25
Criminal justice system
  conflict of ownership in, 15–16, 28, 66, 71
  dissatisfaction with, 5
  example, in RJ City case study, 181, 182, 183,
    184
  focus on offender, 5
  incorporation of restorative justice into,
    30–31
  inefficiency and ineffectiveness of, 10
  opportunity for active involvement in, by
    victims, offenders, and communities,
    47
  resistance to change by, 146–147
  restorative justice
    as a community-based alternative to, 32
    as viable part of, 33
  security maintenance function of, 12
  victim as civil claimant in criminal cases, 75
  victims' inclusion and role in, 26, 28, 67–75.
    See also Victim inclusion, in criminal
    justice proceedings
Criminal law
  failure to recognize harms, 139
  healing as purpose of, 3–4
  norms of society and, 172
  practitioners, as healers, 3
  restorative justice, torts, and, 17
  values clarified by graduated punishment,
    15–16
Criminal Law Forum, 26
Criminal proceedings. *See* Victim inclusion, in
    criminal justice proceedings
Criminal-civil separation, 26
Criminology, 18
Criminology as Peacemaking (Pepinsky and
    Quinney), 18

Crisis
   intervention, 116–117
   phase, of victimization, 127
   services, 126
Crook, Frances, 53, 59
Cultural reconciliation, 31
Cushing, Robert Renny, 71, 78
Customary approach, to justice, 16
Czech Republic, restorative justice principles
      and practices in, 33t–38t

D
Daly, Kathleen, 51–52, 59
Danieli, Yael, 102, 111
Daubney Committee (Canada), 32–33, 33t–38t
Davis, Robert C., 129
de Bono, Edward, 4, 19, 170–171, 176
Death sentence, 8
Debtors' prison, 8
Decentralization, of the justice system, 14–15
Declaration of Basic Principles of Justice for
      Victims of Crime and Abuse of Power
      (United Nations), 68
Declaration of Basic Principles on the Use
      of Restorative Justice Programmes in
      Criminal Matters (United Nations), 31,
      33t–38t, 95
Delegalization, of the justice system, 15
Deliberative accountability, 94
Demeanor, in apology, 101
Demographics, of victims, 115
Depression, 115
Deprofessionalization, of the justice system, 15
Desegregation of public schools, 48
Deterrence, through enforcement or
      punishment, 25
Dialogue, usage of term, 28, 83. *See also*
      Victim-offender mediation programs
      (VOMs)
Dialogue-driven programs, 28
Dickens, Charles, 99, 110
Dignity, respect for, as reintegration element,
      114
Dignity Denied, 71
Direct harm, 13–14
Direct injuries, 106, 108

Direct victims, restitution and, 105
Directness, principle of, 106
Discretionary power, of prosecutors, 156
Disharmony, 169–170
Disorientation, of victims, 116
Dispassionate justice, 172
Dispute Resolution Foundation (Jamaica),
      33t–38t
Distributive justice, 23–24, 39
Diversion, programs offering, 157
Diversionary mediation, 33t–38t
Domestic violence shelters, 115
Drunk Driving Impact Panels (MADD), 87–89
Dual-track model, of restorative justice, 154
Due process model, of criminal justice, 169
Duff, Antony, 52, 59, 105, 111
Dünkel, Frieder, 28, 40
Dwight, Louis, 124

E
Economic and Social Council (ECOSOC;
      United Nations), 31
Eglash, Albert, 23–24, 39, 104, 111
El Salvador, restorative justice principles and
      practices in, 33t–38t
Elder-assisted hearings, for Aboriginal
      offenders (Canada), 159
Elmwood, Kate, 111
Emergent values, 49
Emotion
   in encounter, 88–89, 88b, 160
   in training of facilitators, 89
   of victims, 115–116
Emotional injuries, of offenders, 46–47
Empathy, 85
Employment problems, of released prisoners,
      117–118
Empowerment, 82
Encounter
   accountability for conduct and outcomes,
      94–95
   in assessment framework, 161–163, 161t–162t
   circles, 85–86
   conception, of restorative justice, 43–45
   and consent, 149
   elements of, 88–90, 161

Encounter (*Continued*)
  empowerment in, 82
  example (*The Iliad*), 81–82, 88–89
  facilitators in, 90–92, 94
  family group conferencing (FGC), 84–85
  follow-up meetings in, 83, 103
  in fully restorative system, 160–161
  goals and objectives in, 83, 92
  government representatives in, 93–94
  as hallmark of restorative justice, 174
  impact panels, 86–87
  issues in, 90–95
  mediation and, 43–45
  meeting, narrative, emotion, understanding, and agreement in, 88–90
  minimizing coercion, 90–91
  offenders in, 93
  as operational value in restorative process, 50
  parties involved, 91–94
  privacy of, 94
  restrictions on, 82
  review of agreement by referring party, 95
  support persons/community members in, 93
  victim-offender mediation programs (VOMs) and, 82–84
  victim-offender panel (VOP) and, 86–87
  victim-offender participation in, 140
  victims in, 92–93
  voluntary participation in, 90, 90b
England
  adult-offender mediation in, 156
  conferences conducted by police officers, 156
  conferencing in, 31
  early reform movement, 8
  Leges Henrici Primi in, 7
  mediation in, 156
  restorative justice principles and practices in, 33t–38t
  Sycamore Tree Project, 87
  Thames Valley Police, restorative justice use by, 31, 33, 33t–38t, 156
  victim-offender mediation in, 28

victim-offender panels in, 86
victim-offender reconciliation programs in, 32
Essentially contested concepts, 59
Euller, John, 18
Europe
  restorative justice principles and practices in, 31, 33t–38t
European Commission for the Efficiency of Justice (CEPEJ), 33t–38t
European Forum for Victim-Offender Mediation and Restorative Justice, 31, 33t–38t
European Forum on Restorative Justice, 137, 145
European Union (EU), 31, 33–39, 33t–38t
Evaluation
  guidelines for, 143–144
  impact, 142–144
  realignment of vision and practice and, 144–145
  of restorative justice policies and programs, 69–70
Evans, T.D., 131

F
Facilitators
  accountability of, 94
  in circles, 85
  emotion in training of, 89
  in encounter, 91–92
  in family group conferencing, 84, 84b
  functions of, 91–92
  poorly trained, 90
  training and selection of, 92
Faget, Jacques, 97
Fairness
  victims' experience of, in encounter, 92
  victim's understanding of, 74
  in visual model of restorative justice, 54–57
Faith communities
  Circles of Support and Accountability (Canada), 120–121
  examples, 130
  history, 124–125

Judeo-Christian tradition, 125
    limitations to, 123
    presence of, 126–128
    as reintegrating communities, 124–128, 142
    results of works by, 123–124
    victim and offender assistance from,
        126–128, 141
Faith factor, reintegration and, 125
Families and supporters, for victim/offender
        reintegration, 121–122
Family group conferencing (FGC), 33t–38t
    creation of model of, early days, 33t–38t
    development of, 145
    evaluation studies of, 85
    participants in, 84, 84b
    process of, 84–85
    reintegrative shaming in, 26
    as relational justice, 26
    victim-offender mediation programs
        (VOMs) distinguished from, 29, 84
    without victim, 155. *See also* Conferencing
Family model, of criminal justice, 169–170, 174
Feminist values, restructuring of criminal
        justice and, 17–18
Fielding, Henry, 8
Fines, 7–8, 7b
Finland
    restorative justice principles and practices in,
        33t–38t
    victim-offender mediation in, 28, 157
First Nations people (Canada), circles
        tradition in, 16, 29–30
Florida Atlantic University, 30
Follow-up meetings, in encounter, 83, 103
Forfeiture laws, restitution and, 108
Forgiveness, 25–26
    as emergent value, 49
    limited, 83
    Sycamore Tree Project and, 87
Formal justice, 25–26
Foundation Center for Attention to Victims of
        Crime (Mexico), 33t–38t
Four-dimensional justice, 39
France, victims' right to civil action in
        criminal cases, 75

Freeman, Richard B., 131
Fresno Pacific University, 33t–38t
Fuller, John R., 18, 21
Fully restorative system, 160–161, 165, 166f
Fundamental rights, as a restorative system
        condition, 150–152

G
Gacaca (traditional courts; Rwanda), 33t–38t
Galaway, Burt, 20, 39–40, 59, 98, 111
Gallie, W.B., 59
Gangs, 158–159
Gartner, J., 131
Gehm, John, 98
Generosity, amends and, 100b, 101, 104, 160
"Genesee Justice" program (Batavia, New York,
        Sheriff's Department; 1981), 33t–38t
Germanic tribal laws, 6
German Juvenile Justice Act (1990), 156
Germany, victim-offender mediation in, 28
"Get tough" measures of punishment, 10, 136
Gilman, Eric, 90, 98
Gittler, Josephine, 78
Globalization, restorative justice and, 31–39,
        33t–38t
"Golden age of the victim", 16
Goodwin, Catharine M., 111
Government
    adversarial relationship with offenders, 6
    apology and restitution by, 102
    community, public safety, and, 47
    conflict of ownership of crime and, 66
    crime as offense against, 6
    faith-based programs and, 128
    faith communities and, 123–124
    force by, 48, 59
    investment in restorative justice programs,
        30–31
    monopoly of, in response to crime, 30, 47
    order, as responsibility of, 48, 94, 173–174
    as primary victim, 47
    relationship with victims, offenders, and
        community, 30–31
    representatives of, in encounter, 93–94,
        105–106

Government (*Continued*)
    restorative programs for juveniles, 31
    support of restorative justice processes,
        33–39
    in visual model of restorative justice, 54–57
Governmental power, imbalance and, 173–174
Grauwiler, Peggy, 168
Great Britain. *See* England
Griffiths, John, 169–170, 176
Guidelines Governing Restitution to Victims
        of Criminal Conduct (ABA), 70–71,
        107–108

H
Habilitation, 46–47, 56, 136
Hadley, Michael L., 59
Hagel, John, 17, 20
Handbook on Justice for Victims (United
        Nations), 68
Handbook on Restorative Justice (United
        Nations), 33t–38t
Harding, John, 28, 40
Harland, Alan T., 146, 148
Harm
    from crime, 105–107
    from victimization, 13–14, 13b. *See also*
        Restitution
Harris, M. Kay, 17–18, 20
Harris, R.L., 19
Hay, Douglas, 20
Healing
    circles, 29
    community-based programs as aid in, 27
    as justice requirement, 45
    as purpose of criminal law, 3–4
    through encounter programs, 89
    through victim-offender panels, 87
    in visual model of restorative justice, 56
Hearn, Michael Patrick, 110
Hebrew justice
    restitution in, 6–7
    shalom, 47
Help, 114, 118–119, 122, 126, 129, 141–143
Helping Crime Victims (Roberts), 13
Hennessey, Hayes, 111
Herman, Susan, 120, 130

Hollow Water Community Holistic Circle
        Healing Program, 30
Holzer, Harry J., 131
Homer, 81–82, 88
Homicide survivors, 105
Hong Kong, restorative justice principles and
        practices in, 33t–38t
Hope, 17, 126, 129
Hostility, 89
Howard, John, 8
Howard League of Penal Reform, 53
Huculak, Bria, 30, 40
Hudson, Joe, 20, 39–40, 59, 98, 111
Hugo, Victor, 113, 129
Huikahi Circle, 121–122
Hulsman, Louk, 14–15
Human Kindness Foundation, 130
Human rights abuses, apology, restitution,
        and, 102
Humiliation, 8
Hybrid model, of restorative justice, 154
Hypocrisy, 174–175

I
Idler, E.L., 131
Iliad, The (Homer), encounter in, 81–82, 88–89
Ilivari, Juhani, 28, 40
Imbalance, in power structures, 173–174
Impact
    evaluations, 142–144
    panels. *See* Victim-offender panels (VOPs)
    stage, of victimization, 127
Impartial justice, 172
Imprisonment
    idea from Christianity, 8–9
    as last resort, 17
    restitution and, 16–17, 74, 109. *See also*
        Prison
Incarceration. *See* Imprisonment; Prison
Incentives for good behavior, 150
Inclusion
    in assessment framework, 160–162,
        161t–162t, 162f
    of community members, 76–78
    elements of, 64–65, 66b, 77, 161t–162t
    example (David and Goliath), 64, 63–65

in fully restorative system, 160–161
of offenders, 75–78
as operational value in restorative process, 50
restorative justice and, 65–67. *See also*
    Victim inclusion, in criminal justice
    proceedings
Independent attorney advocates, 71
Indifference, 175
Indigenous justice, contributions to
    restorative justice, 16
Indigenous peoples, restorative justice
    among, 7. *See also* Aboriginal peoples;
    Maori people
Indirect harm, 13–14
Inequity, 173–174
Informal accountability, 94
Informal justice, 15–16
Information needs, victim inclusion and, 67–68
Information-sharing, 33
Injuries
    to community, 45–47
    crime and, 3–4
    direct and indirect, 106
    of offenders, 46–47
    specific, 106. *See also* Victims
Injustice
    identification of, 83
    as moral problem, 174
Innovation, 24–25, 53, 82, 147
Institute for Conflict Resolution (Bulgaria),
    33t–38t
"Institutionalized mentality", 118
Insurers, restitution and, 105
Interest, local community, community of care,
    and shared, 46
Intergovernmental bodies, restorative justice
    by, 31
International Conference on Prison Abolition,
    14–15
International Institute for Restorative
    Practices, 33t–38t
International Network for Research on
    Restorative Justice for Juveniles, 145
Internet resources
    for faith-based organizations, 130
    for restorative justice topics, 33t–38t, 168

Intervention, 116–117
Investigation
    alternative approach (Minnesota), 73
    European system, 73
    victim inclusion in, 72–73
Invitation element, in inclusion, 64–65, 160
Islamic programs for prisoners and
    ex-prisoners, 130
Isolation
    of offenders, 118, 126
    of victims, 116, 118, 123, 126, 139
Italy
    mediation in, 157
    restorative justice principles and practices
    in, 33t–38t

J

Jails. *See* Imprisonment; Prison
Jamaica, restorative justice principles and
    practices in, 33t–38t
Japan
    amends, importance of apology in, 101–102
    compensation theory and restoration of
    community peace in, 7
    probation officers' use of restorative justice
    processes, 157–158
Jesus Christ, 39, 175
Jewish law, ancient, 47
Jewish Prisoner Services, International, 130
Johnstone, Gerry, 43–44, 59
Judeo-Christian tradition, in reintegration, 125
Jurisdiction, royal, over certain crimes, 7
Just Alternatives, 97
Justice
    as allocating blame and punishment, 25
    antiseptic construal of, 172
    commutative, 39
    connection with love, 39
    dispassionate, 172
    distributive, 23–24, 39
    formal, 25–26
    goal of, 6, 54
    healing of victims, offenders, and
    communities injured by crime and, 45
    impartial, 172
    indigenous, 16

Justice (*Continued*)
 informal, 15–16
 parallel, 120
 participatory, 15–16
 "passionate construal" of, 172
 relational, 24
 reparative, 16–17
 retributive, 23–24, 39
 social, 17–18
 theories and theorists of, 23–25
 three- and four-dimensional, 39
 traditional, 53
 transformative, 24
 Zehr's definition, 24
Justice Fellowship, 32–33, 33t–38t
Justice for Victims and Offenders (Wright), 25
Justice Without Law? (Auerbach), 15
Justification, 130
Juvenile Justice and Welfare Act (Philippines; 2006), 33t–38t
Juvenile justice system
 among the Maori people, 28
 Balanced and Restorative Justice Project (BARJ), 30, 33t–38t
 custodial facilities replaced by community-based programs, 14
 German Juvenile Justice Act (1990), 156
 governmental restorative programs for juveniles, 30–31
 International Network for Research on Restorative Justice for Juveniles, 145
 in Japan, 157–158
 in New Zealand, 28–29, 31–33
 New Zealand laws revised, incorporating Maori practices, 32–33
 police use of restorative justice processes and, 156
 prosecutor-referred restorative processes, 156–157. *See also* Family group conferencing (FGC)

K
Kairos, Inc., 130
Kasl, S.V., 131
Keeper (facilitator), 85
Kelly, John, 3–4, 45

Kilpatrick, Dean G., 115, 129
Kindness House, 130
King
 as paramount crime victim, 8
 peace of, 7
King David, 19
Knopp, Fay Honey, 14–15, 25

L
Lampman, Lisa (Barnes), 131
Larson, D.B., 131
Latin America, restorative justice principles and practices in, 31
Law of the Twelve Tables, 6
Lawbreaking, 4–5, 12, 25, 138
Laws
 ancient, 6
 codes of, 6
 Germanic tribal, 6
 Roman Law of the Twelve Tables, 6
Laws of Ethelbert, 6
Lazare, Aaron, 111
Lee, David, 40
Legal standing, of victims in criminal proceedings, 67, 70
Leges Henrici Primi, 7
Leibrich, Julie, 101, 111
Lerner, Melvin J., 19
Les Miserables (Hugo), as reintegration example, 113–116, 118–119, 123–124, 129
Lex Salica, 6
Lipkin, R., 111
Limits to Pain (Christie), 15–16
Littell, M. Sachs, 111
Local communities, 14, 45–46, 105–106
Lord, Janice Harris, 97
Love, connection with justice, 39
Lurigio, Arthur J., 129

M
Machiavelli, Niccolò, 146, 148
Mackey, Virginia, 25, 40
MADD. *See* Mothers Against Drunk Driving
Maguire, Mike, 111
Mandatory restitution, 67, 103

Maori people
    conferencing tradition among, 16, 28–29, 84
    influence on juvenile justice laws of
        New Zealand, 32–33
    practices of, incorporated into New Zealand
        juvenile justice laws, 32–33
    redress for violations against, 31
    Whanau conference, 84
Marriage, damage to, due to spousal
        incarceration, 118
Marsh, Frank A., 17, 20
Marshall, Tony, 24, 39
Massachusetts Department of Youth
        Services, 14
Material help, in reintegration, 114, 160
Mathiesen, Thomas, 14–15
Matthews, Roger, 20
Maxwell, Gabrielle, 29, 40
McCaslin, Wanda D., 40
McCold, Paul, 29, 40
McDonald, William F., 14, 20
McHugh, Gerald Austin, 17, 20, 125, 131
McKelvey, Blake, 20
McKillop, Sandra, 40, 97
McWhinnie, Andrew, 130
Meaningful work, in prisons, 109
Media, 137
Mediation, 25, 28, 77
    by community-based nonprofit organizations
        and judicial authorities, 97
    diversionary, 33t–38t
    in encounter, 82–84
    facilitators in, 91
    global use of, 156–157
    meeting element of, 88
    participants in, 85–86
    protective, 159
    usage of term, 28. See also Victim-offender
        mediation programs (VOMs)
Mediators. See Facilitators
Meeting, in encounter, 88–89, 88b, 160–162,
        161t–162t
Mennonite Central Committee (Canada), 27,
        120–121
Mennonite tradition, 17
Mercy, 25–26

Mexico, restorative justice principles and
        practices in, 33t–38t
Middle Eastern codes, ancient, 6
Miller, Jerome, 14, 174–175
Miller, Nick, 20
Miller, Susan L.,
Mills, Linda G., 168
Minimally restorative system, 165, 167f
Minnesota Crime Victim Justice Unit (CVJU), 73
Minnesota Department of Corrections, 33t–38t
Minnesota Office of Crime Victim
        Ombudsman, 73
Minorities
    discrimination of released prisoners, 117–118
    racial, imbalance of power and, 173
Moderately restorative system, 165, 166f
Monetary payment, restitution and, 103, 109
Moore, David, 26, 40, 89, 97
Moral and spiritual guidance and care, as
        reintegration element, 114, 129, 160
Moral injuries, of offenders, 46–47
Moral problems, 174–175
Moral reconciliation, 110–111
Morality, 105, 110, 114, 117, 119, 124, 129, 151,
        160–161, 164–165, 173–175
More, Thomas, 103
Morgan, Rod, 111
Morris, Allison, 29, 40
Morris, Norval, 20
Morris, Ruth, 14–15, 24, 40
Moses, R.V., 41
Mothers Against Drunk Driving (MADD),
        Victim Impact Panels/Drunk Driving
        Impact Panels of, 87–89
Municipal Mediation Act (Norway), 33t–38t
Murder Victims' Families for Reconciliation
        (MVFR), 71
Muslim and Islamic programs for prisoners
        and ex-prisoners, 130

N
Narrative, in encounter, 86b, 88–89, 160
Nathanson, Donald, 26
National Institute for Crime Prevention and
        Reintegration of Offenders (South
        Africa), 33t–38t

National Institute of Corrections, 30
National Moratorium on Prison Construction, 14–15
National Organization for Victim Assistance, 26–27
National Parole Board (Canada), 159
NATO Advanced Research Workshop on Conflict, Crime and Reconciliation, 33t–38t
Negative self-identity, of victims, 116
Negotiation by proxies, 88
Neiderbach, Shelley, 122–123, 130
Neighborhood Watch programs, 48
Netherlands, The, 14–15
Neto, Virginia V., 78
Networking, 33
New South Wales
    Department of Corrective Services, 159
    protective mediation, 159
    Wagga Wagga family group conferencing and restorative justice in, 26, 29, 33t–38t
New York, "Genesee Justice" program (Batavia), 33t–38t
New Zealand, 7
    adult-offender mediation and processes in, 31, 156
    Children, Young Persons and their Families Act (1989), 28, 31, 33t–38t, 155
    conferencing tradition in, 16, 28–29, 84
    Parole Act (2002), 159
    redress for violations against Maori people, 31
    restorative justice principles and practices in, 33t–38t
    restorative processes
        for adult offenders, 31, 156
        implementation, 32–33
    Sycamore Tree Project, 87
    Youth Court, 28, 155
Nolan, Pat, 130
Norman Conquest, 7, 10
Norms of society, criminal law and, 172
North America, 7, 17, 28
    circles among aboriginal peoples, 85
    indigenous peoples, 7
    victim-offender mediation in, 28

North Carolina, 128
    mediation in, 157
Norway
    adult diversionary mediation, 33t–38t
    diversion mediation project, 33t–38t
    mediation in, 156
    restorative justice principles and practices in, 33t–38t
    victim-offender mediation in, 28
Notification, of victims, about the status of offender prosecution, 68

O
Observers, of encounter, 95
O'Connell, Terry, 29
Offenders
    ability to pay restitution, 108–109, 140–141
    adversarial model of criminal justice and, 169–170
    adversarial relationship with government, 5
    alienation of families by, 158
    apology by, 101–102
    changed behavior of, 102–103
    in circles, 85–86
    coercion to participate in encounter, 90–91
    contributing injuries to, 46–47
    crime as defining moment for, 114
    crime of, as offense against victim, 7–10
    in encounter, 93, 140
    faith communities as help to, 126–128
    after family group conferencing, 84–85
    family model of criminal justice and, 169–170
    focus on, 5
    guarantee to confront their accusers, 82
    healing of, 45
    humanizing of victims by, 89
    inability to pay restitution, 74, 108–109
    inclusion of, 75–78
    injuries of, 46–47
    "institutionalized mentality", 118
    Internet resources for, 130
    involvement in the justice process, 47
    isolation of, 118, 126
    labeling of, 117
    needs upon release from incarceration, 117–118, 118b, 127

obstacles faced by, 117–118, 118b
parallel justice and, 120
power imbalance with victims, 173
practical assistance for, 127
public retribution against, 8
recidivism of, 117
re-entry of, victim involvement in, 159
re-entry process, 123, 127–128
reintegration by, 117–118
reintegration help for, 141–142
resources needed by, 120–121
resulting injuries to, 46–47
retribution, recompense, and, 52
shift in thinking about, 7–10
spiritual resources for, 128
stigmatization of, 114–115, 117, 117b, 126,
    126b
support groups for, 123
in victim-offender panels (VOPs), 86–87
in visual model of restorative justice, 54–57.
    See also Apology; Circles; Conferencing;
    Encounter; Restitution; Victim-offender
    mediation programs (VOMs)
Office of Crime Victim Ombudsman
    (Minnesota), 73
Office of Juvenile Justice and Delinquency
    Prevention, 30
Ohio, workplace (prison) conflict programs,
    158–159
Online resources. *See* Internet resources
Order
    defined, 47
    government responsibility to provide, 48,
        94, 173–174
    peace vs., 47
    in visual model of restorative justice, 54–57
"Out of court offense compensation"
    (Austria), 156
Overcrowding, "get tough" measures and
    prison, 10

P

Packer, Herbert, 169–170, 176
Pali, Brunilda, 147
Paradigms, Zehr's descriptions of, 4
Parallel justice, 120

Parents of Murdered Children, 122–123
Parliamentary Standing Committee (Daubney
    Committee; Canada), 32–33, 33t–38t
Parole
    hearings, victim statements at, 69
    officers, use of restorative justice processes
        by, 159–160
    violation hearings, victim inclusion in, 74
Parole Act (New Zealand; 2002), 159
Participatory justice, 15–16
Passive responsibility, 104
Past, crime handling in, transformation of
    perspective and, 171–172
Patterns of thinking
    ancient (restitution and vindication), 6–7
    defined, 4
    described, 4–5
    discounting of restorative justice, 19
    for reflection on alternative approaches, 5
    restorative justice antecedents, 12–18
    shift to government and offender model, 7–10
    transformation of perspective and, 170–173
    usefulness of, 4
    weakness of, 4, 4b
Peace
    as avenue for achieving safety, 48
    community's responsibility for creating, 47,
        94, 173–174
    in visual model of restorative justice, 56f–57f
Peacemaking
    Aboriginal circles and, 85
    as social justice, 18
Peace table, in Bellavista Prison, Colombia,
    158–159
Pedophiles, 117–118
Peel, Sir Robert, 10
Penitentiary
    defined, 8
    Quakers as founders of, 14, 124
    vision and practice realignment, 144–145
    Walnut Street Jail, 8–9, 14. *See also* Prison
Pennell, Joan, 29, 40
Pennsylvania approach of corrections, 124
Peold, Nicole, 168
Pepinsky, Harold E., 18, 21, 176
Personal responsibility, 17

Persons, transformation of, 174–176

Perspective, transformation of, 170–173

Peters, Tony, 40

Philadelphia (Pennsylvania)
magistrate's courts in, 11
prisons and restorative justice processes in, 158–159

Philadelphia City Prisons, 158–159

Philadelphia Society for Alleviating the Miseries of Public Prisons, 9

Philippines, restorative justice principles and practices in, 33t–38t

Physical injuries, of offenders, 46–47

Plea agreement, victim statements and, 69

Plea bargaining, 73, 107

Poland, restorative justice principles and practices in, 33t–38t

Police, 10–12
information provided to victims, 68
Thames Valley (England), 31, 33, 33t–38t, 156
use of restorative justice processes, 156

Policy change, 135–137, 147

Pollefeyt, D., 111

Pollock, Frederick, 20

Portugal, restorative justice principles and practices in, 33t–38t

Positive reinforcement, 103

Post-sentencing, victim inclusion in, 74

Post-Traumatic Stress Disorder (PTSD), 115

Poverty, imbalances in criminal justice and, 173

Power imbalance between the victim and the offender, 151–152

Powerlessness, of victims, 19, 173

Practical and material help, as reintegration element, 114, 160

Practice of Punishment, The (Cragg), 25–26

Pranis, Kay, 30, 33t–38t, 40, 97, 111, 136, 147

Prenzler, Tim, 111

Presbyterian Church (USA), Criminal Justice Program of, 25

Presence in court, right to, in victim inclusion, 67–69

Presentencing, victim inclusion in, 73

Pretrial diversion, 157

Primary victims, 45, 47

Prince, The (Machiavelli), 146

Prior conditions, 46–47

Prison
abolition movement for, 14–15
emergence of, 8–9
failure at rehabilitation, 14
as last resort, 17
meaningful work in, 109
overcrowding and "get tough" measures, 10
use of restorative justice processes by, 158–159. *See also* Penitentiary; Punishment

Prison Ashram Project, 130

Prisoners, alienation of, 158

Prison Fellowship, 125, 158

Prison Fellowship International, 33t–38t, 87, 145, 154

Prison Moratorium Project (New York), 14–15

Private prosecution, 10–12

Private remorse, 101

Probation
in Japan, 157–158
officers, use of restorative justice processes by, 157–158
offices, victim-offender mediation and, 28
violation hearings, victim inclusion in, 74

Probation and Mediation Services Act (Czech Republic; 2001), 33t–38t

Problem-solving courts, 24–25

Prosecution, victim inclusion in, 14

Prosecution of Offenses Act (1879), 10

Prosecutorial diversion (Austria), 156–157

Prosecutors
decision to prosecute by, 72–73
discretionary power of, 156
use of restorative justice processes by, 150
victims and, 70–72

Protective mediation, 159

Psychological trauma, crime-related, 13–14, 115–116

Psychology of reintegrative shaming, 26

Public defense, 79

Public harms, 105

Public opinion surveys, 136

Public order, 12

Public police force, 11

Public policy, restorative justice as source of, 32–33

Public–private prosecution, hybrid process, 11

Public prosecutor, 10, 72–73

Public retribution, 8

Public safety, government and community responsibility for, 47

Punishment
  corporal, 8
  denial of victim participation in, 23–24
  deterrence through, 25
  "get tough" measures, 10, 136
  model, 23–24
  as replacement of restitution, 8
  restitution approach to, 17
  retributive justice and, 23–24, 39. *See also* Prison

Punishment and Restitution (Abel and Marsh), 17

Q

Quakers (Society of Friends)
  as founders of the penitentiary movement, 14, 124
  penitentiary philosophy, 144–145
  prison abolition movement, 14–15

Quinney, Richard, 18, 21, 138, 176

R

R. v. Moses (sentencing circle case; Yukon Territory Court, Canada; 1992), 33t–38t

Racial minorities, as powerless victims, 173

Radzik, Linda, 110

Real Justice, 33t–38t

Recidivism
  beating the odds, 127
  defined, 5
  as failure of rehabilitation attempts, 5
  rate of, 5
  reasons for, 117

Recompense
  defined, 52, 53b
  in Hebrew justice, 7, 19
  restitution and, 103
  in visual model of restorative justice, 54, 56

Reconciliation, 49, 87
  cultural, 31
  Murder Victims' Families for Reconciliation (MVFR), 71
  objection to term, 28, 83
  in place of prison, 14

Redemption, 110

Redress, in visual model of restorative justice, 56

Re-entry process, for offenders, 123, 127–128, 159

Reform
  as contributor to restorative justice theory, 12–18
  of prisons, early days, 8–9, 125
  restitution as initiative of, 16–17
  restorative justice as dynamic for, 33–39
  for victims' rights, 13–14

Regret, expression of regret, and apology, 101

Rehabilitation
  early prison reform and, 8–9
  "get tough" measures vs., 10
  impossibility of, 9, 125
  peacemaking and, 18
  prisons as failure at, 14
  recidivism as failure of, 5
  restorative justice compared to, 51–53
  victim's view of, 102–103

Rehabilitation model
  of criminal justice, 3–4
  of sentencing, 8

Reiman, Jeffrey H., 173, 176

Reiner, Robert, 111

Reintegration
  in assessment framework, 160–161, 161t–162t, 164, 165f
  building, 119–121
  communities
    and demands on, 119
    faith communities, 124–128
    families and supporters, 121–122
    support and assistance groups, 122–124
  defined, 119
  elements of, 114b, 160, 161t–162t
  example (*Les Miserables*), 113–116, 118–119, 123–124, 129

Reintegration (*Continued*)

    faith communities as help to, 175

    in fully restorative system, 160–161, 165, 166f

    guidance and care element, 114

    help element, 114, 114b, 129

    help for victims and offenders, 141–142

    material help in, 114, 114b

    moral and spiritual direction in, 114, 129

    of offenders, 117–118, 141–142

    as operational value in restorative process, 50

    parallel justice, 120

    relationships, 119, 121

    respect element, 114, 129

    safety element, 114

    stigmatization vs., 114–116, 126, 126b

    victims in, 115–117, 141–142

Reintegrative shaming

    re-entry for both victim and offender and, 119

    restorative justice linked to, 26

    stigmatizing shaming distinguished from, 130

Relational harm, 110

Relationalism, 26

Relational justice, 24, 26

Relational Justice (Burnside and Baker), 26

Releasing circles, 159

Religious-based services. *See* Faith communities

Remorse, 49, 101

Renewal, 85–86, 175–176

Reorientation in sentencing (Canada), 31

Reparation, in victim-offender mediation programs, 83

Reparative conception, of restorative justice, 44–45

Repentance, 7, 9, 9b, 87, 130

Research Institute of Crime Prevention and Control (China), 33t–38t

Resistance, to restorative justice, 146–147

Resolution in visual model of restorative justice, 54, 56

Respect, 47

    as reintegration element, 114, 119, 129, 160

Responsibility, 87

    acceptance of, 93

    active, 104

    assumption of, 47

    passive, 104

    personal, 17

Restitution, 25

    abandonment of, 8

    as active responsibility, 104

    as "add-on" to real sentence, 74

    agreements of, in family group conferencing, 85

    amends and, 100–101, 100b, 103–104, 160

    in ancient codes, 6, 19

    calculation of, 105

    community service as, 104, 106

    compensation compared to, 111

    compliance rates, 74

    creative, 39, 104

    defined, 103

    direct injuries, 106

    direct victims, 105

    in dismissed cases, 107

    early enthusiasm for, 146

    feasibility and unfeasibility of, 74, 108–109

    historic background of, 103

    impediments to, 108

    imprisonment replaced by, 17

    incarceration of offenders and, 74, 109

    injuries requiring, 107–108

    injury to society, 105

    in later times, 7–10

    mandatory, 103

    meaningful, 74

    monetary payment and, 103, 109

    offender's ability to pay, 108–109, 140–141

    offenders identified but not convicted, 107

    as passive responsibility, 104

    prisons replaced by, 14

    rationales for, 16

    as reform initiative, 16–17

    replacement of, by fines to state, 7

    requirements of, 103

    resistance to, 146

    restorative justice based on, 23–24

    secondary victims, 105

in sentencing, 74
seriousness of offense and, 107
specific injuries, 106
as strategic goal, 141
victims' right to pursue, in criminal cases, 141
who should receive?, 105–107
Restoration, 17, 25, 52, 88, 105, 110, 128–129, 142–144, 151, 161
Restitution in Criminal Justice (Hudson and Galaway), 39
Restorative and Community Justice Programme (Jamaica), 33t–38t
Restorative community justice, 24, 26–27
Restorative Community Justice: A Call to Action (Young), 26–27
Restorative justice, 88
    accountability and, 51, 51b
    antecedents of, 12–18
    Christianity, the Bible, and, 39
    circles as, 29–30
    citizen-government conflicts and, 31
    as a community-based alternative to the criminal justice system, 32
    conceptions of, 43–45, 57
    conditions for, 149–153
    conferencing as, 28–29
    contemporary criminal justice compared to, 53–54, 58
    criminal justice systems and, 30–33
    critiques and reform efforts, 12–18
    defined, 43–45
    development of, 12–18, 31–39, 33t–38t
    direct involvement by parties, 47
    discounting of, 19
    does it work?, 53–54
    encounter as hallmark of, 174
    encounter conception, 43–45, 154
    explorers of, 25–27
    focus of, 23–24
    four parties in, 54
    fully restorative, 160–161, 165, 166f
    fundamental principle, 160–161
    globalization of, 31–39, 33t–38t
    goal of, 56
    government investment in, 30–31

inclusion in, 61–80
increasing the use of, 137–138
indigenous justice and, 16
informal justice critique, 15–16
innovations in, 24–25
intergovernmental bodies, 31
as an international reform dynamic, 33–39
key features of, 54–57
models, 153–155
person transformation and, 174–176
perspective transformation and, 170–173
principles of, 45–48
prison abolition movement, 14–15
processes
    in contemporary criminal justice, 156–160
    court use of, 157
    parole officer use of, 159–160
    police use of, 156
    prison use of, 158–159
    probation officer use of, 157–158
    prosecutor use of, 156–157
programs offering, 27–30
promise of, 64–65, 64b
proponents' selective use of history, 19
as public policy source, 32–33
reparative conception, 44–45, 154
restorative practices vs., 50
retributive justice and rehabilitation compared to, 51–53
social justice movement, 17–18
strategies
    assessment and evaluation, 142–144
    build support for, 135–137
    coalition development, 138–139
    impact evaluation, 142–144
    learning, collaborating, and challenging, 145–146
    resistance to, 146–147
    strategic goals, 139–142
    vision and practice realignment, 144–145
    vision review, 142–144
structure transformation and, 173–174
systems
    access to, 165
    aspirations in, 165
    assessment framework for, 160–165

Restorative justice (*Continued*)
    elements of, 160
      fully restorative, 160–161, 165, 166f
      minimally restorative, 160–161, 165, 167f
      models, 153–155
      moderately restorative, 165, 166f
      substantially restorative, 161
    term usage, 23–25
    theories and theorists of, 25–27
    timeline of, 31–39, 33t–38t
    transformation as hallmark of, 170,
      175–176
    transformation conception, 44
    transformative conception, 154
    value of, 39
    values of, 48–50, 58
    victim-offender mediation as, 27–28
    victims' rights and assistance, 13–14
    visual model, 54–57. *See also* Restitution
Restorative Justice Online (http://www.
    restorativejustice.org), 145, 33t–38t
Restorative Justice: The Evidence, 33t–38t
Restorative practices, 50
Restorative Resolutions Project (Canada),
    157
Restorativeness assessment, indicators, 150
Resulting injuries, of offenders, 46–47
Retail Theft Initiative (England), 33t–38t
Retribution
    defined, 51–52
    in Hebrew justice, 6–7
    public, 8
    shillem and, 6–7
Retributive justice, 23–24, 39, 51–53
Revenge, 6
Rich Get Richer and the Poor Get Prison, The
    (Reiman), 173
Richards, Kelly, 19
Risk, 109–110, 140–141
RJ City project (case study), 154–155,
    177–188
Roach, Kent, 59, 111
Roberts, Albert R., 13, 20
Roberts, Julian, 59, 111
Robinson, Gwen, 60
Roche, Declan, 93–95, 98

Romania, restorative justice principles and
    practices in, 33t–38t
Roman Law of the Twelve Tables, 6
Rosen, Cathryn J., 146, 148
Rössner, Dieter, 28, 40
Rothman, David, 20
Rowland, Judith A., 78, 127
Royal Canadian Mounted Police, 33, 33t–38t
Rucker, Lila, 176
Rwanda, restorative justice principles and
    practices in, 33t–38t

S
Safety
    public, 47
    as reintegration element, 114, 114–115, 160
    as restorative system condition, 150–152
    in visual model of restorative justice,
      56, 56f
Safety net model, of restorative justice,
    153–154
Salvation Army, 130
Sangrey, Dawn, 13, 20, 116, 129, 131
Scandinavia, victim-offender mediation in, 28
Schafer, Stephen, 16, 20
Schiff, Mara, 59, 111
Schluter, Michael, 40
Schneider, Carl D., 101, 111
Schönfeld, Walther, 39
Schrey, H., 39
Schweigert, Francis J., 176
Secondary victims, 45, 105
Security, 48
Self-control, 169–170
Self-help groups, for victim/offender
    reintegration, 122, 122b
Sentencing
    circles, 29–30, 33t–38t, 85–86
    incorporation of restorative justice
      principles in, 31
    rehabilitative model of, 8
    reorientation in, 31
    restitution in, 74
    restorative processes for, 157
    victim impact statement at, 69–70
    victim inclusion in, 14, 74

Settlement-driven programs, 28
Seventh Day Adventist church, 128
Shalom
  in ancient Jewish law, 47
  meaning of term, 6–7, 47
Shame, apology and, 101
Shaming, 26, 119, 130
Shapland, Joanna, 60
Shared interest, local community, community
  of care, and, 46
Shattuck, Michelle, 131
Sheffer, Susannah, 78
Sherman, Lawrence, 53–54, 59
Shillem/shillum, meaning of term, 6–7
Shuttle diplomacy, 88, 97
Skelton, Ann, 39
Skogan, Wesley G., 129
Skotnicki, Andrew, 20
Snyder, Francis, 20
Social, political, and economic inequities,
  power imbalance and, 173–174
Social justice movement, 17–18
Social services, 123–124
Social support, 137
Social welfare model, 29
Society, restitution to, 105–107
Society of Friends. *See* Quakers (Society of
  Friends)
Solidarity, 49
Sorsby, Angela, 60
South Africa
  Child Justice Act (2009), 33t–38t
  Community Peace Committees in, 156
  National Institute for Crime Prevention and
    Reintegration of Offenders, 33t–38t
  restorative justice principles and practices
    in, 31, 33t–38t
  Truth and Reconciliation Commission, 31,
    33t–38t
Soviet-bloc countries, restorative justice
  principles and practices in, 31
Specific injuries, 106, 108
Specificity, principle of, 106
Speedy Trial Act, 96–97
Spiritual and moral guidance and care, as
  reintegration element, 114, 129

Spiritual injuries, of offenders, 46–47
Standard of living, quantifications of harms
  and, 105
Standards, 49
Standards Relating to the Prosecution
  Function (ABA), 70–71
Steinberg, Allen, 11–12, 20
Stereotypes, 137
Stern, Vivien, 19
Stigmatization, of victims and offenders,
  114–116, 126, 126b
Stigmatizing shaming, 130
Stott, John, 20
Strang, Heather, 53–54, 59
Strategic goals, 139–142
Structures, transformation of, 173–174
Struggle for Justice, 14
Stuart, Barry, 30, 40, 86, 97
Stubbs, Julie, 168
Support groups, for victim/offender
  reintegration, 122–124
Support persons, in encounter, 93
Supreme Court of Canada, 31
Sycamore Tree Project, 87, 158
Sylvester, Douglas J., 19

T
Texas
  early victim-offender mediation, in prisons,
    28
  prisons and restorative justice processes
    and, 158
Thailand, restorative justice principles and
  practices in, 33t–38t
Thames Valley Police (England), restorative
  justice use by, 31, 33, 33t–38t, 156
Therapeutic treatment, of offenders, 23–24
Three-dimensional justice, 39
Toews, Barb, 130
Tomkins, Silvan, 26
Tort law, 17
Traditional approach, to justice, 16, 53
Traditional justice, 53
Training
  of facilitators, 89–90, 92
  on restorative justice, 30–31

Transformation, 169–176
   as hallmark of restorative justice, 170,
      175–176
   of persons, 174–176
   of perspective, 170–173
   of structures, 173–174
Transformation conception, of restorative
   justice, 44, 154
Transformative justice, 24
Trauma, psychological, crime-related,
   115–116
Treatment, of victims, 116
Treaty of Waitangi (1840), 31
Trials, victims' presence at, 68–69
Tribunal of Restorative Justice (El Salvador),
   33t–38t
Truth and Reconciliation Commission (South
   Africa), 31, 33t–38t
Tutu, Desmond, 31
Twelve-step programs, 128
Twelve Tables (Roman Law), 6

U
Uganda, restorative justice principles and
   practices in, 31, 33t–38t
Umbreit, Mark S., 18, 27, 40, 79, 83, 86, 97–98,
   111, 137–138
Understanding, in encounter, 86b, 88–89, 160
Unitarian Universalist Service Committee,
   National Moratorium on Prison
   Construction, 14–15
Unitary model, of restorative justice,
   154–155
United Kingdom. *See* England
United Methodist Church, 130
United Nations
   Declaration of Basic Principles of Justice for
      Victims of Crime and Abuse of Power,
      68
   Declaration of Basic Principles on the Use
      of Restorative Justice Programmes
      in Criminal Matters, 31, 33t–38t, 95,
      150–153, 168
   Economic and Social Council (ECOSOC), 31
   endorsement of restorative justice, 33–39

Handbook on Justice for Victims, 68
Handbook on Restorative Justice, 33t–38t
   restorative justice principles and practices
      in, 33t–38t
United States
   amends, importance of apology in,
      101–102
   churches as reintegrating communities, 124
   criminal justice system, 11
   early victim-offender mediation in, 27
   "Genesee Justice" program, 33t–38t
   Justice Fellowship in, 32–33, 33t–38t
   legal standing of victims to address court,
      70
   prisoner ministry in, 130
   prisons and restorative justice processes in,
      158–159
   public defender, 79
   restitution established in, 103
   restorative justice principles and practices
      in, 33t–38t
   social services in, 123–124
   victim-offender panels in, 87
   victim-offender reconciliation programs in,
      32
   workplace (prison) conflict programs,
      158–159
University of Pennsylvania, 123–124
U.S. Association for Victim Offender
   Mediation, 33t–38t
U.S. Department of Justice, 30
U.S. Office for Victims of Crime, 125
U.S. Office of Juvenile Justice and
   Delinquency Prevention, 33t–38t
Utopia (More), 103
Utrecht School, 14–15

V
Values
   changed, 103, 103b
   changed behavior and, 103
   clarified by graduated punishment, in
      criminal law, 15–16
   communicated by the state through the
      infliction of pain, 15–16

feminist, restructuring of criminal justice
    and, 17–18
of restorative justice, 48–50, 160. *See
    also* Amends; Encounter; Inclusion;
    Reintegration
Van Ness, Daniel W., 17, 20, 26, 43–44, 59, 96,
    145, 199
Victim bills of rights, 67
Victim compensation funds, 67
Victim inclusion, in criminal justice
        proceedings
    at arraignment through presentencing, 73
    example (David and Goliath), 64, 63–65
    information needs, 67–68
    at investigation stage, 72–73
    legal standing of victim to participate,
        67, 70
    notification of victims, about offender
        prosecution, 68
    in offender re-entry, 159
    plea bargaining and, 73
    at post-sentencing, 74
    presence in court, 67–69
    prosecutor and, 70–72
    restitution and, 141
    restorative justice and, 65–67
    at sentencing, 74
    at stages of proceedings, 72–74
    victim as civil claimant in criminal cases, 75
    victim impact statement, 67, 69–70
Victim Offender Meeting Program
        (Washington), 90
Victimization
    costs of, 13–14, 115
    crisis phase, 127
    harm resulting from, 13–14, 13b
    impact stage, 127
Victim–offender dialogue (VOD), 97
Victim-offender mediation (VOMs) programs
    arbitration distinguished from, 82
    community-based, 27–28
    conferencing distinguished from, 29
    court process distinguished from, 82
    family group conferencing (FGC)
        distinguished from, 84

future intentions, 83
goal of, 83
identification of injustice in, 83
participant empowerment, 82
participants in, 91, 93
power of, 83–84
pre-encounter preparation, 84
purpose of, 27, 82–84
as relational justice, 26–28
reparations (making things right), 83
as restorative process program, 27–28
structure of, 83
support persons/community members in, 93
terminology variations in, 83
transformation and, 174
victim-offender panels (VOPs)
    distinguished from, 86. *See also*
    Encounter
Victim-Offender Mediation Association
        (VOMA), 145, 33t–38t
Victim-offender panels (VOPs)
    benefits, 87
    examples, 86
    meeting element of, 88–89
    participants in, 86
    purpose of, 86
    victim-offender mediation and
        conferencing distinguished from, 86
Victim-offender reconciliation programs
        (VORPs)
    first use of, in Canada, 33t–38t
    history of, 27–28
Victims
    absence of, in family group conferencing,
        155
    advocates, 75, 137, 139
    alienating effects on, of offender-oriented
        system, 14
    apology to, 101–102
    assistance, 24–25
    during bail procedure, 73
    biblical justice concerned with, 17
    bills of rights, 67
    in circles, 85–86
    as civil claimant in criminal cases, 75

Victims (*Continued*)
    common needs of, 45
    community distinguished from, 59
    compensation fund, 108
    compensation programs, 13–14
    concerns of, about restorative justice,
        136–137, 137b
    contemporary rediscovery of, 13
    crime as defining moment for, 114
    crime as offense against, 6–7
    in crisis, 115–116
    crisis phase of victimization, 127
    declining role of, 10–12
    defined, 45
    demographic characteristics, 115
    direct, 105
    dissatisfaction with criminal justice system, 5
    in encounter, 92–93, 140
    fairness concept and, 74, 92, 92b
    faith communities as help to, 126–128
    goals of, in encounter, 92
    harm to, extensiveness of, 13–14
    healing of, 3–4, 27–28, 45
    humanizing of, by offenders, 89
    impact stage of victimization, 127
    impact statement, 67, 69–70
    information provided by police, 68
    as injured parties, 3–4, 12
    innovations for, 82
    Internet resources for, 130
    involvement in the justice process, 47
    isolation of, 116, 118, 123, 126, 139
    legal standing of, to participate in criminal
        proceedings, 70
    life in the new "normal" patterns, 117
    movement, 13–14
    negative self-identity of, 116
    negative view of, by others, 116
    parallel justice for, 120
    participation, in the prosecution and
        sentencing of the suspect, 14
    plea bargaining and, 73
    post-sentencing and, 74
    powerful vs. powerless, 19, 173
    power imbalance with offenders, 173–174
    practical concerns of, 116

    primary, 45, 47
    prosecutors and, 70–72
    reintegration by, 115–117, 141–142
    reintegration help for, 141–142
    right to pursue restitution, in criminal
        cases, 141
    right to speak at felony sentencing, 74
    right to speak in court, 82
    rights and assistance, 13–14
    role of, in criminal justice process, 26, 28
    safety need of, 115
    secondary, 45, 105
    sentencing and, 14, 74
    shift away from restitution to, 7–10
    spiritual or moral crises of, 117
    stigmatization of, 114–116, 126, 126b
    support, 177, 179
    support advocates, 83
    support for restorative justice, 137
    support groups for, 122–124
    in victim-offender panels (VOPs), 86–87
    in visual model of restorative justice, 54, 56
    as witness, 66, 68–69
    witness assistance, 67
Villmoare, Edwin, 78
Vindication
    in Hebrew justice, 6–7
    as victim need, 45
    in visual model of restorative justice, 54, 56
Virginia Acts of Assembly, 168
Voluntary participation, in encounter,
    90, 90b
VOMs. *See* Victim-offender mediation
    programs (VOMs)
von Hirsch, Andrew, 59, 105, 107, 111
VOPs. *See* Victim-offender panels (VOPs)
Vulnerability
    in apology, 101
    of victims, 115–116

W
Wagga Wagga, New South Wales, Australia
    family group conferencing programs in, 26,
        29, 33t–38t
    restorative justice practices in dealing with
        juvenile offenders, 29

Wales, Sycamore Tree Project, 87
Walker, David, 102, 111
Walker, Lorenn, 121, 130
Walnut Street Jail, 8–9, 14
Walz, H., 39
Washington (state), 90
Web sites. *See* Internet resources
Wedge, Mark, 40, 97
"We-they" attitude, between community and
    justice system, 138
Whanau conference, Maori people and, 84
Whitehouse, W., 39
Wilbour, Charles E., 129
William the Conqueror, 7
Wineburg, Robert J., 130
Witness
    presence at trials, 68–69
    statements, 68–69
    victim's role as, 66, 68–69
Worth, Dave, 27

Wortley, Richard, 111
Wright, Martin, 24–25, 28, 40, 97–98
Wrongful acts, 105

Y
Yantzi, Mark, 27
Young, Marlene A., 24, 26–27, 40
Youth Court (New Zealand), 28, 155
Youth Criminal Justice Act (Canada), 31
Youth Justice and Criminal Evidence Act
    (England; 1999), 33t–38t

Z
Zedner, Lucia, 111
Zehr, Howard, 4, 19, 24–25, 27, 39–40, 51–52,
    59, 89, 97–98, 130, 148, 170
Zimbabwe
    Prison Fellowship in, 158
    restorative justice principles and practices
        in, 33t–38t